D1448330

IDEAS MAN
SHERIDAN SIMOVE

**The Amazing Real-Life Adventures
of a Modern Day Creative Genius**

CORGI BOOKS

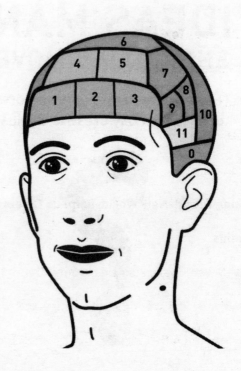

THE IDEAS

'*A book about your ideas? What!? Are you stupid?! . . .
Do you really think anyone is going to be interested in your
pathetic escapades! Of course not!*

*And they're certainly not going to care about your
crazy theories, like the way you think
"every person can be a creative powerhouse" . . .
Don't be ridiculous . . . ha ha!*

*Anyway, it's such a hassle sitting down to write –
so why even make the effort! Watch some TV instead.
The Simpsons is on – you like that . . .*'

IDEA 0

My Attempt To Get You Hooked

So. Hello. Great to meet you – even though I'm not really meeting you, more that you're meeting me I suppose. It's a pity I can't meet you, as I love encountering interesting new people, but unfortunately I just can't – the technology for books to do that isn't quite there yet. Ah well, not to worry. I'll introduce myself quickly anyway.

My name is Sheridan Simove. But please call me 'Shed'. I know 'Shed' sounds weird, but to me it's my name. Everyone calls me that, even my parents, the people who came up with the shortening. I wonder if they realized I'd have a lifetime of people being puzzled and making jokes when I introduced myself? Probably not.

'No, my brother is not called "Greenhouse",' I often remark when I've just told someone my name and they question whether it's the same as the place in a garden that stores tools. I always half chuckle after they've made that same joke I've heard so many times before. I explain that the only time I've ever been called 'Sheridan' is when my parents told me off as a child – 'Sheridan! Stop your nonsense!' – and so to me 'Shed' is absolutely what I'm called. So that's that.

Anyway, I hate books where there's a load of waffle at the start. So let's plunge straight in ...

The ideas started relatively small, but even the early ones changed things, as you'll soon see. It would take a while until I came up with larger, more ambitious schemes, and it would be a very long while before I had 'the big one', the 'bright' idea for a TV programme that really changed my life and landed me on the front pages (I'm the guy bottom right on the newspaper below).

I made the programme when I was thirty and posed as a sixteen-year-old to try to attend high school for the second time round. To my surprise, the plan worked and I spent a whole term as a sixth-former. When I finally revealed my true age to the teachers and my fellow pupils, a whole town wanted to lynch me. But, hey, I'll get to that story a bit later . . .

So, what's this book all about then? Well, here's my cunning plan:

I'm hoping to keep you interested with the tales that have arisen from an amazingly simple two-stage process. It's something we all do and it goes like this:

First: you think about doing something . . .
and then . . .
. . . you make it happen.

This empowering, life-affirming couple of steps has taken me on all sorts of adventures – adventures I'm about to share with you.

I am chronically addicted to having an idea, no matter how ludicrous (and it's been mentioned that some of the ideas you'll read about here are certainly ludicrous), then acting upon that idea until something happens. You'll see what occurs when I turn thoughts into reality: sometimes the consequences are great, sometimes not so wonderful. You'll be the judge of which ones you reckon are any good. Hopefully you'll find all of them vaguely interesting. They just might even be a little bit inspiring to you (if you're in need of inspiration, of course), because if *I* can make these things happen, then anyone can.

Anyway, nice to have you with me, in spirit if not in body. Enjoy the trip.

*'Thousands of people want to work in television . . .
loads of candidates applying for this amazing job
will have more experience than you . . . and . . . ha ha! . . .
you're rubbish in interviews! . . .
the application form is huge . . .
why even bother? . . . you won't get the job . . .
give up now and save loads of time . . .'*

The Pizza That Changed Everything

'Cheesy' self-promotion at its finest

I didn't know it then, but it was going to be a special day. It started normally enough: my dad shouted from the hall, waking me from my beauty sleep.

'Shed! Shed! Come on Shed – don't stay in bed all day!'

My dad hated me sleeping in, believing it to be a waste of the day. I wearily dragged myself downstairs to find a solitary piece of mail from my college. Bless the people who work there, for in that envelope was a piece of paper that would change my life.

Ripping open the envelope, I instantly recognized the contents: a white A4 booklet covered in black print. A careers newsletter. I scanned it with a heavy heart, having seen many similar bulletins in the last few months. I just didn't want to go through yet another one, reading all the jobs that were on offer – the dozens of accountancy firms offering great salaries, the law practices, the merchant banks – and then guiltily realize that none of them turned me on in the slightest.

So now I stared at the newsletter, daring it, willing it to come up with something that would vaguely capture my imagination. I scanned the first page, ballpoint-pen poised, ready to ring any job that was even vaguely sexy.

Nothing on page one. Nor on page two. Oh dear. A position in an ad agency on page three got me slightly excited, but not ecstatic.

Then, on page four – bingo! I saw it, the paragraph that held my future. If this scene had been in a movie, angels would have sung and the block of words on the page would have shone brilliant gold.

But it wasn't a movie. I was in Cardiff, the capital of Wales and my home town, and it was raining outside. Yet these words were now catching my eye and my imagination at the same time. They seemed like a wondrous portal into another world, one I wanted to jump right into.

Ten years later, when I started to write this book, I tried to find out exactly what this life-changing advert had said. I called up the university careers service. Even though they told me that old newsletters weren't on computer in those days (how old did that make me feel!), they thought they still may have a hard copy in their archives. After a labour-intensive search, they found the newsletter and the advert in question. It was sandwiched between an opportunity to work at a merchant bank and an offer to join a systems personnel firm (whatever the hell that is). Here's the ad that had such a big impact on my life:

5th Floor, Cavell House, 2a Charing Cross Road, London WC2H 0NN. EAF.

Planet 24

Television Production Trainees.

Further to their presentation on 27 April at The Old Fire Station, Planet 24 will be taking on two graduate Production Trainees. The company produces Big Breakfast, The Word, and Surf Potatoes. They are interested in 'people with wit, originality, talent - and the capacity for lots of hard work'. Successful applicants will spend a year from September 1994 at their London offices. To apply send a stamped addressed envelope to Mary Durkan at the address overleaf. Don't call.

i+B

Salary: £13,000
Apply to: Mary Durkan, Personnel Manager, Planet 24, Norex Court, 195 Marsh Wall, London E14 9SG.
Letter. Closing Date: 05-MAY-94

Professional Systems Personnel

Now it's fair to say that back then Planet 24 was the hottest television company in the UK. They specialized in making highly entertaining and highly original television shows. The oft bandied-about word 'groundbreaking' was frequently used in the same sentence as their name and this was well deserved.

Planet 24's first breakout programme was *The Word*, a frenetic, spiky, late-night, live show packed full of memorable hosts, great music, outspoken guests and shocking features. In one notorious segment called 'The Hopefuls', the producers exploited the fact that people would do anything for the chance to be on TV. Viewers were invited to appear on the show only if they would perform extreme tasks in return for airtime. The grim images of a young man puking up into a beer glass and then promptly drinking his puke back down stay with me even now.

Predictably enough, the *Daily Mail* and indeed anyone over thirty-five hated the show – which, in turn, made it even more attractive to young people. It was a programme for the young, made by the young – a no-rules paradise of unpredictability. To many of the nation's youth, it felt as if a gaping hole had been filled – finally this was television that directly engaged with a younger generation. It spoke to me too. I watched in awe at this seemingly glamorous world crammed full of gorgeous, naughty and amusing shenanigans. I was, like many other people, wowed. Little did I know I'd be standing in the studio as part of the production team only four years later, feeling the hairs on my neck stand up as the show's opening music started.

As if making one groundbreaking show wasn't enough, at the time the ad came out Planet 24 had also recently launched another seminal programme that changed the face of British TV for ever. Fresh from the success of *The Word*, the Planet 24 bosses joined the race to win the lucrative breakfast-show slot on Channel 4. They managed to attract hot, new, talented presenters and set their programme in a real house. Their pitch document was delivered in a specially created cereal box, a detail that I learned when I saw the box in one of the bosses' offices years afterwards. Planet 24 won the contract for the breakfast show, despite competition from much bigger companies, and so *The Big Breakfast* was born. It was a two-hour non-stop burst of energy that included the biggest celebrity guests, hilarious gags and two alien puppets. It also dared to do something that had never been seen before – it crossed the 'fourth wall'. *The Big Breakfast* turned the camera round to show the crew. They in turn became characters on the programme. It was daring, exciting, fresh – and a massive success.

So to say I was excited at the idea of getting a job at this company was an understatement. After reading the advert, I knew it was the place for me. Suddenly everything was clear. I wanted to work there. No, it was stronger than that – my whole soul yearned, ached, screamed to work there.

My heart sank as I read the ad. It mentioned a presentation that Planet 24 had given at my uni before the ad was placed. I'd heard nothing about this and so hadn't attended.

It was frustrating that I couldn't travel back in time so I could show up to gather any tips. I felt I was already playing catch-up to the people who had been there, because I reasoned that any knowledge about a goal you're aiming for is always helpful. Would everyone who attended have a much better chance than me? I couldn't let that bother me. I just had to power on.

I immediately wrote off for the application form and was on tenterhooks the whole time I waited for it, completely stressed out. All my hopes seemed invested in this one dream. I didn't want anything else.

My obsession with getting the job just grew and grew. This all-consuming focus would reoccur at other times in my life when I really wanted to get something done. Once a new idea or goal has captured my imagination, I find myself hurtling almost uncontrollably towards the completion of that goal. It is an enjoyable state of being, but it's also scary, as it sometimes seems as though I'm not the master of my own destiny. It's not just a case of wanting to do something; it suddenly becomes clear to me that I *have* to do it.

I sometimes beat myself up in a psychological way to spur myself on to try harder to make something happen. I play a perverse game with myself which goes like this: I imagine that somebody (it doesn't matter who) says to me, 'Shed, in one year's time I will cut off your arm unless you have achieved X'. In place of 'X' I put any one of my dreams: writing a book, launching a toy, doing an amazing speech, winning an Oscar.

Is that weird? But my logic does sort of make sense, doesn't it? If someone really *was* going to cut off your arm in a year's time unless you had succeeded in some goal, then you'd spend every waking moment making that goal happen, wouldn't you?

So that's the sort of focus I had when I was trying to get the Planet 24 job. My obsession started to accelerate out of control. When I say I became obsessed, I really was consumed, like you'd poured some strange kind of idea gasoline over me and set it alight. Virtually every waking thought was concerned with working out how to get the gig. I began to formulate a detailed plan.

I figured a lot of people would be going for this job. The world of TV was, and is, a draw to many. The Planet 24 position was an opportunity for someone to be fast-tracked through a company making the two best youth shows in the country. The same advert appeared a week later in the *Guardian* (a friend of the family cut it out for me) and that meant even more people would apply. I knew I had to raise my game in order to get noticed by the Planet 24 team. I also wanted to give the bosses some physical proof that I was a good bet, rather than relying solely on the application form.

The form finally arrived. It was five pages of questions with huge gaping spaces for me to fill in my answers. One of the spaces asked about 'the most interesting thing you've ever done'. I talked about the year I'd just spent in Florida working for Disney as a sixteenth-century gentleman. But there were two more tough spaces to fill that were going to pose me a much bigger challenge. The first one was headed 'Write down an idea for a new segment on *The Word*'. The second was even harder: 'Come up with an original concept for a TV show.'

There I was, someone who'd never worked in television before, and I was being asked to come up with a new programme. How the hell was I going to do that? Sure, I'd watched a lot of TV, but just because you come into contact with something doesn't automatically make you an expert in it. Even though I *now* know it's not exactly brain surgery coming up with a new TV show, it's most certainly an identifiable skill that involves specific techniques and knowledge.

Anytime you're looking to come up with something new, you have to know what has been done before. This is important for all original idea creation – you need to immerse yourself in the subject, see what's been done before and then do something different! It's as simple – or as difficult – as that.

So I tackled the first challenge first – a new strand for the cutting-edge youth show *The Word*. I approached this in a strategic manner, with the following thought processes:

a. *The Word* is a TV show that likes to shock
b. it's a sexy show
c. it's also a show with a sense of humour

Therefore, my strand needed to fit in with these three qualities. My final offering (at which I now cringe) was this:

Strand Idea for The Word:

True or Falsie?

The idea: Ten female models dressed in bikinis stand in a row. One celebrity guest must then go along the line and judge whether the girls' breasts are real or false just by looking at them.

After each guess, the girl reveals their boob status by holding up a sign which says '100% GENUINE' if they're real – or 'YOU'VE BEEN SILICONNED!' if they're false.

I groan at the thought of this idea now, and yet I'm sure I've seen it on cable TV sometime in the last five years.

My suggestion for a new TV show also involved a cringeworthy play on words. In fact, a lot of my ideas do, as you'll see. But it was rather less tasteless. At the time, the cookery show *MasterChef* had been running for a while. It was a hit programme that involved members of the public cooking meals for a celebrity judge. Working on the premise that 'cookery' shows were about to be big in the UK, I just twisted this idea into another form, or 'ripped it off' if you prefer! My entry read:

FasterChef

A chef creates a fantastic meal while under time pressure. The expert has just half an hour to cook a three-course meal. This would show the viewers that it's possible to cook good food in a short amount of time.

Now, unknown to me at the time, a half-hour programme with a slightly similar theme was in development at a rival television company. It hit the air soon afterwards and was hugely successful. The show is called *Ready Steady Cook* and involves two members of the public giving two chefs some ingredients that they've purchased to a budget. The chefs must create a wonderful meal in just twenty minutes out of the food they've been given. The studio audience then decides which chef's meal is more impressive. It has been an extremely popular daytime programme ever since it launched and is still shown on BBC2 and in many other parts of the world today.

I remember watching *Ready Steady Cook* soon after it aired, feeling delighted that it was slightly similar to my 'FasterChef' idea. I was at least thinking along the right lines.

Back then I was unaware that getting a TV programme on the air involved far more than just having a basic idea. But still, the idea of ever creating a TV show from scratch was so completely thrilling to me that I took pleasure in the fact that, because my idea wasn't a million miles away from something that was now being broadcast, perhaps I could just possibly make my own show one day. Little did I know then that one day I *would* get that chance.

I typed out the ideas for the application form on to a computer, printed them out, stuck them on to the paper so it would look beautifully neat (yes, I've always been anal) and proudly sent off the application. Then I waited.

I called Planet 24 a couple of times to see if there was any news and spoke with the busy but polite girl on reception. I could hear in her voice that she was rather stressed by similar calls that she'd received from other super-keen applicants. She told me that there had been a huge response to the advert and that someone would get back to me. It was my first experience of the old 'don't call us, we'll call you' routine so prevalent in the media.

While I waited impatiently, my obsession raged onwards. I wanted the job so badly I could feel it in my bones.

During this period I was doing part-time jobs to keep myself financially solvent. It was while I was working in a novelty shop stacking luminous condoms that I felt a strong surge of desperation go through me. I knew at that point that I had to spend my life doing something fulfilling (and stacking luminous condoms was definitely not doing it for me). I had to chase my dreams. So it felt like every cell in my body ached to get the Planet 24 job.

I began to worry about how I could get the powers-that-be at the company to notice me and how I could prove to them how much I wanted the job. So I started to hatch a plan to find out everything I possibly could about Planet 24.

I needed to find out every detail about the people who ran the company, so that then perhaps I could know what would impress them. A job interview is an exercise in selling yourself. In fact, you literally are 'selling yourself' because you're the product and you need to sell that product to prospective buyers. Now I've always believed that it most certainly makes sense to know who you're selling to, so you can address their needs and give them a product that they're looking for.

At the time, I felt completely detached from the television world and pretty much alone in Cardiff with my hopes and dreams. I had no connection to the media whatsoever – my mum was a dentist and my dad ran bingo clubs. So when I decided to try to get hold of information on Planet 24 I had to think laterally. My thought process was this: 'Who would know about this TV company?', and given that the internet wasn't around at the time, there were only three sources for getting information about Planet 24: the company itself, friends and families of the bosses, and, lastly, the press.

Now I didn't know how to reach anyone personally connected to the bosses' families at that stage (and also that's called 'stalking', isn't it?), so first off I called the company. I was getting to know the receptionist quite well by now and asked her to send me any company information that they had. A glossy brochure arrived, listing their programmes and displaying gorgeous shots of all their presenters and the celebrities that had appeared on their programmes.

Unfortunately, it didn't really contain anything I didn't already know from watching the programmes. But just holding it felt glamorous and strengthened my steely determination to work there.

The only route left to me at the time was to try to obtain all the press information written about Planet 24 and its bosses. But how was I going to get a dossier of all the articles published about this relatively young company? I wanted all the press cuttings I could find. On a hunch, I rang Directory Enquiries and was surprised to find there were a number of companies that ran a press-cuttings service. The name they gave me was for a firm in London called Cutting It Fine (another great pun, I'm sure you've noticed). I excitedly tapped in the numbers, getting that adrenalin rush that comes when you feel you're making progress.

'Hello, Cutting It Fine,' a polite female voice said.

I launched into my spiel. 'Yes, hi. I'm applying for a job – my dream job – and I need to find out everything about Planet 24. Can you help me please?'

The person on the line explained that, yes, they could perform a search on Planet 24 and that yes, they could find many articles about the company, compile them into a file and send them to me. Superb. She also told me that this service would cost a fair amount of money, much more than I had saved at the time from my mindnumbing temporary jobs. Demolishing fruit machines and sweeping hair up in a hairdresser's are jobs that unfortunately just don't bring in the big bucks.

My heart sank.

'Oh,' I sighed when I was told how much it would cost.

I really needed that information, but it seemed out of my reach. And then something amazing happened.

The lady on the other end of the phone must have heard the desperation in my voice and felt sorry for me.

'Give me your address and I'll see what I can do,' she said. So I did.

Two days later an A4 envelope dropped through the letterbox. It was an inch thick and bore the postal stamp of Cutting It Fine.

Hallelujah praise be! My heart sang. I immediately knew it was the Planet 24 cuttings and ripped open the envelope as quickly but as carefully as I could. Inside were pages and pages of photocopied articles about the company I was so obsessed with. I laid them out on the floor near my front door and started reading them eagerly.

I never knew who that kindly person was who sent me the articles for free, but years later, whenever I was working in a company where the opportunity arose to choose between using one press-cuttings service or another, I would always use Cutting It Fine and tell everyone around me that they were the best in the business. That one act of kindness secured my eternal loyalty.

When you're moving towards a goal there will always be a lot of obstacles, not only the practical ones involved in making something happen, but also hurdles created by other people. Some people may not want to be involved with your project; much worse, others may submit reasons why you can't reach your goal. So when you find someone who's willing to give you a leg up with no thought to how it will affect them, then that person really shines. The kind lady at Cutting It Fine who sent me the articles helped alter the course of my life and I'll never forget that.

I devoured the press cuttings voraciously, poring over every word, drinking them in ten to the dozen. I started to learn a great deal about Planet 24 and it was fascinating.

I learned that the company had been founded by three men. The first was named Charlie Parsons, a visionary, energetic producer with a passion for groundbreaking TV. After building up and eventually selling Planet 24, he made even more millions from creating the hit reality show *Survivor*. The next founding partner was Waheed Ali, a financial whizz-kid who'd made his fortune in the City at the age of sixteen. Soon after setting up Planet 24 he was made the youngest Lord ever, and now sits in parliament as Lord Waheed Ali no less. The triumvirate was completed by Bob Geldof, who of course you probably know: he's the ex-pop star turned businessman and Live Aid 'Give us your fucking money' maestro.

The press cuttings delivered great bits of detail on all these three clever power-players, but I wanted even more information. By a stroke of luck, one source of research was very close by.

Companies House is a building where the records of every company in the country are kept. By a wonderful coincidence, it's based in my home town of Cardiff. Even back then I'd always been interested in setting up my own company, so I knew exactly where it was and what it could offer me.

I called them up and asked them what information they could send me on Planet 24. They said they could only release the company accounts and the annual report for a small fee. At the time, I didn't even know what these formal documents were, but I readily agreed and paid for them over the phone with my mum's credit card, which she had kindly permitted me to use.

When the envelope from Companies House arrived two days later, I thought they'd made a mistake. The envelope was so small and thin that I figured it must contain a letter telling me they were unable to find the information. Instead, I opened it to find four postcard-sized pieces of wafer-thin clear plastic covered in blue squares. Each square contained a slightly different intricately etched pattern. I held the plastic sheets up to a window and could make out that the pattern was in fact tiny words and tables. This *was* the information – it was a microfiche, a clever way of storing a lot of information in a small space. Marvellous. There was just one snag. I needed a microfiche reader to read it.

Another call to Companies House told me that microfiche readers were available for use on their first floor. I quickly jumped into my mum's car and she whisked me off to decipher the little plastic squares. I rushed up the stairs to find the microfiche machines lined up in two rows of three. They looked quite space-age, rather I should say 'retro space-age': huge, deep, sloping screens with plastic fronts and lots of knobs everywhere. A friendly woman on reception showed me how they worked and at last I could unearth the treasure of information in the blue squares.

As I studied the Planet 24 records, I was confronted with lists of business figures which weren't that interesting. Far more fascinating, though, were the nuggets of info littered through the miniature files. I discovered that the name Planet 24 came from an amalgamation of two previous companies, 24 Hour Productions and Planet Productions. I learned that Bob Geldof's middle name was 'Xenon' and I found out that Charlie Parsons lived in the Islington area of London. I began to feel much closer to the people I was trying to get a handle on, much more armed for the way I was going to impress them.

Back home, I started to formulate a plan about how to use all the information I'd gathered.

I figured that if you're applying for a popular job and your aim is to get noticed, then all you have to do is have a look at what everyone else is doing and then work out a way to raise your game above theirs.

Most people just send a CV or fill in the application form. How could I do something that would mark me out for special attention so that I could have the very best crack at getting the job? I didn't know how I was going to wow them, but I felt sure that my research would reveal the answer.

So I went back to the press cuttings and decided it was time to try to create something very personal for the top boss, Charlie Parsons. One of the gems of information hidden in the press cuttings was the fact that Charlie was an avid *Coronation Street* fan. It was mentioned in many articles that he loved populist television and that he believed that some of the characteristics of this northern British soap opera could be found in all great TV.

Up until the point of reading the cuttings, I'd never really liked *Coronation Street*. I had flippantly dismissed it as being visually unappealing; it was a bit 'brown' looking and full of old people. However, once I learned Charlie was a worshipper of 'The Street', as it is commonly called by fans, I wanted to see what all the fuss was about. I started watching the show, hoping to spot the allure that makes millions upon millions of avid viewers tune in every week, putting it consistently at the top of the viewing polls.

Even today, when I'm trying to think up new TV programmes, I try to break *Coronation Street* down into its basic components to find out exactly why it engages so many millions of people. Then I apply these principles to my shows. Is it so popular because it deals with people the audience identify with? Perhaps it's enjoyable for people to watch the characters having a worse time in life than they themselves are? Is it the wonderfully camp humour that runs through the show? Or maybe it's the superb writing that creates the wonderful drama? Whatever it is, Charlie was a fan, and his love of the show would lead me to think up my first promotional stunt.

One article about how Charlie Parsons adored *Coronation Street* contained the answer. It offered a key piece of information: that Charlie's favourite character in the soap was a middle-aged wheeler-dealer and ladies' man named Mike Baldwin. The character was played by a seasoned actor called Johnny Briggs.

My mind immediately started working on how to use this information and out sprang an idea. I thought it would be fun to write to Johnny Briggs and get him to sign a photo endorsing me for the job. I thought Charlie would be impressed that I'd found out that his favourite character was Mike Baldwin and perhaps he'd be amused that I'd bothered to write off to get a photo from the actor who played him.

Thus began my quest to reach Johnny Briggs. It wasn't easy and I only partially succeeded, but sometimes the partial fulfilment of a goal can still lead to success.

Here's what happened: I drafted a letter to Mr Briggs, asking him to send me a photo with a message for Charlie. I managed to track down the address of the *Coronation Street* studios, but I was concerned my letter would just get lost in the sacks of fan mail I imagined all the cast received. So to be sure, I sent another letter to the Press Office, hoping they'd feel sorry for me and circumvent the usual route.

In the end it took a while to achieve any result, but eventually I received two separate envelopes, each containing the same thing – a standard signed postcard photo of Johnny Briggs, the traditional cards that many actors are given by the show so they can give them to adoring fans. These 'autograph cards' traditionally show a slightly cheesy photo of the actor, and in those days they usually had a separate section at the bottom with a space for the actor's signature.

I was a bit gutted that I hadn't achieved exactly what I'd set out for, but I just had to think laterally to finish the personalized idea to my satisfaction. So I stuck the Mike Baldwin postcard to a sheet of A4 and printed out a speech bubble in which I'd typed some words. I then sent the finished montage to Charlie.

I've managed to find an autograph card on eBay like the one I used back then, so I can show you what I sent all those years ago. Hold your sides and brace yourself for the joke:

Hire Shed - He's right up your 'Street'!

Best Wishes
Johny Burgis

I carefully placed this cracker of a Baldwin joke with all the photocopies I'd made of the microfiche and popped them into a neat little folder. I hoped this collection of paperwork would show the bosses that I was committed to their company in some sort of way, and that I was different to all the other candidates who simply completed the application form. I just wanted them to see I was going the extra mile.

Looking back, the microfiche-postcard folder was simply a way of me screaming, 'HERE'S PROOF THAT I REALLY WANT THE JOB!' In fact, that wording may have been an appropriate label on the envelope itself, but hey, I didn't want to appear *too* desperate! Instead I just labelled it up 'Research On Planet 24' and sent it off to Charlie Parsons.

Then came another agonizing wait. About a week later, I got a call. It was Planet 24 and they wanted me to come to London for an interview. Abso-bloody-lutely brilliant. I was ecstatic.

I nervously travelled up to London in my sober Marks & Spencer suit to the barren industrial wasteland of Docklands. When I was called in for the interview I was taken past a glass door behind which

I spied dozens of staff working in an open-plan hive of activity. I sucked in this brief glimpse – everyone rushed around with such determination and seemed so young, trendy and gorgeous. It looked like a thrilling place to work.

I was interviewed by one of the top guys in the company, a blond Adonis specimen of a man in his mid-twenties named Adam Wood. He took me into a small office on the third floor. As we got out of the lifts, there were numerous huge pictures of celebrities lining the wall. Very 'showbiz' indeed.

We sat down in his office and Adam tried to put me at ease. 'So Sheridan, welcome to Planet Twenty-four.'

'Um . . . please call me "Shed",' I nervously requested, then I quickly blurted out the whole 'Shed' thing – that 'Shed' was my real name as I'd never been called anything else, blah blah blah.

'OK . . . Shed,' he chuckled.

He then went on to say how he'd been impressed with my application. As he did, I was thrilled to spy the proposal containing the microfiches and the Baldwin postcard in front of him on his desk.

Adam was delightfully warm (what a relief!) and proceeded to ask me questions about the application form I'd sent in. He asked me about my recent year working for Disney.

I told him how I'd recently got back from Florida after working as a sixteenth-century gentleman in the Epcot Center theme park, where I sold British goods to Americans who often hadn't considered that anywhere outside the States even existed. We Brits were quite a novelty in our costume of Olde Worlde frilly shirts, short trousers with long (itchy) socks, buckled shoes and of course our very own one-hundred-percent-genuine British accents.

I told Adam that I would often get asked the most astonishing questions by American tourists.

'Oh my gaaad, Sheridan – do you really talk like that?' they'd drawl.

Sometimes I'd cheekily reply with a completely straight face, 'No, Madam, I'm really from Ohio – and Disney has trained me to talk like this.'

I used this line one day on a male tourist who was wearing an oversized Goofy hat. He paused after I'd said it, computing the false information, then seemed to accept its plausibility:

'Gee, that's so awesome! Aren't Disney amayyyzing! They can do anything!'

Quite.

I told Adam that after the best year of my life up to that point, partying hard in Disney World, I had actually bought in to some of the Disney way of thinking. The scope of the wonderful, inspirational ideas the Disney 'imagineers' (short for 'imagination engineers') had put into the theme parks and the attention to detail in the name of entertainment was simply phenomenal.

I had started out very cynical, assuming that the organization was a lucrative money-making operation. But then I began to see first-hand the amazing standard of entertainment on offer and, more powerfully, the effect it had on kids and adults alike. I suddenly reached a very significant conclusion. I reasoned that, if you're going to run a business, then why not run one where you can have fun coming up with new concepts and give others pleasure at the same time? Disney made great films, yes, but I saw much more in my year away: the stunningly huge theme parks, the beautifully lavish parades, the imaginative rides and the educational but also fascinating, engaging themed pavilions. Everything, from the Mickey Mouse shaped butter on the dinner table to the sprawling amusement parks, was done with panache.

With my socialist ideals still reverberating from my Sociology A-level years, it seemed that in the grand scheme of capitalism it wasn't the worst way to go. Even more significantly, my time at Disney World showed me that anything was possible given the starting point of a thought.

I rambled on to Adam about my American adventure, hoping he didn't think I was mentally unhinged. My passion for the core values of Disney was sincere – it totally inspired me to believe anything was possible, especially in the entertainment arena. Even to this day, I still draw strength from Walt Disney's quote: 'If you can dream it, you can do it'.

Call me cheesy, but I truly believe it. (I even included this powerful ethos on a banknote I created when I launched my own currency years later.)

Adam then asked me to explain how I'd put together the programme ideas I'd written about, so I dissected each one, getting rather embarrassed when I had to describe my silicone-breast guessing game, 'True or Falsie?'

I recall that I had to dab my forehead with a handkerchief I carried in my inside pocket because I was so nervous. Apart from that, though, the interview was fairly uneventful and was over incredibly quickly. In half an hour I was out and back on the train to Wales.

In the hours and days that followed, a huge insecurity weighed heavy on my mind. I constantly worried that I'd come across very weakly in the interview and that I'd blown the chance to go to the final round of interviews with the big bosses. I was concerned that, perhaps due to my nerves, I hadn't shown them the best of me, whatever that is. These thoughts hounded me so badly that I decided there was only one thing to do: I had to prepare something else, anything to get the people at Planet 24 to see my passion again, just in case they were wavering about putting me through to the next stage. Once again I started to rack my brains.

The answer came after a chance conversation with a friend. We were out in a pub in Cardiff. It was one of those faux pubs with lots of random objects on the wall like fishing rods and American licence plates, placed there to give the atmosphere of a characterful drinking hole that has been open for years, when in reality it had probably been put together by a corporate interior designer six months ago.

The American licence plates were strangely appropriate, because the friend with me was a guy from the States named Scott, one of the blokes I'd worked with at Disney World. He was over in Wales on a flying visit and decided to look me up. I suppose I should have taken him to a traditional British pub to show him a bit of real 'culture', but he didn't complain. We were happily chatting away over a drink and I mentioned that I was applying for a job sought by many people and that I needed to get noticed.

Scott said that a friend of his had been in a similar situation and apparently had sent a box to the office of a big-shot boss he hoped to work for. When the boss opened the box, loads of balloons floated up, each one bearing a picture of the friend's face. I can't remember how the story ended, but I do remember that my own internal angels started singing again and an inspirational light hit me. I quickly became excited about how this person had thought of another way to challenge the 'normal' rules of applying for a job.

This was a pivotal moment that crystallized my thinking. The thought that there was one common way of doing something, and then another completely novel way, really caught my imagination. It has stuck with me ever since. I didn't quite realize it at the time, but sending the *Coronation Street* photo had been the start of many attempts to get something done by simply doing something unexpected.

So now my mind started firing in a million different directions. What could I do next? I didn't want to repeat the 'balloons in a box' idea – I figured that if I'd heard of it, then maybe the people at Planet 24 had as well. I needed something original.

Over some more drinks we tossed around various ideas and I suppose this was my first 'brainstorm' – a managerial word for what is essentially a positive interchange of thoughts that moves in a direction to solve a certain challenge, or at least that's what it should be. I've been in many brainstorms that were decidedly non-positive, if that's a phrase, but that night I was just excited that the door of possibilities was open. I decided that I too would send something, this time to the guy who had just interviewed me.

My budget was low so I had to think cheap, but I also needed the idea to be highly attention grabbing. I wanted to send the team at Planet 24 a message and to do it in a new and hopefully amusing way.

We chatted for a bit, but couldn't come up with a good idea. Then Scott said something out loud, almost to himself.

'Hmm . . . what could you deliver to them that they'd like?'

That was the spark. I replayed his words in my mind: '. . . what could you deliver . . .' The word 'deliver' leapt out at me. It was the key. My mind instantly leapt from 'deliver' to 'delivery', then to 'pizza delivery'.

Once this trigger had popped into my mind, it stuck fast. Ideas tumbled in at lightning speed.

'I've got it!' I blurted. 'I'm going to send them a pizza!'

'Um – go on,' Scott replied, sounding not entirely convinced.

I quickly explained that I didn't want to send just any pizza. Oh no – I wanted the decision-maker at Planet 24 to receive a hot pizza, ready to eat, with a message on. And I wanted the message written in olives.

Once I'd decided on this goal, I began to take the steps to make it happen. First, the logistics needed to be worked out. I was in Cardiff and the company was in London. So I called Directory Enquiries once again and found the nearest pizza-delivery place to the Planet 24 offices. Next, I called the pizza place and explained what I wanted. It wasn't a call they were used to receiving.

'Hi there. I'm trying to get a job and, uh . . . I want to write a message on a pizza in olives . . . and then please can you deliver it to a company around the corner from you?'

A short pause on the end of the line.

'You want to do what?' the pizza guy said, puzzled.

I repeated my odd request for a pizza greetings card and once the guy realized I was serious, he began helping me. But there was a snag. When I told him the message I wanted, he said it wouldn't fit and that anyway, olives might sink into the cheese, making the message very messy and hard to read.

So, OK, a small challenge to overcome. The pizza man suggested I write the message on the box. 'Hmmm, not bad . . .' I thought. But I needed something with a bit more finesse. I said I'd get back to him.

Thinking cap back on, I decided to follow his advice and use the pizza box as the location for the message. But I wanted a twist. I expanded on the idea that I was going to send this out of the blue, with no real explanation except the message. I thought it had a tiny connection with how a ransom note would arrive. I'd found my inspiration.

The traditional movie image of a ransom note is a piece of paper covered in letters cut from newspapers – the concept being that the villain doesn't then use his handwriting to create the letter and thus leaves fewer clues to connect the criminal with the crime. I decided to create my own ransom note that could be stuck on the pizza box. I rushed over to my parents' magazine rack and began plundering the glossy publications, spreading dozens of papers and magazines over the floor and painstakingly cutting out different letters to make my message. I made swift progress, enjoying putting the oddly differing letters next to each other.

My mum came into the messy room and asked me what I was doing. When I told her I wanted to put a ransom message on the front of a pizza box with the person's name on and another one on the underside of the box lid, she looked at me quizzically for a second, then asked something very perceptive.

'But won't the tomato sauce from the pizza go all over the message and ruin it?'

Well, sometimes my mum is absolutely right. So, once I'd stuck all my letters down on two pieces of card, I walked down to a nearby printing shop and got them both laminated in clear, wipe-clean plastic. Now even the sauciest of sauces couldn't harm those beauties and nothing would stop my messages being read. The two beautifully laminated ransom-note cards looked really neat.

Another quick phone call to the pizza man in London and I was set. I asked him if I could send him a cheque, the laminated cards and some instructions where to stick the cards. He agreed, saying he'd deliver the pizza whenever I wanted. I excitedly packaged up the laminated messages, wrote out the cheque, drew instructions describing where to place each bit of card and then took the full envelope down to the post office where I sent it on its way.

I called the pizza place next day, but they hadn't received my package. I was so impatient for the pizza message to be delivered, completely revved up about this one little stunt. To me it was part of a bigger goal that I just had to reach.

The next morning I called the pizza shop again and discovered that my package had arrived. I decided to have the pizza delivered just before lunch, settling on a time around 12.15 p.m. when it was unlikely the bosses would be out. Only later would I discover that most of them never went out to eat anyway – the hard-working TV executives usually worked through lunch and often dinner too.

I was told that the Italian message meal was to be delivered that day and I waited all afternoon for a phone call from Planet 24. No one rang.

The next day my mind raced. I fretted that perhaps the pizza hadn't been delivered, so I phoned the pizza man again (who by now must have thought I should be committed to a mental asylum), but he confirmed that the pizza had indeed been delivered the day before.

I called the receptionist at Planet 24 who recognized my voice. I asked her if they'd received 'anything'.

'Hi Shed. Yes, we got your pizza. Thanks a lot.'

I scoured the tone of her voice for any hint of enthusiasm, but she was quite matter of fact. I asked her if the powers-that-be had liked it, but she said she didn't know. At least I knew it was there. Then, once more, I waited.

The pizza stunt certainly couldn't have harmed my case because two days later I got a call for the final round of interviews. Superb.

I was so close to my dream job that I could taste it. That just made me all the more anxious. When you want something so badly, it's exhausting. But the adrenalin was also pumping. I knew that I couldn't blow this chance and felt that I had to have some more proof of my passion for this post to take to the next interview. I started compiling a list of new programme feature ideas.

When the day of the interview arrived, I donned my only suit once again and British Rail helped me get to the Planet 24 offices for the big final meeting with the top echelons of the company. I was ushered into a large boardroom this time. Uh-oh.

Sitting at the table was the big cheese himself, Charlie Parsons, plus three of his top people. I was rather star-struck to be in Charlie's presence for the first time. Here in front of me was a man I'd seen in countless photos, obsessed about for hours and idolized from afar as a TV genius. I remember my heart beating like the clappers and that the people in front of me kept laughing whenever I spoke. Afterwards I wondered if they were laughing with me or at me. Perhaps I was just laughably rubbish in the interview. I just couldn't work it out.

During the grilling, one of Charlie's sidekicks asked me if I would accept the position of 'runner' at Planet 24, rather than a position on the Graduate Trainee course. I didn't know it then, but this was a test. At the time, I was really thrown by the question. Frankly, I would have been delighted by any position in the best television company in Britain, but I hesitated before I answered and then remembered all the work and thought I'd put into reaching the goal of a place on the fast-track scheme. Nervously, I spoke.

'I came to get a place on the Graduate Scheme and that's what I'm focused on,' I replied.

The faces in the room didn't give me a clue whether they were pleased with this answer or irritated.

As with my previous meeting at Planet 24, the interview seemed all over quite quickly. As I left the room, I handed Charlie the folder containing my new programme ideas, hoping that at least if I'd mucked up the final interview, they'd know I was still super keen to do the job. The folder was full of bits of script I'd written for *The Big Breakfast*, brand-new items for *The Word* and various formats for new TV shows.

I caught the train back home, sitting there completely dazed. Well, at least I could say that I'd given the job application my best shot over the last three months. I'd invested so much of my mind, body and soul into one goal. I'd been a man possessed.

I didn't dare think about getting turned down for the job – the thought chilled me to the bone.

A few weeks after the final interview, I got a phone call to say I'd landed the role. I was to start as a Graduate Trainee Producer in four months' time. I was ecstatic. All at once, my life seemed to have direction and meaning.

I later found out that over two thousand people had applied for that job. And Charlie later told me that my pizza trick was one of those things that could work both ways – a risky strategy that, luckily, in my case was part of an overall package that got me the job.

Thus began a new chapter in my life. I thrived on working with the voracious ideas-eating monster that is magazine television. It gave me the most incredible schooling in the skill of taking a thought and then making it happen in a structured and, hopefully, entertaining way. This skill would come in very useful after I left. But I loved it so much I stayed there for six years.

'An invention? Get out! . . . You reckon you can think up
something and get it made? Don't make me laugh!
My sides are splitting . . .
who do you think you are – Thomas Edison?
Please! . . . just forget it . . .'

A Champagne In The Arse

Is this a corker of an idea?

The years at Planet 24 passed quickly while I made fast-paced youth television every day. I began to realize the sheer power of 'ideas' and how they could be translated successfully into the real world. However, it was one thing to turn a mere concept on paper into a feature on a TV show, but quite another to turn a thought into something more lasting, more solid.

As a lowly researcher on a youth magazine show, I was constantly being sent package after package of the latest toys, games and novelty goods, their senders all hoping that their product would end up on air and receive some free publicity. This flood of plastic novelty nonsense amused me, sometimes amazed me and then began to inspire me.

I began to wonder whether the skills I was learning at Planet 24 could be transferred to other areas of business. My time working on *The Big Breakfast* gave me a fantastic schooling in the art of transforming a thought into a television programme segment. The way this fast-turnaround, daily morning show was made meant that it ate up ideas very quickly. I wondered whether the process could, in fact, be used for something slightly different. I started to become engrossed with the idea of getting a product made.

My first attempt at trying to turn an idea into a product was to teach me a vital lesson.

The idea, inspired by the king of drinks, champagne, was born when I was lying awake in bed thinking about the year 2000, which at the time was just under three years away. I'd read an article that day about how sales of champagne were going to hit the roof over the millennium and this intrigued me greatly. My immediate reflex was to dream about launching my own brand of millennium champagne to make a quick killing.

I pondered on how you could launch a new champagne that would capture the public's imagination. I reasoned that it would need to offer the customer something more than normal champagne. Most manufacturers rely on brand recognition to sway customers, or on the quality of the bubbly inside, but I was trying to create another reason you'd want to buy one champagne over another.

So I thought, 'What if a certain champagne bottle had an extra feature that made it more attractive than another one?'

Lying in bed, I began to go through the features that currently made up a champagne bottle: the bottle itself, the champagne, the label on the bottle, the foil around the cage bit, the cage, the cork – *the cork*! Eureka! It popped (yes, good gag) into my head: 'Let's make *the cork* different!'

So now my mind began firing again: 'What happens to the cork on a champagne bottle? Well, it flies through the air most of the time . . .'

In my mind's eye, I saw the cork exploding out of the bottle, flying upwards and then falling back down. Ding! An idea appeared: 'What if, on the way down, the cork was slowed by a parachute?!'

And so, praise the god of lame ideas, the concept for 'The Paracork' was born – a champagne cork with a tiny parachute attached so that once the cork was popped it would float down to the ground.

I fantasized that maybe the Paracork could be customized to relate to a specific person. I thought it would be fun if you could order a champagne bottle for someone called Russell so that when the cork was popped the parachute read 'Happy Birthday Russell!'

Immediately, a couple of other cork ideas sprang into my mind, and boy were they tacky: a cork covered in beautiful, twinkling coloured lights that started flashing once the foil and wire cage were removed, and a musical cork that played a tune relevant to a special occasion.

I wanted to protect these ideas, and having heard that you have to get a patent for new ideas in order to stop other people just copying them, I called the Patent Office.

The man on the end of the phone explained that there are a number of stages involved in being granted a patent, plus loads of forms to fill in. He went on to explain that if these forms weren't drafted correctly with the technical wording, then the product wouldn't be adequately protected. I commented that the process seemed rather complex, so the Patent Office guy suggested that I should find a patent attorney to draw up my application.

Out came the Yellow Pages and to my delight I saw that there were three companies near me listed under 'Patent Attorney'. I called one up and arranged a meeting right away. The whole patent arena was new for me and I found it exciting that I was about to meet a professional with such a niche expertise.

The patent attorney was located above a posh women's shoe shop in an old shopping arcade. The man who came out to greet me introduced himself as Mr Eric Barnard. He was around fifty, shorter than me, with a shiny bald head complete with neat bits of hair by his ears. His cuddly build was housed in a well-worn dark brown suit. I instantly liked him.

We sat down in his small, cream office and I described my wondrous cork ideas. Mr Barnard explained that he'd have to draw up the application carefully and that we needed some diagrams as well, ideally technical drawings. He also told me that we'd have to avoid any words in the title of the application that limited the effectiveness of the patent. For example, he said that the word 'cork' shouldn't be used because then it would allow someone to make a stopper for the champagne bottle out of plastic and thus dodge the patent. Mr Barnard suggested the term 'closure member' instead, as that would encompass any material used to seal the champagne. He also said that the word 'bottle' was similarly constraining, so this became 'a pressure vessel'. So my 'champagne cork' ideas suddenly magically transformed into 'closure members for a pressure vessel'. Little details like those really rock my world.

There's something marvellous about working with someone who's very passionate about a business that hitherto you haven't come across. It always makes me chuckle to think that certain people have jobs where they make something really obscure, say rivets, and that this person is an absolute expert in that product. When they were young, did that person know they'd work with rivets? Is there a magazine called *Rivet World*? Who are the innovators in the rivet market? And does the rivet expert go home and talk to their family about rivets? How on earth do you end up working with rivets anyway? There certainly wasn't a career option for it when I was coming up through the system.

But I was more interested in corks than rivets. Armed with the clear goal of working up the patent application for the champagne corks, I forged ahead with rewriting the wording and preparing the drawings for Mr Barnard. Budget was tight, so I bashed out some diagrams on the computer as best I could and put my obsession with ClipArt to good use.

As I'm sure you know, ClipArt is the name for the prefabricated illustrations that were bundled with Microsoft software in the early days of computers. They're now available all over the internet, of course. With the invention of ClipArt, suddenly anyone who couldn't draw could be a designer, because it was easy to incorporate the ready-made diagrams and drawings into a presentation.

Thus, they got used and abused in boring PowerPoint presentations and on home-made posters all over the world. Just in case you're interested, here are my favourite pieces of overused ClipArt:

Coincidentally, when you place them together like this, they make up a tableau of what normally goes on when I meet someone and pitch them my ideas.

I may mock the wonders of ClipArt, but the myriad illustrations available on the internet have helped me enormously many times. My cork application was no exception. With a couple of deft clicks, I suddenly had some great pictures of corks, marvellous parachute diagrams and some delightful musical note images with which to grace my application write-up.

Mr Barnard added the technical specs in his patent-attorney language and I filed off my first patent application. You can see it below.

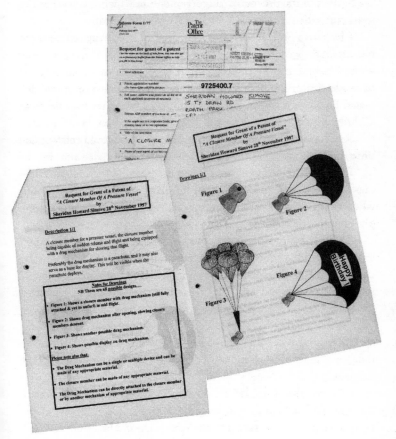

I would deal with the Patent Office again several years later, this time to register the trademark for my brand-new range of rude confectionery, which was part of a huge number of products I came up with for the 'adult' market. I'll tell you all about them in the next chapter. Bet you're excited.

Once I'd lodged the cork applications with the Patent Office, I tackled the next stage of the plan to get the Paracork and the other novelty cork concepts to market. I spent every spare moment I had compiling a huge folder of research all about champagne and sparkling wines. Slowly, I became an expert in the whole production process of bubbly, from the pressing of the grapes to the turning of the bottles, to the process of 'disgorgement' in which the yeast in the sparkling wine is frozen and removed as a solid clump.

I began to realize that the lead time in producing champagne meant that there was little chance I'd get the cork ideas off the ground in time for the millennium. It takes years for champagne to be made, simply the time for the whole *'champenoise'* process to take place. This was a tough realization to swallow, given that the year 2000 had inspired the ideas, but I swiftly moved on, believing that the core concepts could still be something people would enjoy at any time.

Other issues cropped up too. As I researched the champagne market more and more, I began to have nagging doubts about whether my novelty corks were exactly right for an upmarket drink like champagne anyway.

So, as with any journey towards a goal, there was a need to adapt to overcome the challenges. I changed direction slightly, aiming at the cheaper end of the sparkling wine market. A shopping trip to my local Tesco furnished me with a crate of various cheap sparkling wines that sat on my desk, inspiring me.

At that stage, what I really needed was a prototype of one of my cork ideas, but it would require a technical build to produce such a thing, which would cost money. I decided to find some help with the finances.

I figured that I needed a backer who knew the ins and outs of business, plus someone who would also be willing to invest in the project, enabling us to take it to the next stage and hopefully beyond.

So who the hell was I going to get to invest in ideas that were just on paper? Sitting at my desk at *The Big Breakfast* late one night, I drew up a list of criteria for a potential partner: they had to be a business expert and, most importantly, someone I'd like working with. I realized that the process of making a new idea happen is full of stresses and hurdles and so it's vitally important to have someone you get on with so you can face these challenges together and have fun whenever possible.

This brings up one of my fiercest beliefs – that 'work' should be enjoyable. It may seem like an obvious statement, but I feel the need to shout this philosophy from the highest mountains, because sometimes in our culture we forget to let our kids know that it's one of the ultimate prizes in life to reach a position where you can do something you're paid for and also find the activity you're doing exciting, fulfilling and really fun. The concept of 'work' is far too often given negative connotations. Certainly in the UK work is often seen as a necessary evil, an activity getting in the way of life, rather than as a pursuit that can enrich and fulfil. I've spent a lot of my life trying to turn my 'play' – activities I thoroughly enjoy – into 'work', so that the end result will mean I get paid for having fun. If you're fortunate enough to be able to choose what you do (and I realize not everyone can), then shouldn't you choose something that you adore doing? After all, 'work' takes up so much of our time, and we have only a limited time on the planet, so shouldn't we tell our kids to aim to spend it pleasurably?

As well as having to find someone who was a business expert and great to work with, I needed someone who believed in me. The list of people I knew who fulfilled all these requirements was worryingly short.

At the top of the list was a man named Gerry McGuinness. Gerry was very high up in the echelons of Planet 24 – a financial wizard who was the right-hand man of one the founders, Waheed Ali. He'd helped Waheed build the firm up from nothing and now it was worth millions. So it was no surprise that Gerry looked like he'd had a good life so far. He was a short man in his early forties with a little pot belly which he carried well and which had probably come from lots of very fine, very expensive business lunches. He had a round face with a good head of hair, neatly parted at the side and slightly greying round the sides. He had a sort of Santa look about his face, with rosy cheeks and a twinkle in his blue eyes.

Being a lowly researcher at the time, I hadn't had many dealings with Gerry – he was far too high up in the company – but I'd watched him and the rest of the board in awe from afar. I hoped that they had noticed me too.

I'd been working my socks off in the company for a couple of years and it was starting to pay off. The genuine unbridled passion I had for making TV, and especially an ideas-hungry show like *The Big Breakfast*, had meant I was constantly in the office with the rest of the team, trying to make the best programmes possible.

Gerry in particular had always been very kind to me, stopping in the corridor for a brief chat about the latest crackpot segment for the show I was working on, and he seemed genuinely interested in my progress. I hoped that maybe he'd listen to me witter on about my corks.

I found his name on the internal company email and sent him a cryptic message about wanting to show him an idea. Gerry emailed straight back and said I should arrange a meeting with his PA, then pop upstairs to the fourth floor to see him. The fourth floor was where the top brass worked and it had a real buzz about it.

A week later I was in his office – a small but neat room with a view of the water and some industrial cranes. Gerry greeted me warmly. I began my pitch.

'I won't take much of your time Gerry. I'm here to tell you about an idea I've got and I need your help.'

I was pleased to see he looked slightly intrigued. He was smiling, so at least that was a good sign. I then told him briefly how the millennium celebrations had got me thinking about champagne and excitedly described the idea of a cork flying upwards with a parachute popping out of it as it flew through the sky.

'I call this contraption the "Paracork" Gerry,' I said enthusiastically.

Gerry let out a small 'Ha!' It was going well.

With a flourish, I pulled out my lever arch file overflowing with champagne research. I used the tabs on the side to find the patent applications and unclipped them as I spoke. Gerry listened carefully as I told him how I'd filed for the patents and that my aim now was to get his help to make some prototypes so we could get the cork ideas to market. Then I paused. A beat passed.

'Shed, you've come here today . . .' Gerry started. Oh no – was he going to go mad with me for wasting his time? '. . . and you've brought me something really special. I love it!' he said, his eyes wide.

'Oh yeah!' I thought. 'Bullseye!'

We discussed what to do next. Then Gerry said the magic words: 'Yeah, Shed, I'll invest in this project.'

Nervously, I broke the news that we'd need a four-figure sum to enable us to get a good prototype made. Amazingly, that didn't scare him off. We hammered out a deal for our share of any profits from the cork and, hey presto, Gerry was on board.

He agreed to put in the seed money – the most cash anyone had ever invested in me until that point. That was daunting because I didn't want to let him down. But that wasn't all. He also said his brother had contacts in Hong Kong with whom we could liaise for the prototype build.

The meeting had been a joyous success. I left the office on cloud nine. The next part of the story then played out over nearly a year. It took a long while to source the right partner in Hong Kong. We ended up working with a man called Mr K. T. Lam who had a small electronics factory in the fishing district of Kowloon. I'd speak with him at very odd hours of the day (given the time difference between the UK and Hong Kong), trying to convey my vision for the new corks. Mr Lam told me that the first stage was to produce some technical drawings. I sent him my rough ClipArt designs, but what came back pretty much blew them away.

An envelope arrived at my offices one day, addressed to me and covered with Chinese symbols in red ink. That got me very excited. Inside were some beautifully produced drawings illustrating the 'musical cork' idea. You can see them over the page.

Gerry and I met whenever we could, but even though we worked in the same building the meetings were few and far between as we were both incredibly busy. I often had to get a show together for the next day and he was running the finances of a

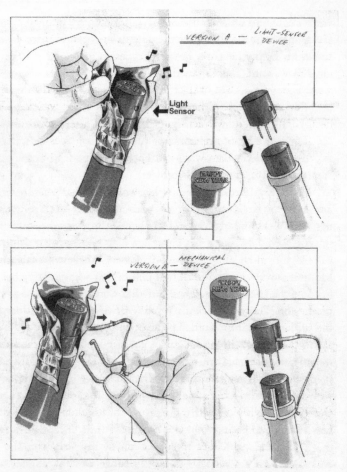

multi-million-pound organization. This meant it was months before we were ready to commission any prototypes.

In our discussions with our Hong Kong technical wizard Mr Lam, it transpired that it would be exceptionally complicated to produce the Paracork itself. Apparently there were just too many variables. How did the parachute know when to deploy? What if the cork didn't go high enough? Would this version be useless if someone popped the champagne indoors? Of course, all these challenges are solvable, it's just that, at the time, we didn't have enough time or resources to tackle the problems doggedly enough.

Undaunted, I decided that we should concentrate on the most tacky (and most promisingly mass market) version of the cork ideas: the musical, flashing cork. I called Mr Lam.

'Hi Mr Lam. Thanks for the drawings – they're great. So now we want to build a version of the musical flashing cork. Is that possible?'

'Sure, no problem!' he replied. The phone line was remarkably clear considering he was across the other side of the world. We chatted for a while about important considerations such as materials and functions until Mr Lam was satisfied he had enough information to start manufacturing a mini cork.

Six weeks later, a brown box not much bigger than a shoebox arrived at my flat. Once again, the Chinese writing on the outside got my heart beating faster. I carefully opened the box. Inside, I found lots of plastic bubble-wrap taped up in a bundle with something deep in the middle. I peeled back the layers, finally revealing a small, but quite lovely, contraption.

I held it in my hands. It was a traditional cork with a solid brown plastic top. The words 'HAPPY NEW YEAR' were carved into the top of the plastic top. A small piece of clear acrylic protruded from a slit in the side of the plastic and a gold ribbon was attached to it. I pulled the plastic tag out with a feeling of great anticipation.

Wonderfully, very tinny music started to play. I immediately recognized it as an electronic version of 'Auld Lang Syne'. What's more, the 'HAPPY NEW YEAR' wording on the top of the plastic attachment started to flash. Wow! Cool! I loved it.

This is the marvellous creation that Mr Lam sent:

The prototype was perfect. It was a simple physical manifestation of the idea. Of course, when we eventually went to market, the extra part of the cork would be much smaller or even built into a plastic cork so it was hardly visible, but for the moment this was a wonderful proof of concept.

I'm rather embarrassed to tell you that my pursuit of the novelty champagne corks pretty much stalled at this point. We discovered that in order to launch in America (a large target market) any 'closure member' had to be approved by the FDA – the Food and Drug Administration – and this is a process that takes years. What we didn't realize then was that there was another solution to the problem that would have circumvented the annoying FDA bureaucracy. It's just frustrating that it was solved by someone else . . .

Some years later, a friend of mine called me up with some interesting news.

'Shed, have you seen the *Daily Mail* today?' she asked.

It certainly wasn't my usual newspaper of choice, so I hadn't.

'No. Why?' I asked, puzzled.

'Look in the centre pages,' she said.

'What? Go on – why?' I countered.

'Just have a look Shed!' and she was gone.

I put the phone down and jumped up. I was working at Channel 4 at the time and my department always had the whole rack of daily newspapers readily available. I grabbed the *Daily Mail* and started flicking through the pages. There on the centre spread, underneath a big headline which read 'NAFFY CHRISTMAS', I was bombarded with dozens of images of various novelty goods. Centre page was a plastic Jesus action figure and top right were some sumo wrestler 'fat suits'. The article was about gloriously tacky presents you could buy for Christmas. As my eyes scanned the page more carefully, they settled on something at the bottom.

Oh. That was it.

There, in all its glory, was a picture of the neck of a champagne bottle, complete with cork. Stuck on to the cork was some kind of attachment that had a parachute on the end. Crikey.

The text next to the photo explained that the product was called the 'Champi Chute' – great name – and that the item simply stuck on to a normal cork. When the champagne was popped the cork would shoot out of the bottle with the Champi Chute attached, then the cork would float to the ground and display the message on the parachute at the same time. Here's the picture that graced the article:

So there it was. Someone had not only had the same idea independently of me, but they had also successfully cracked the problems I'd encountered in order to make the idea work. Impressive.

The powerful lesson this taught me was that even though it may seem that an idea has hit a very high brick wall, there's always a way round the wall. I'd approached the problem of getting my Paracork from the point of view that I needed to make a closure member – either a cork or plastic stopper – with a mechanism already attached. This plan had caused me to encounter the hurdle of needing to get approval from food and drink safety boards. The absolute genius of the Champi Chute was that the contraption was attached to the cork of a shop-bought bottle of champagne. This meant there was no need during manufacture to alter the closure member of the champagne at all. It was an elegantly simple solution to the problem. Ingenious.

I kicked myself for being so shortsighted. Why hadn't I thought of that? Well, to be fair, I had considered an external attachment – in fact, the very first prototype had stuck into the cork with metal prongs. I'd just been blind to the possibility of its working and so ditched that route early on.

Although I was gutted not to have solved the many challenges myself and not to have launched a product, I was actually delighted to see the problem solved at all. The Champi Chute looked like an extremely well-made item. I ordered a couple immediately and vowed to be even more open minded the next time I hit a snag while trying to get something off the ground.

Next up though, some ideas that I did manage to launch . . .

*'Oh, here we go again . . . You still reckon you can try your
hand at designing products do ya? Pah! . . .
but you failed last time!
It takes years at college to be a proper product designer –
and even if your ideas are any good (ha!),
you'll never find someone who likes these concepts . . .
They're just . . . so . . . tacky . . .'*

IDEA 3

Adults Only

Is a rude poem a . . . perverse?

It's incredibly childish I know.

The first 'adult' idea that I came up with spurred a whole slew of related products and it seemed to come from nowhere in particular.

If I were an amateur psychologist, I'd hypothesize that the ideas you're about to hear about come from the primal side of my brain, but maybe that's just an excuse. Perhaps, like all men, I'm just inherently, perpetually juvenile.

After I left Planet 24, I worked at various production companies, developing new shows and producing established ones, like the huge reality franchise *Big Brother*. This work not only provided the much-needed stimulation of having bright minds around me, it also gave me the chance to pursue my personal projects in the periods between contracts.

One day, while I was travelling home on the tube after a day at the BBC creating new television programmes, I had an idea out of the blue. It was an idea for a new range of 'rude' sweets.

I don't know where the inspiration came from. It's certainly unusual to be inspired on the rat-infested, smog-clogged, moving sardine can that is a London Underground train, but I was. Well it has been said that innovation comes from adversity, I suppose.

I'd like you now to imagine a drum-roll, please, before I tell you the idea. Here we go:

It was a sweet range called 'Clitoris Allsorts'.

The joke was a simple one, based on the famous confectionery brand Liquorice Allsorts. With another pun coming into my head came another all-consuming obsession. The idea of making a sweet in the shape of something socially taboo with a rude name ticked all my strange boxes.

Plus, I did actually believe that a line of sweets called Clitoris Allsorts was a commercially viable prospect – I reckoned that some people might find the range mildly amusing and would therefore buy them for their gimmick value, or even for hen nights and parties. I got to work straight away.

The first challenge I tackled was protecting the brand name. The idea was simple and copiable, so I had to try to get as much protection for it as possible. It amused me to think that if I asked the Trademark Office for a trademark for this brand name, then someone in a grey building sitting at a desk under fluorescent lights would have to process my odd request. So that's what I did.

I employed a trademark specialist and filed straight away, hoping to become the extremely proud owner of the words 'Clitoris Allsorts®'. The big aim was to obtain the tiny 'R' in the circle – this denotes a registered trademark rather than the '™' which indicates an unregistered trademark.

While I waited for the bureaucratic process to go through the motions, I turned my attention to designing a prototype for this new type of sweets. I knew at some point I'd have to show my concept to someone working in the adult novelty-gift sector, so I needed something tangible to get them excited. My vision was a classily packaged confectionery range that would be sold in adult shops such as Ann Summers, with the actual sweet resembling the female private parts with an extended appendage at the top, the anatomical embodiment of the brand name.

I designed a logo immediately and coined an appropriate strapline for the range – another play on words. It looked like this:

Clitoris
Allsorts™
The Original Bush Tucker

A couple of months later, I got a phone call from the trademark specialist. The result of the first stage of the application had come back. Bad news.

It was a flat rejection. In the opinion of the Trademark Office, there were two main reasons why I was to be denied the trademark. First, they said the name was 'obscene'. Second, they said that because the product was confectionery, there was a chance that kids could come into contact with it and therefore the name might potentially 'warp' youngsters.

I discussed these points with the trademark specialist, who recommended we write back pointing out that the term 'clitoris' was actually a correct anatomical term, therefore it wasn't technically 'obscene'. We'd also explain that we'd always intended that the sweets would be sold only to over-eighteens in 'adult-only' outlets. I mean, please! Did they really think I'd try to sell them in the local newsagent's next to the Mars Bars?

'I'll have a pint of milk, two Lottery tickets . . . and, oooh – give me a packet of those Clitoris Allsorts please,' says the old lady in the corner shop. Hmm. Not likely.

We sent the letter off to the Trademark Office, hoping that we had addressed the objections that they'd raised so that they would reconsider and grant us the mark.

But they weren't reassured at all. Once again, they rejected the mark on the grounds that it was offensive. Determined not to let the bureaucracy scupper the goal, I deliberated whether to throw good money after bad and pay for a hearing with the Trademark Office. At a trademark hearing, a patent attorney gets to argue the case with a trademark officer in person.

I knew I could fund a hearing by taking advantage of a healthy overdraft facility. The cycle of 'boom' (when I was gainfully employed in the TV industry) then 'bust' (as I pursued my personal passions) was to become a common pattern in my life. To this day, it's a nerveracking situation to be in, never really knowing whether I'll get a job to take me back into the black and pay my mortgage. But I try not to worry about money – I always believe that it will arrive if I follow my passions. My theory is this: if you love doing something, it means you'll most likely become good at it – and people will always pay for someone who's good at what they do.

The whole process of getting the name trademarked was really dragging on. It had already taken months and months, and I was no further forward. However, it was a big decision to carry on, and I deliberated for days. Was I mad spending money on a lame gag? And for a product I hadn't even launched yet?

Well maybe, I concluded. But I wanted to complete this goal. So I paid for my patent attorney to attend a hearing. Later he relayed to me that the meeting hadn't gone well. Apparently, the trademark officer had explained how the Trademark Office had received a huge amount of flak for granting the infamous and inspired FCUK® name. This trademark had brought UK fashion brand French Connection huge global success, allowing them to emblazon the subversive (and thus attractive to the young) slogan all over their garments. Some people deemed the FCUK® slogan offensive: it was clearly an anagram of a rude word. For the very reason that young people liked the idea that they could wear a swear word without it actually being a swear word, some critics found it obscene. A furore ensued and the Trademark Office was blamed as part of the problem because they had granted the trademark and thus, in the critics' eyes, endorsed it.

Therefore the trademark officer was now extremely cautious about granting any trademark that was even slightly contentious. For him, 'Clitoris Allsorts' was certainly not worth the potential aggravation.

Gutted, but still determined to win after nearly a year of trying to get the name protected, I asked the patent expert I worked with what to do next. She said the only option open to us was to file for a European trademark. This would be granted by another department and might stand a better chance of being approved. It was expensive, though.

At this time I hadn't worked for a while and my finances were getting very low. Nevertheless, I again took my usual approach to money and gave the word for the attorney to apply for the European trademark. It would be another six months before I heard anything.

Meanwhile, I powered onwards, deciding to create some actual sweets in the correct shape and get them packaged up beautifully.

I started the challenging process of tracking down suitable companies who might help me get the range off the ground, then cold-called them to see if they would take a meeting with me. This took a lot of time and persistence, but eventually a few did agree to see me.

At every company where I pitched the range, the decision-maker would say the sweets were a funny idea, but they wouldn't be prepared to make them because they were either too rude or too 'niche'. Person after person said, 'They just won't sell, Shed.' After being told this repeatedly, and with no backers to help me turn the idea into reality, I made a swift decision.

Whenever I'm told a thing won't work, something clicks in my brain. I have a really strong emotional response to someone saying 'It can't be done.' It's a mixture of annoyance (that one person can be so absolutely sure that something that's never been tried before definitely won't work), mild amusement (that the person is closing themselves off from learning and having an adventure) and also determination (to prove them wrong).

It's my solid belief that *any* challenge is solvable. Crikey, the human race has put a man on the moon. So anything less ambitious than that, including creating a range of stupid rude sweets, is eminently possible. Whether something works or not simply depends on how you go about it. So, when someone says 'It'll never work!', my mind rejects these words as if they're a virus trying to bore their way in.

If no one was willing to launch the idea, there was only one option. It was up to me to make the sweets on my own.

I took stock. I was able to invest only a tiny amount in this range. I decided on a strategy that would fit with my finances. I planned to manufacture a small batch of Clitoris Allsorts so I could bring the range to life and then use these packets to obtain some concrete orders.

This was my first naive assumption. I *thought* I would be able to get a small batch of confectionery made. It actually ended up being a lot more than tiny.

I began an intensive trawl for manufacturers that took me weeks of research, trying to find a company that could make some jelly fruit gums in the shape of a woman's lower regions. I started with confectionery manufacturers in my home country, but quickly discovered that no UK company could help given my limited budget. The cost was simply way out of my reach.

Undaunted, I then tried the Far East. Harnessing the magic of the internet, I searched for suitable confectionery companies and sent message after message to over fifty firms in a three-month period. Soon I started receiving dozens of emails in broken English from entrepreneurial companies in Hong Kong and China. Unfortunately, many of them refused to produce the small amount I could afford. Even when I did eventually get positive replies from a few companies, once I revealed the specific shape of the sweets I needed, they refused to work with me.

'I am sorry we cannot make this candy. We make fun sweets for children,' one email explained.

Added to this, I kept coming up against the problem that my budget was still too small. Because of the tooling costs of making a new mould for the confectionery and the set-up charges involved in starting a new production line, I was constantly being asked to order thousands of packets of sweets.

I imagined my flat stuffed floor to ceiling with boxes of miniature clitorises. Um . . . no, I didn't want to live in 'Fanny Towers', thanks very much.

Exasperated after another day of phone-bashing and email-writing, I decided to change tack.

During my search for a manufacturer of jelly sweets I'd stumbled across a website selling products called Jelly Boobs and Jelly Willies.

I'd ordered some immediately so I could see how they'd been made. A padded envelope duly popped through my letterbox containing two boxes covered with simple designs. The Jelly Willies box was purple and adorned with a drawing of a funny little character in the shape of a penis with a smiley face. The Jelly Boobs box was red with an illustration of a busty brunette in a red corset. I tore the boxes open hurriedly and found that, true to the packaging, they contained lots of different-coloured fruit-gummy sweets in the rough shape of a willy or a pair of boobs.

When my search for manufacturers for my Clitoris Allsorts was going badly, my attention went back to those colourful boxes on my desk. First off, I emailed the company, Spencer & Fleetwood, and asked them how much it would be to produce some of my own jelly sweets. A nice guy called Chris Lee answered my emails, explaining that he could indeed help make a new range of sweets, but that the cost would be high. Yet again, the budget and amount I was required to produce meant I couldn't proceed.

I stared at my computer screen, let out a deep sigh, and considered whether to abandon this arguably frivolous business idea. Then I pushed the thought of giving up to the back of my mind. I decided I just needed to change my approach again and asked myself an important question:

'Why am I busting my balls trying to make these sweets myself? Perhaps I should start all over again and try harder to find a company that currently makes adult novelty sweets and ask them whether they'd like to license the idea from me ...'

I logged on the net, found Spencer & Fleetwood's number and picked up the phone. I spoke to Chris Lee, the guy whom I'd been emailing, and found out that he was the boss. Straight to the top – excellent! I managed to persuade Chris that I wasn't a complete joker and that he needed to see me. I explained that I'd send a 'confidentiality agreement' for him to sign. (When I first began thinking about showing my ideas to others, I had this one-page contract drawn up by a brilliant lawyer I'd met while working on a TV show. The agreement demonstrates to the people I pitch to that I'm slightly professional and gives me some protection against being ripped off. But asking someone to sign one is often a risk. Some companies have a flat policy of not signing because of the chance that they are developing something similar, which means you can't move forward. Plus, I also think it's like saying to someone 'I don't trust you', which isn't the best sentiment to project at the start of a business relationship. It's a tricky one . . .) Fortunately, Chris said he'd be happy to sign the agreement that I emailed over, so we arranged to meet the following week.

The day came round quickly. I travelled down to Epsom with three ideas to show Chris. The first one was Clitoris Allsorts; the other two were products I'd been working on since I had been inspired by the adult novelty sector.

The first of my two new ideas was the 'Pubik's Cube' – a six-sided square that unfolds with a picture of a different penis on each side.

I spent hours downloading pictures of penises from the internet (not a regular occupation for me), delighting when I found an unusual one like the image of a willy that had been fully tattooed like a black-and-green-striped snake. Ouch, that had to have hurt! I then carefully created a prototype that displayed the penises on a pre-existing cube I'd found in a gift shop. I now had a physical manifestation of the first ever Pubik's Cube in all its glory (or should that be 'gory'?).

My second masterpiece also came from the dark recesses of my sordid mind. While working on the Clitoris Allsorts range, I started brainstorming about other concepts relating to the female privates. (Well, some of us are accountants, some people are architects and some are the brain surgeons that give something back to society. And me? I'm Shed Simove and I like to spend quite a considerable amount of my precious time on this wonderful earth thinking about rude body parts. You just know my parents are so proud.) Inspiration struck me one day when I was thinking about the latest craze in waxing bikini lines. It amazes me how women's hairstyles are now not only confined to their heads. How could I turn this trend of 'shaving your privates' into a novelty item? It was this simple question that caused the brainwave.

I suddenly remembered a toy that I used to love as a child which consisted of a picture of a bald man's face packaged behind a see-through plastic sheet. Inside the plastic sheet was a large amount of minuscule black iron filings that could be moved with a magnetic wand provided with the toy. The idea, of course, was to drag the iron filings on to the man's face and head so that they resembled hair or whiskers. Small pictures around the edge of the packet displayed suggested styles of moustaches, beards and hairstyles. It was a fun, innocent little toy. I was amazed to find it still in production today.

Flash forward twenty years, and there I am sitting at my desk, perverting this symbol of childhood by creating . . . tah-dah . . . the 'Designer Beaver'.

This novelty adult-toy concept was to be an up-to-date version of the magnetic-hair toy whereby the person using the toy has to move the iron filings to create a particular pubic style. I know you're applauding me right now. Thank you.

Using the original toy as a template, I carefully knocked up a crude prototype:

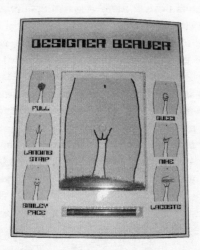

Now I was ready to pitch these two gems, along with the sweet range, to Chris Lee at Spencer & Fleetwood.

I found Chris's offices easily enough. They were in a rather faceless business park in Epsom, just outside London. As I had arrived early, I took the next ten minutes to sit in the car park calming myself down and thinking about the pitch.

When I walked in with my bag of ideas, I was interested to find myself feeling that the offices of Spencer & Fleetwood were surprisingly normal. I must have been subconsciously expecting something else from the premises of one of the biggest sellers of adult novelty goods. Maybe rubber walls or leather ceilings? Whips and chains everywhere perhaps? It certainly wasn't like that. The offices could have been the headquarters of any company, complete with off-white walls, purple carpet squares and polystyrene ceiling tiles. The only rubber in the offices was on the ends of the pencils standing in the traditional black plastic desk tidies plonked next to every computer screen.

I shouldn't have been nervous about the meeting, because when I walked through the door Chris smiled a broad smile and offered his hand in welcome.

'Hi Shed – great to see you,' he said cheerfully.

Chris looked as normal as the offices he worked in. He wasn't some overtly sexual deviant covered in multiple piercings or lewd, brightly coloured tattoos. Instead, he was a tall man in his forties with a slim build and slightly balding head. He wore a plain blue open-necked shirt with slacks and looked a little bit like a jovial middle-aged golfer, I suppose.

I proudly pitched the Designer Beaver, Pubik's Cube and the Clitoris Allsorts to Chris. It was a quick meeting. All three got rejected instantly.

The sick feeling in my gut that happens when I get an idea turned down happened again. But instead of taking it deeply personally and getting upset (as I did at the beginning of my pitching life when someone shot down my ideas), I listened. I've learned that when your ideas are knocked it's not really a personal slight, even though it may be the natural reaction to view it as one. Your ideas are so closely linked to you as a person, that it's very easy to mistake someone saying 'No' to mean 'Your idea is bad, therefore you're not talented in any way and also you've got bad judgement'. This is not often the reality, however. There are a million reasons, both rational and irrational, why someone might reject your idea and these are rarely related to the fact that *you* came up with it or pitched it.

The fact is, often the person you are pitching to knows their business very well and so, even though it hurts being turned down, I try to remember that the person rejecting the ideas often has very valid reasons for doing so. That doesn't mean you have to give up, however. Quite the contrary.

It's good to be dogmatic and focused on a goal; however, it's also useful to listen to any objections to your ideas because often they are valid and, more importantly, frequently they help you make the concept better. But sometimes, when you truly believe in a concept, you you have to stick to your guns and just take it to someone else.

Chris explained that the products were simply far too explicit for the market he sold into. He patiently went through his range, which adorned the meeting room we sat in, showing me many of his products in detail, like the Chocolate Willies, TitBits (biscuits in the shape of boobs) and his completely genius creation Stressticles – a squeezable stress toy in the shape of a pair of testes (wish I'd thought of that one).

Chris said that all these products were just on the safe side of 'saucy'. My eyes were opened even wider when he emphasized that another hugely significant part of a product's being successful for him was the packaging. The Chocolate Willies, for example, had a cartoon penis with a smiley face on the cover. This made the box look like a fun novelty gift rather than an explicit adult product. He'd been selling them like this for over ten years. Chris told me that this approach was vital if the products were to sell in the high street (and the mass market was where serious sales could be made, so this was very important). Unfortunately, he said that my ideas were just too rude for the shelves of high-street stores. I could see that this made sense.

Driving back home, I felt gutted. It's horrible getting ready for a pitch, getting all revved up and then striking out. It's happened to me so many times that you'd think I'd be used to it, but I'm not. Even as I drove home, however, my brain cogs were whirring and seeds of new ideas were beginning to form.

Chris had kindly given me the contact details of a couple of other companies who might appreciate my novelty-product concepts. This was a pretty decent thing to have done, given that they were his rivals. Over the coming days, I spent hours chained to my computer, designing a lot of brand-new products and collating them into a long proposal.

This was one of the periods when I was lucky enough to be able to take a few weeks off between TV jobs. These times are when I pour my energy into my various little dreams. I call them 'the vampire weeks' because of my sleeping patterns, which go something like this. I work through the night when the phone doesn't ring and I can just happily bash away on my computer. During these nights, I often gorge on trash TV packed full of programmes sandwiched between cheaply made adverts for 'Love Albums' and thigh exercisers. Often I feel sleepy at about 7 a.m., then sleep until around 11 that morning before jumping out of bed to attend meetings and work on some TV ideas or prototypes. Maybe I'll have an hour's nap around 6 in the evening, then work right through the evening and early hours, when the cycle starts again. I actually love this schedule; it feels very natural to me. Often when I take a job, it's hard to get back into a traditional 'nine till five' routine where I have to wake up at the time I normally go to bed.

After a particularly intensive vampire week, lots more adult novelty-product concepts proudly shone out from my computer monitor.

I followed up the contacts Chris had given me and managed to persuade one of his rivals to see me. I travelled down to a huge warehouse in Brighton to meet them, my bag bulging with new prototypes jammed together with a twenty-page proposal. The team there said they thought quite a few of the ideas were great and for days afterwards I was elated, thinking I'd cracked my goal of launching an adult novelty product. How wrong I was. The first inkling that something was wrong was when the company didn't return my emails. Boy, that's frustrating.

Then, after I politely pestered them with phone calls, I was eventually told that none of my ideas was suitable. I was completely baffled and, actually, a bit annoyed. It's one thing to be told your ideas aren't right, but quite another to be told straight away that they're great, but then to learn over the phone a week later that in fact they're not actually even worth developing a bit more. This sequence of events happens so often these days that, even though it still brings a sick feeling, I've learned to force myself to keep the faith.

It was time to take the fall, jump back on the horse and get ready for the next opportunity . . . which was about to present itself.

I knew that the adult-entertainment industry was soon to convene for their annual trade fair, called 'Erotica'. This was a great chance to meet new companies and wow them with my 'adult' ideas. I printed up some flyers proclaiming my status as a product designer with a portfolio of adult gifts ready for licence.

By coincidence, my mother decided to come to visit me the weekend of the trade fair. After much thought, I decided to take her along to the Olympia Exhibition Centre for the Erotica fair. I'd never been before and didn't know whether my mother would be offended; she was normally very open-minded and encouraging to me in all my ventures, but would she baulk at a 'sex exhibition'?

We entered the fair and straight away a man dressed head to toe in shiny rubber, complete with a gimp mask, passed right by us. Then we spotted a group of women in French-maid costumes, closely followed by a man trotting along in full horse leathers. In fact, many of the visitors had donned their very own sexy outfits – I'd never seen so many G-strings indoors.

My mum, being my mum, loved it of course. We both marvelled at the decorative stalls with their ornate penis metalwork, the explicit oil paintings, the varied restraints and all manner of dildos.

The fair was rather disappointing from a business point of view, though. I was looking for companies producing adult novelties, but they were very thin on the ground. I didn't use the promotional flyers I'd made or the reams of confidentiality agreements I'd printed up, as there were only three companies there who actually traded in the type of products I was creating. Out of those three, I'd already been to see two before the fair and the third one wouldn't sign a non-disclosure agreement, which meant I didn't pitch to them.

However, there was a real glint of hope amid the rubber-clad bustle of the fair. I visited the Spencer & Fleetwood stand and met Chris Lee. He was rushed off his feet when I arrived, talking business to one person after another. I hovered like a stalker for a while, waiting for an opportunity to reinforce myself in his mind. Luckily, there was a stand nearby selling poles for home pole-dancing and various semi-clad females were trying them out, so I had something to watch while I waited. This sight would normally have been quite sexy, except for the fact that it was happening in a huge, draughty exhibition hall with strip fluorescent lighting and dirty grey carpet tiles on the floor.

Finally my window of opportunity opened. Chris was standing with a lady in a very sober pinstripe suit who was enquiring about his range of candy G-strings. These are beautiful creations made from tiny ring-shaped sweets which Chris told me are hand-stitched together by a roomful of hard-working women in China. Chris handed the lady his business card and I dived in like a whippet.

'Hi Chris – Shed here,' I reminded him. 'Just wanted to say hi.'

'Oh, hi Shed! Good to see you!' Chris was reassuringly welcoming and calm amidst the throng of people milling around his stall.

Time was short, so I began a spiel designed to let him know I still wanted to be in the game if he'd let me. I splurged at the poor man: 'Chris, since our last meeting I've been hard at work making more products. I think some are really up your street and if you'll see me again then—'

'Of course I'd love to see your ideas Shed,' he interrupted. 'I'll sign another confidentiality agreement if you like. Can you send them by email?'

Always believing that personal interaction is way better than a cold electronic message, I tried to get him to meet. 'I can swing by your office if that's OK with you? I'll be quick again!' I explained.

'Sure! No problem Shed. Give me a call and we'll arrange a meeting,' he replied.

'I'm determined to bring something you like Chris! Thanks a lot,' I said with a smile.

He laughed, probably at the fact that this freaky bloke was so dogged, then we shook hands and I left. Great. That went well.

During this time, the legal wranglings with the Trademark Office over my application to trademark the brand name for Clitoris Allsorts were, annoyingly, still going on. They kept rejecting the application. Apparently they felt it was still an offensive word. I can't believe they didn't see the fanny side – I mean the funny side (ha ha). But I wasn't giving up. No way. We sent numerous letters again and again, trying to argue the case, but they were all followed up by yet more rejections.

The issue became all the more important when I learned that another company was planning to launch a range with exactly the same name. It was vital that I had some legal protection if I was going to produce my own Clitoris Allsorts. But I hadn't heard from the European Trademark Office yet, so there was still hope.

Three weeks after the Erotica trade fair, I visited Chris Lee at the Epsom office of Spencer & Fleetwood for the second time. I pitched thirteen new ideas, including one inspired by my mum, of all people. While we were at the trade fair together, browsing at a stand that sold chrome penises, Mum whispered that she had an idea for a new product I could make. 'Here we go!' I thought sceptically. But I was being hasty. Mum had indeed thought of a gem. Once we were outside the stand, she suggested that we create bronze doorknobs in the shape of penises and call them 'Door Nobs'. Ha ha! Awesome! Obviously my gift for awful puns had a genetic basis. The idea really caught my imagination and began sinking into my brain. As we walked through the rest of the conference centre, something niggled me, though. I was very concerned that, although the gag was excellent, the market for penis doorknobs wasn't that huge. I mean, would *you* have a penis doorknob in your home? I certainly wouldn't.

I thought the name and the general idea were great, but I needed a more mass-market product. The answer arrived pretty quickly while I lay in bed that night. Here's the journey my brain took. The name 'Door Nob' is a good gag. Therefore, to work, I needed a product that referred to both doors and nobs (willies). How about a penis that sticks on the door? OK, but why? For what purpose? Well, how about a penis with a message printed on it that you could hang up? It would be a willy-shaped door sign. Hmm, not bad. I was close, but no cigar. There had to be something just a tiny bit cleverer (although 'clever' is all relative when talking about nob gags). Then it came to me: this time I got the cigar, the lighter and the humidor.

From door signs, my brain made the connection to hotel-door signs. I'd just been to Orlando, staying in a lovely hotel in a place called Celebration – a rather freaky town completely built by Disney. It was the culmination of Walt's dream to build a 'perfect' community with white picket fences and safe places for children to play. It's an odd place – there are loads of rules you must adhere to if you live there, like the colour you can paint your house and the need to keep all public places constantly maintained. This had the effect of making the town look brand spanking new even though it was actually years old. It had the eerie feeling of a picture-perfect town film-set, even though people actually lived there permanently.

I stayed in the Celebration Hotel, a lovely colonial-style boutique hotel with whirring leaf fans spinning above your head and huge pot plants dotted everywhere. True to form, while I holidayed there I often slept erratically through the day. On a number of occasions when I took an afternoon kip, I didn't want the maid to clean my room, which naturally meant I employed the traditional hotel 'Do Not Disturb' side of the door-hanger that graced the handle of every room in the hotel. And yes, you've guessed it: this was the answer to my Door Nob conundrum. The Door Nob range would be a set of door-hangers in the shape of a penis proudly displaying messages. In keeping with the shape, I felt these slogans should reflect suitably saucy goings on inside the room.

I immediately wrote all this down at the top of the huge block of notepaper that's lived under my bed for years, faithfully recording many a late-night scheme. I couldn't sleep though. I was so excited at having cracked this lame idea. Even though it was 5.30 in the morning, I jumped out of bed and spent the next hour and a half designing and meticulously cutting out a positively perfect penis-shaped prototype door-hanger. Mesdames et Messieurs, this is what I made – voilà!

The next day I worked up lots more slogans. It struck me while I was beavering away (or should that be penis-ing away?) that all the slogans I came up with were, not unsurprisingly, very male orientated. Well, it just seemed right that a penis would be hung from a man's door. What could I do for women?

Easy. It wasn't a huge leap to go from Door Nobs for men to a female version called . . .

'Door Knockers'.

When I drove back down to Chris's office on a dark winter's afternoon, once again I came prepared with a beautifully printed and bound proposal. But this time the proposal had thirteen ideas in it. All of them were carefully thought through, the result of much brainstorming and chucking out of any concepts I thought were just far too poor or plain unsuitable. Thirteen ideas. I would be over the moon if Chris agreed to take just one of them and get it on the shelves.

I'm ushered into the meetings room, which is packed full of boxes containing candy thongs recently arrived from China, plus some new samples of candy bras, which Chris proudly shows me.

We sit down at a small round glass table and I pitch my ideas swiftly one by one. I open my proposal to page one, proudly presenting the first product concept, a festive item called 'Nut Crackers' – Christmas crackers with shiny gold plastic testicles on. He hates it. Oh dear. (Or perhaps more appropriately, 'Bollocks.')

He also hates the second concept, an idea for a range of underwear printed with the flags of the European Community members and called 'A Thong for Europe'. He's not even convinced when I bring out the thongs I've mocked up, printed with colourful flags and European Union logos. They look great, but he's not buying. I tell him I reckon they'd sell like wildfire around Eurovision time. He remains completely unconvinced. Maybe he's anti-Europe? Yes, that must be it.

Still, two down, eleven to go. I hesitate before pitching the third one, because it's a product I designed specifically to fit in with Chris's product range. I start my spiel . . .

'This product is an "emergency nookie kit", Chris. It's a novelty item designed to be used when you unexpectedly need to get frisky. The packaging is a tin container in the shape of a penis, with a cute

willy character on the front and a red cross printed across his "waist".
Inside this tin willy is a condom, a small bottle of massage oil, some
breath-freshener mints and some chocolates. So, Chris, may I present
to you this emergency nookie kit in the shape of a penis: it's the
. . ."Parame*DICK*".'

I stress the last syllable, 'dick', then I immediately feel like an
idiot for doing so because of course Chris will get the gag. He
hesitates. I flip open my proposal to show the logo I've designed for
the product:

I wait as Chris takes it all in. 'Come on my son . . .,' I think to
myself.

'I like it Shed,' he says. Hurrah!

The rest of the meeting rattles along. Chris rejects the Door
Nobs and the Door Knockers, which he says are too tacky for him.
He rejects idea after idea, mostly because he's either had experience
with something similar or he doesn't think it would sell in his market.

At the end of the pitch, Chris had identified just one product
idea he liked. Even though he liked the Paramedick, he carefully
explained that the route to market would be a long and rocky one.
First, he had to pass any idea by his team. Presuming they didn't put
the kibosh on it at that stage, Chris still had to source the materials,
check the safety of the product, and (crucially) ensure the item could
be made profitably. He said he'd get back to me after Christmas, in
three months' time.

*

During this time, I still burned to launch my rude sweet range, Clitoris Allsorts. All my enquiries about ordering some packets myself had led to nothing, plus I couldn't find a company willing to take on the idea and invest in making them themselves. Now what?

Undeterred, I decided the only way forward was to make this happen on my own. I went back to the internet and enlisted the help of the Hong Kong Trade Council, posting numerous calls for help on their messageboards, which are read daily by many businesses in the Far East. I targeted Hong Kong as I knew that tooling and manufacturing costs were much lower there than in the UK, plus many people spoke great English, making communication a breeze.

A steady trickle of companies responded to my postings. It was pretty exciting to receive emails from company directors thousands of miles away who wanted to help. I sent a detailed proposal to every company who wrote to me, complete with technical dimensions, design drawings and visualizations I'd mocked up on the computer.

Once again, as soon as I explained that I only wanted a small order of one thousand packets, many companies refused to proceed. It seemed it just wasn't worth their while.

Then, one day, just as I was nearing the end of my tether, I received an email from a lady called Clare Li. She worked at a medium-sized Hong Kong company called Leadsky Candy – a Kowloon-based manufacturer of many different confectionery products. My heart did a little leap when I looked at her website and saw that Leadsky made gummy candies of the sort I wanted. But I didn't let myself get too excited as I hadn't sent the full product proposal yet. Many companies had refused to work with me when they'd seen what shape I wanted the candy to be.

Clare emailed me back after receiving the proposal. It was incredibly good news. I hadn't yet told her the small quantity my budget demanded, but she explained that Leadsky could indeed make the sweets in the shape I required. However, she then asked about how many shipping cartons of packets I wanted.

'Boy, is she in for a shock,' I thought.

Holding my breath, I typed out an email requesting a quote for just one thousand bags in three different packet weights – 15g, 50g and 100g. Most confectionery wholesalers deal in huge unit orders, often in the tens of thousands of packets, so to a candy factory my order was tiny.

An email came back giving me a price for three thousand bags, in one thousand of each weight. I couldn't quite believe it.

Although at this stage Clare incorrectly thought that I needed three thousand packets, I was delighted to receive this email for two reasons. First, I felt it was a good sign that Leadsky would make as few as three thousand packets – perhaps they'd make just one thousand. Second, the price quoted was in US dollars, which at that time was a very weak currency compared with the British pound. This was a huge bonus, given that at the time my finances were a little shaky and I was out of work. But I live a very fortunate life, because whenever it looks like I won't be able to afford the next month's rent, something always seems to crop up. This time I got offered a job on the fifth series of the reality-television phenomenon *Big Brother*. Not only was it an awe-inspiring experience being part of one of the biggest shows on TV, but it also allowed me to get back in the black so that I could carry on chasing my dreams.

Newly confident that I could carry on with my crackpot sweet scheme, I wrote back to Clare at Leadsky to explain the quantity of packets of Clitoris Allsorts I wanted: just one thousand bags. I told her that there would be no need for any shipping cartons just yet, but that I really wanted to work with her. As I sent off the email, I was concerned she'd cancel the order because it was too small and all the hours spent finding a company would have been in vain.

I guess Clare must have sensed my sheer desperation and determination to get these sweets made. Slightly reluctantly, she agreed to proceed with the order of one thousand packets, in the hope that I may order more in the future. I told her I couldn't promise a repeat order but that I'd certainly give it my best shot. She seemed fine with that assurance and agreed to proceed. At last, the Clitoris Allsorts range was about to come alive.

Over the next month, I corresponded with Clare on numerous occasions, making sure we got the order exactly right. I kicked off our correspondence by sending her my drawings and visualizations for the design of the sweet.

front
view

side view

When I first called Clare in Hong Kong, it was exciting to put a voice to someone I'd been emailing for over three weeks. My brain seemed to want to create a visual image of her. She had a bright, perky voice, speaking English very well with a strong oriental accent. She sounded as if she was in her late twenties or early thirties, but I couldn't be sure. I found my mind's eye creating an image of a slender woman with a very smiley face and shoulder-length black hair, wearing a blue (for some reason) two-piece work suit. Clare sounded very efficient and hard working, so I imagined her face looking friendly, but no-nonsense at the same time.

It was exciting liaising back and forth with Hong Kong. When I sent an email over, I often had to wait for a reply until the next day; because Hong Kong is eight hours ahead, any message I sent in the day would not be read until the early hours of our morning, the next day in Hong Kong. Sometimes, when I didn't have meetings or a regular job to go to, I would live my vampire life and Clare and I would talk throughout my night, her day. I wondered if she was ever puzzled that I was up at 5 in the morning.

After sorting out the finer points of the deal, one day I asked Clare to send me some illustrations of the candy she was producing for me so I could approve them and then get a final mould made for the first run of Clitoris Allsorts. Her response arrived while I was on a package holiday in Spain. I managed to check my emails in the slightly dilapidated hotel I'd ended up in, paying for the internet per half-hour.

Three days into the holiday, I noticed an email from Leadsky in my inbox, complete with an attachment. I opened it hurriedly, and up popped something amazing. There, in front of me, was a full-colour photo of three differently sized see-through packets filled with a mixture of red, yellow and green fruit candies, and best of all – zip-a-dee-doo-dah – I could clearly see that the sweets inside the packets looked as if they were in the exact shape of my drawings. I couldn't quite believe it. There in front of me were some actual, real-life Clitoris Allsorts.

Now, this development was way beyond what I'd expected. Even though I'd been working well with Clare for weeks, I hadn't actually signed a contract. Incredibly, she had instructed her team to make a mould of my design and run off some actual candies. This was a large investment from their point of view, as no money had changed hands at this point. I was both impressed and delighted. There's something so thrilling about seeing your creation living and breathing in three dimensions. My Clitoris Allsorts had actually come to life.

When I returned from my Spanish trip, I wired Clare some money to send the samples over so I could examine them carefully before I placed my first proper order. I'd never wired money before to a foreign country, but it was pretty easy. I traipsed down to my bank, filled in a few forms, paid through the nose for bank charges this end and the Hong Kong end, and that was that.

Clare sent the samples over by air mail using the postal carrier UPS, which meant I could track the progress of the samples via their website. It's a totally cool experience to watch your shipment being scanned at each point in its journey from Hong Kong to London. This tracking system also gave me information that appealed to my childish sense of humour. I chuckled when I discovered the name of one of the destinations the package of sweets visited en route. It seemed highly appropriate that my candy vaginas left Hong Kong from an airport called 'Chek Lap Kok'.

A week later the samples arrived. They were great. I had in my hand some brand-new sweets. I immediately fired off an email to Clare thanking her for the samples and asking her to put in an order for me. I thought my ambition to break into the rude confectionery business was complete. But the challenges weren't over just yet.

First, I changed the colours of the actual sweets. After showing the samples to a few of my trusted friends, their feedback pointed to the fact that the sweets needed to be pink – a colour more associated with the real-life part of the anatomy in the name of the sweets. So

I chose three shades of pink, created a colour card and sent it over to the factory. A week later I saw photos of the new samples. I could immediately see a problem, seemingly caused by the language barrier and my inability to represent a colour as see-through. The new Clitoris Allsorts were pink, but they were no longer transparent. I quickly emailed Clare to ask her about changing the gummy mixture.

Poor woman. I bet she never thought she'd have this much trouble in her lifetime with mini candy vaginas. On many occasions after I'd spoken with her in the middle of the night I thought to myself how goodnatured and professional she was. It also made me chuckle to think of her going home after a hard day's work to her husband/boyfriend/significant other and him saying, 'How was work dear?' Clare would reply, 'Well darling, this afternoon I created thirty thousand miniature clitorises for an odd man in London . . . And how was your day?'

Eventually, after a few weeks of trying a number of combinations of colouring and gummy mixture, Clare created three distinct translucent pink versions that I was happy with. They were resplendent:

It also seemed there were a few hurdles to overcome with the packaging. The first set of designs I'd sent over didn't cut the mustard, so I had to learn hastily how to use new graphics software to produce a 'cutting guide' – the technical term for the template used on the factory production line for packaging. It was thrilling discovering new terms and processes. Accumulating tiny titbits of knowledge is really fun. I enjoyed looking up the meaning of business terms I hadn't yet encountered, like the day when the phrase 'T/T Transfer' appeared in one of my emails. I Googled 'T/T Transfer' and found out it meant 'telegraphic transfer', an old term that now means the wiring of money from one bank account to another.

Although many complications cropped up to frustrate me, I was learning the sweet-manufacturing business at a rate of knots, which was very exciting. Eventually, with the help of a friendly man who worked in the print shop down the road, I managed to produce the correct template for the packet designs. Complete with colour bars and cut-marks dotted all over it, the cutting guide looked like a work of art to me.

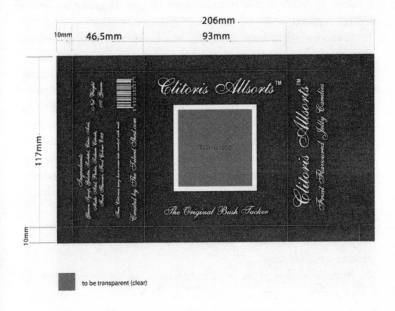

to be transparent (clear)

Just before I sent it to the Far East, I stopped myself, wondering whether to add just one more strapline to the packet. Underneath the words Clitoris Allsorts, so far I'd created the subtitle for the sweets: 'The Original Bush Tucker'. Now I wondered whether to add another line that I'd been deliberating about for weeks. The idea for this new wording came when I was marvelling to myself at how the sweets were a truly international collaboration, with the creator in the UK and the manufacturer in Hong Kong. It therefore seemed rather appropriate to mention this on the back of the sweet packet, with a joke built in for good measure. I scribbled the line I'd come up with on a piece of paper. It read:

CLITORIS ALLSORTS ~
PRODUCE OF MORE THAN ONE
CUNT RY

In the end, I decided not to include it – it was just a bit too rude. The line of decency had to be drawn somewhere.

I proudly sent the finalized cutting guide off to Hong Kong, knowing that soon I'd be the proud owner of one thousand packets of deviant confectionery.

Lots of niggling little stumbling blocks still managed to crop up. First off, the computer files I emailed couldn't be read by the factory in Hong Kong, so we spent days emailing back and forth until finally they could open the cutting guide. Then the bar code on the packet held things up because the factory found that it wouldn't scan properly and I had to explain that it was just there for design purposes.

Finally, Clare helpfully spotted that I'd forgotten to include the 'TM' symbol next to the name of the sweets, so a new printing plate had to be made to compensate for that too. All these tiny things were frustrating, but we got over them one by one and the momentum of the project carried us onward.

It was such a thrill when I eventually saw a photo of the first packet proofs. It took the project to the next step of reality. Things were moving fast now.

Just a week later, I received a cardboard box in the post that contained the final approval packet full of the pink candies. The whole ridiculous concept was right there in my hands and it looked bloody great. It was time to give the order that I'd been waiting to make for so long – to roll forth the production of the first one thousand packets of a brand-new confectionery called Clitoris Allsorts.

I typed out the email confirming to Clare that I wanted to go full steam ahead. This moment held real significance for me. In my little life, getting anything produced from the starting point of a simple thought is the most wonderful thing. It had taken just over a year and a half to get these babies made and I was pretty proud of my small triumph.

During the next few weeks, I'd often think about my sweets being made in the factory in Hong Kong. Somewhere, thousands of miles away, in a place that only existed for me in my imagination, there were hundreds and thousands of tiny little miniature representations of women's genitals being pumped out of a machine on to a production line. I imagined the factory workers on the production line doing the quality control:

'How are the fannies today Janice?'

'All good Bob – another batch of clitorises have just come out, and they look lovely . . .'

Although the workers in Hong Kong were probably not called Janice and Bob.

One month later, a courier arrived at my flat in south-west London. Blow me down, the sweets had arrived. I thanked the delivery bloke profusely, grinning like a deranged idiot as he unloaded seven huge brown boxes.

I immediately tore open a box to find yet more boxes inside, each containing fifty packets of Clitoris Allsorts. There, in front of me, was my creation, finally realized in wondrous three dimensions. The 'idea' that had been just a thought was at last now an actual, touchable reality.

The euphoria subsided after a few hours and I set about thinking what the hell I was going to do with one thousand packets of miniature clitoris sweets.

I decided that I'd use the first run of limited-edition packets in three ways. First, I'd try to persuade a large, well-known company to sell them in its shops. The high-street adult-goods store Ann Summers was at the top of my list. I thought they might appreciate the sweets and believe they might sell well to people with a rude sense of humour, or for hen nights perhaps.

Second, I was going to send quite a few packets out as promotional gifts to people and companies with whom I liked to work. Well, a packet of Clitoris Allsorts is different to a branded mousemat isn't it?

However, these two methods wouldn't dispose of many packets and, more pressingly, certainly wouldn't generate any income to cover the cost of getting them made. I needed a way of selling hundreds of packets quickly.

I hit upon the idea of selling the sweets on eBay and concocted a twist to make them more desirable. I wouldn't just sell them as packets of jelly-gum confectionery. In order to be able to charge more for them, I added the promotional spin that each packet of these sweets was part of a limited-edition series of edible modern art. I'd always been fascinated by the gaudy trinkets and ceramic plates that appear in the Sunday magazines, labelled 'limited editions' in the hope that the simple fact that the number of plates created was 'limited' makes each object more valuable.

I figured that as there genuinely *would* be only one first run of Clitoris Allsorts, I could use this as a feature in their marketing. I posted the advert for my sweets on eBay for the world to see. And then I waited.

Meanwhile, something exciting and unexpected happened that would bring me my very first order.

Three days after the Allsorts arrived, I happened to bump into a TV producer friend I'd worked with in the past. During our chat, I proudly mentioned my new range of confectionery. Her eyes lit up and she immediately suggested that I should send the sweets to a lesbian magazine called *Diva* because of their prominent link to the female form. What's more, a friend of hers was the editor of the magazine. Superb.

I managed to track the editor down, sent her some packets and was delighted when she called me to say that not only would they like to run a feature on the sweets, but that she'd also like to buy fifty packets to sell on the magazine website. Wow!

My first order wasn't exactly huge, but it was a welcome start, especially since the eBay sales weren't going that well – I'd sold only eighteen packets after two weeks.

Meanwhile, I was striking out finding other mainstream outlets. The Ann Summers chain didn't want to sell my sweets. When I contacted them, I found out that they'd been planning to sell their own range of Clitoris Allsorts for over a year. I was proud that I'd managed to get mine out in the world before theirs, though. They eventually released their sweets under a different name – Clit Bits.

I might have struck out with the biggest adult chain in the UK, but their nearest rival, a chain of shops called Harmony, did take an order. After sending a couple of samples to their head buyer, she called me up to place an order of thirty-six. Again, the quantity was small, but this development was another step forward – the range was now being sold in high-street stores.

There was another twist in the story a few weeks later. *Diva* magazine called me up. By then, the issue with the feature about the Clitoris Allsorts had hit the newsstands. Here it is:

BUSH TUCKER
When ordinary chews won't do, reach for a Clitoris Allsort, new from The Talent Shed. More than 50 confectionary companies worldwide refused to make the cute, fruit-flavoured jellies – they're now made in China. Clitoris Allsorts have been thoroughly tested (ok, greedily snaffled) and approved by the *Diva* team. *Clitoris Allsorts are available from www.divadirect.co.uk*

I asked the head buyer how sales were. Good, came the response. Before I could ask if they wanted to order any more packets to sell on the website, he launched into a mini speech: 'Hey, Shed. We want to run a promotion this month . . . and give away a packet of your sweets with every order . . .'

Brilliant! Then I momentarily panicked – a thought flashed through my mind: 'He's not going to ask me to give him some for free is he?'

'. . . so I want to order some more from you . . . but I want a deal,' the buyer said.

Fantastic. My worries were unfounded. This was sounding good.

'How many do you want?' I asked.

'Four hundred,' he replied. I paused for a second, taking the good news in. Crikey. What a result!

We quickly discussed a deal. It was fun batting figures back and forth until we were both happy. I'd managed to land my first substantial order. It got rid of three huge boxes full of sweets that were clogging up my flat. Now I only had another three left.

In the end, getting the first batch of Clitoris Allsorts made cost one-fifth of what I was quoted by British companies. A few months after they'd arrived from Hong Kong, I had managed to sell the whole thousand packets. Even though I didn't make a profit on that first thousand, I ordered another 2,500 packets for the second batch, hoping to make money on those.

Unfortunately, a freak shipping incident involving a metal container that got left in the sun meant that when I opened most of the boxes in the second batch I found a rather shocking sight – all the Clitorises had congealed together. I was totally gutted on discovering this 'clit-astrophe', but there was still something comedic about the whole sorry episode.

Tragically, I hadn't taken out insurance on my confectionery fannies. With the privilege of hindsight, it's easy to think I should have done so. But naturally I didn't think that my shipping container full of gelatine clitorises would be placed next to a super-heated engine or on a blazing hot deck. Would you? So I stood to lose a lot of money through this debacle.

Sitting on the floor of my flat, I spent hours sorting through box after box, trying to salvage any packets that I could sell. Luckily, I managed to find around six hundred pristine packets in the end and sold these off very quickly. This meant I broke even, but learned a hard (and important) lesson about the need for refrigerated shipping containers when importing foodstuffs from abroad.

All in all, though, I count the whole Clitoris Allsorts venture as a huge success. I got my own range of adult confectionery made, garnered media coverage, plus I clearly demonstrated to the companies I was approaching at the time that I was a do-er and not just a dreamer.

Just as I was thinking I was getting nowhere with my other adult novelty-product ideas, a most wonderful bolt from the blue occurred. It was five months since I'd had a lukewarm meeting with Chris Lee from Spencer & Fleetwood. Although Chris had been welcoming and friendly, he'd turned down pretty much my full portfolio of product ideas, which had rather knocked the wind from my sails. But I'd persevered and kept in touch, because he struck me as a decent, professional guy and someone fun to work with.

Then one day, completely out of nowhere, he called me up. After some initial chit-chat, he said something both wonderful and unexpected:

'. . . so I discussed some of your ideas with my team and they really liked one of them.'

'Oh, wow,' I peeped, only half managing to stifle my mixture of surprise and delight.

'Which one is it? The Paramedick?' I guessed. It was after all the idea Chris had liked when I pitched it.

'No Shed, I costed that one out and it's gonna be too expensive,' he said.

'Ah, shame,' I blurted.

'But we do like your other idea – the "Butt Plug",' he countered.

My brain clicked into gear. The Butt Plug was an idea buried deep in the middle of the large portfolio I'd left with Chris. It was my concept for a moulded electric plug shaped like a bare bum, which is called a 'butt' in American slang.

As you may know (my mum didn't), a 'traditional' Butt Plug is the name commonly given to a small plastic sex toy shaped like a miniature traffic cone, designed to be inserted up a person's back passage in the pursuit of pleasure. I traded on the name of this taboo object by playing with the literal meaning of the words.

The first visualization of my new Butt Plug was made by combining a photo of a three-pronged British plug with the image of a plastic novelty bum:

Sometimes, when I have wild flights of fantasy, I imagine that one day my name will appear in *Who's Who*, the much-respected book published yearly listing the movers and shakers in society. Next to the judges, politicians, company heads and medical pioneers, there'll be a small entry that reads something like this:

> **Sheridan Simove** *(b. 1971, Cardiff), Creative Adventurer and inventor of the 'Butt Plug' – groundbreaking novelty electrical socket cover.*

Well, we can all dream.

Even though Chris liked the core idea of the product, there was a problem. Originally I'd designed the Butt Plug to be a functional mains electrical plug in the shape of a pair of buttocks. Chris explained that he'd need to go through elaborate safety procedures before he could produce a mains plug – anything electrical must be certified as safe. This involves the product being awarded a Kitemark, the symbol that indicates to the consumer that the circuitry works properly and won't burst into flames. The process of getting a Kitemark often takes a while and even then there is the chance that the product may fail if it's not made well enough.

This process would be both cost prohibitive and time consuming. So he asked me to come up with a different version of the same idea.

I put the phone down and immediately started brainstorming. I wanted the core joke to work, so the design had to involve a bum-shaped piece of plastic that would plug into a socket. But what product could plug into the mains without being electric?

The answer was staring me in the face. Or at least it was staring me in the side of the face. On the shelf next to my desk was something I'd recently bought on impulse while browsing at the supermarket. It was a plug-in air-freshener.

Eureka!

And so the idea for the Butt Plug plug-in air-freshener was born. The product concept was now developing into a bum-shaped contraption that was pushed into a mains socket. This action would activate the simple internal mechanism, releasing the wonderfully fragrant perfume contained inside.

I drew up the plans for this new version and gave the Butt Plug air-freshener its own strapline: 'The Sweetest Smelling Bum in the Universe'.

Chris loved this new development and said he'd pitch it to his team in the next meeting a month later. The wheels were turning, albeit slowly. But I still had no contract.

A couple of months passed and just when I thought we might have cracked a specific Butt Plug problem, another one swiftly emerged.

Even though a plug-in air-freshener would be easier to make, Chris pointed out that the three-pronged British-style plug configuration was very country specific, meaning that British plug-in air-fresheners would work only in UK sockets. This limited the number of territories the product could be sold in, and definitely ruled out the lucrative American market, as the US have a two-pronged socket. All these objections meant the plug became a less attractive proposition to manufacture from scratch.

The Butt Plug idea was hanging on by a thread, but luckily Chris wasn't deterred. A few weeks later, after much brainstorming, he had cracked the problem. He called me up, excited, to tell me what he was planning.

'Basically, Shed, we knocked it around a bit in the office – loved the concept but wanted to keep it simple . . .' he started.

My brain sparked. I immediately thought about an office boardroom full of grown adults sitting around a huge wooden table, talking seriously about making a plastic arse. Excellent.

'. . . and my moulding guy thought it would be easiest to make a simple piece of rubber shaped like a bum that can be placed over a normal plug,' Chris continued.

This was an ingenious solution to the safety challenge. I thought it was great news. However, Chris hastily explained that there was still a high chance that the Butt Plug would never make it on to the shelves. 'We've got to see if we can get the right factory . . . the silicone may be too expensive to allow us to sell it at a price that customers would accept. And the packaging costs may take the price too high too,' he cautioned.

I thanked Chris for his time, knowing he must have heard the disappointment in my voice. I put the phone down, then played a strange mental game with myself that I often play. It'll probably seem rather odd to you.

When a project that I've been working on for a long time seems as if it won't succeed, I temporarily indulge my demons. I let them persuade me that the success I'm chasing absolutely definitely won't happen. I listen as they cackle in my head: '*Hey, this idea isn't going to work . . . Can't you now realize the idea is rubbish? Silly boy – just give up now . . .*'

Once I've listened to the demons, two things happen in quick succession. First off, I feel better because I'm attracted to what they say. Yes, it would be superb to stop trying and give up now. The realization that I *could* give up makes me feel much better. Giving up would stop me having such downers when things are going badly. It's a strange comfort to know that at any time I could take the option that's always available: do nothing and get a life without downers – certainly an attractive proposition.

Then I quickly realize that I also have the power to make myself *even happier* by succeeding. It'll just involve a bit more trying. So now I see the choice ahead as a 'win-win' situation: if I stop setting myself difficult challenges, then I won't experience the awful feelings of disappointment when they don't work; and if I *do* set myself these goals and never give up, I will absolutely indisputably gain great happiness from succeeding. Both ways hold the promise of my feeling better. Odd logic, eh?

On this occasion, I tried to make myself believe that none of my products was going to happen with Chris. I was preparing for the worst, so I wouldn't feel deflated when I got the confirmation call. This temporary thought strategy also helps me, because it forces me to look for other options. It would be so easy to let months go by hoping that everything will turn out right from one source, all my eggs sitting firmly in one basket, only eventually to find out that the mission had completely hit a dead end, the basket had been dropped, the eggs had broken and that I'd wasted all that time (if you'll allow me to stretch the metaphor to breaking point). Far better to assume that nothing will come of a situation that looks bleak and meanwhile try to make headway elsewhere.

So I did. I went back to the drawing board with a rather heavy heart and tried to find more adult novelty companies who would want to make my concepts. It was a laborious process, not only because there aren't that many in this country, but also because they're scattered all over the place.

Over the next few months, while I tried other avenues, Chris Lee flew to Hong Kong and sourced a factory that could make the plastic bum mould for the Butt Plug. About six weeks in he found one – a medium-sized toy manufacturer with an expert-ise in extruding plastics. Chris immediately commissioned a prototype.

In a strange twist of fate, the factory mistakenly produced the first prototype in a bright pink silicone, even though Chris had asked for the colour to be more of a flesh tone. This was to be a lucky mistake.

When Chris saw the prototype, he instantly loved it.

Even though the factory decided to use a high-grade silicone that was more expensive than the cheap plastic used in most novelty toys, and even though the colour was not what he ordered, Chris thought the bright pink bum was perfect. Packaging designs were swiftly mocked up and the first full prototype was born. Here it is:

Shortly after this conversation, an email arrived that made my heart soar.

It was from Chris and read:

> Dear Shed,
> Sorry for the lack of contact, but I've been really busy since my trip to China.
>
> Butt Plug is a goer! The sample from China in vivid pink silicone looks great. We are finalising the packaging designs and will talk with our artist on Thursday.
>
> We will launch the product this July and start distributing from September.
>
> You can either visit the office to sort out an agreement or I can send you an agreement to sign with sample of piece when I have one to spare!
>
> I'll look forward to hearing from you.
>
> Regards
> Chris Lee

Well, knock me down. Whooo-hooo! When I called Chris to confirm the good news, I was thrilled. We swiftly signed a contract for the licence and six months later the first novelty Butt Plug went on sale.

*

Shortly after this good fortune came some less favourable news. The Clitoris Allsorts trademark ruling from the European Trademark office arrived at last. Since I'd launched the range of sweets a few months earlier, they'd been selling well and I was very keen to get the name officially protected. I'd spent a lot of money in the attempt, and the European Trademark office was the last possible avenue I could explore.

I stared at the letter in front of me. It was a rejection.

My eyes scanned all the way down the page, trying to find out why they'd denied me once more. The reason they gave was as follows: 'The sign making a clear reference to a part of women's genitals is offensive for women and therefore is contrary to accepted principles of morality.'

I instructed my patent attorney to try one final time to appeal for the trademark and, once again, the application failed. Sometimes when you've given something your best shot you have to know when to stop banging your head against a brick wall. During the years I'd tried to get the name Clitoris Allsorts trademarked, I'd spent a considerable sum on lawyers and applications, plus I'd released the sweet range anyway. I didn't strictly need the name officially protected any more, because when a product is out in the public domain it gains some legal protection from the business it builds up.

The sweets had been born into the world and I felt pretty good about that.

However, I still wasn't totally happy about the fact that all these public bodies had deemed my rude sweets unworthy of a trademark.

OFFICE FOR HARMONIZATION IN THE INTERNAL MARKET
(TRADE MARKS AND DESIGNS)

Trade Mark Department

Notice of grounds for refusal of application for a Community trade mark issued under Article 7 of the Regulation and Rule 11(1) of the implementing Regulation

Alicante, 03/06/2005

BROOKES BATCHELLOR

RECEIVED
0 6 JUN 2005

Application N° : 004252821
Your reference : JM/PB/T04285
Trade mark : CLITORIS ALLSORTS
Applicant :

On examination of your application it has been found that the Trade mark applied for is not eligible for registration because it falls under Article 7(1)(f) CTMR to the extent that:

The trade mark applied for consists of the English words CLITORIS ALLSORTS in classes 25, 28, 30.

The expression CLITORIS ALLSORTS applied for consists of *three conjoined* word elements "CLITORIS", "ALL" and "SORTS".

The first word means: "A small erectile part of the female genitals in mammals and some other vertebrates" the second means:" the whole amount, quantity, extent or compass of" and the third means "of different or various kinds" (*The New Shorter Oxford Dictionary*)

The structure of such expression does not diverge from English grammar rules but rather complies with them. Therefore, the relevant consumer will not perceive it as unusual but rather as a meaningful expression: *all kinds of clitoris*.

The sign making a clear reference to a part of women's genitals is offensive for women and therefore is contrary to accepted principles of morality.

Avenida de Europa, 4, E - 03008 Alicante, Spain - ☎ (+34) 965 139 100 - Fax (34) 965 131 344
http://oami.eu.int

And so I engineered a very childish last laugh. I decided to submit a different collection of words altogether to see whether the Trademark Office would approve a brand-new strapline I'd come up with.

I carefully filled in the forms and sent off the application to trademark this new phrase, which read: 'The Trademark Office Has No Sense Of Humour'.

Because I was so clearly having fun with the trademarking process, I thought that this would give the Trademark Office a bit of a challenge. However, I didn't think that they could realistically raise any objections against me having it trademarked – my phrase certainly wasn't used by anyone else and it certainly wasn't morally questionable on any level.

I was ready to fight hard for this one.

A few weeks after I filed, I received a letter saying my application was to be denied because I hadn't filled in the forms correctly. Now this time, because my finances were low, I had decided to file the application myself rather than using my brilliant patent attorney, which meant I didn't have such expertise to help me. It was therefore plausible that I'd made an error filling out the complex forms (there are so many coded categories of business types on the application, it's mind boggling). I was very annoyed that a mistake could halt my chances of getting this one through, so I got straight on the phone and badgered a poor man at the Trademark Office. After a long chat, I managed to discover that I simply needed to change one letter in one box on the form and then send it back so the process could continue. Hmm. Lucky I called.

I made the required change quick as a flash, and had the application back in the post the same day.

Two more weeks went by and another letter arrived.

This one was from a trademark officer who questioned my need for a trademark. It insinuated that I was only filing for a joke and that therefore I'd be denied the mark.

It was my turn to retaliate. I was kind of enjoying this now. I quickly wrote a long letter to this officer explaining why I needed the trademark, stressing the validity of my application. I just told him the truth – that I wanted the trademark for a book (Class 16: Printed Publications) and that part of the book chronicled the trademark process. Therefore, if my writing on the trademarking process was to have any credibility at all, I needed the phrase 'The Trademark Office Has No Sense Of Humour' trademarked.

Again I waited. Surely they couldn't deny me now?

A phone call came the next week. It was from the trademark officer who had written to me. He sounded in his fifties and had a posh accent. He politely introduced himself, then launched into his reason for calling.

'It's about your application for . . .' He paused.

Here we go, I thought. Keep calm.

'. . . "The Trademark Office Has No Sense Of Humour",' he continued.

I tried to detect any waver in his voice that might give away whether he thought this whole scenario was ludicrous. There didn't seem to be any such sign.

'Ah, yes – thanks,' I said.

I deliberately made a huge effort to ensure that my voice sounded even and that my tone was serious too. I was going to play this very straight, because that's what I thought was necessary. I figured that if this man thought I was mucking around, he'd just rip up my application. What was slightly worrying was my realization that I actually didn't know whether I *was* messing around. I wanted the trademark badly – it wasn't just a frivolous jab at the system (although that was part of it, of course). To me it was justice (cue some swelling classical music).

The trademark man carried on. 'Mr Simove, I'm just phoning to check whether you're really serious about getting this phrase trademarked,' he said, half chuckling.

Ah good – a sense of humour.

'Absolutely,' I said strongly. There was no laugh in my voice. 'I need it for a book,' I emphasized, and once more went on to explain the whole reason I needed the phrase trademarked.

After I had finished, the trademark guy thanked me for my time. He seemed satisfied with what I'd said. Sensing he was about to go, I asked if my application could go through now.

'Uh . . . yes,' he said. 'I see no reason why the application would be held up any longer.'

Praise be, that was the last hurdle I encountered.

Remarkably, four months later, I received a letter, stating that my phrase had indeed been granted a trademark.

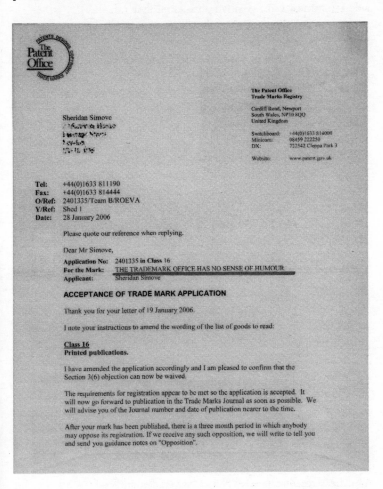

The Patent Office
Trade Marks Registry

Sheridan Simove

Cardiff Road, Newport
South Wales, NP10 8QQ
United Kingdom

Switchboard: +44(0)1633 814000
Minicom: 08459 222250
DX: 722542 Cleppa Park 3

Website: www.patent.gov.uk

Tel: +44(0)1633 811190
Fax: +44(0)1633 814444
O/Ref: 2401335/Team B/ROEVA
Y/Ref: Shed 1
Date: 28 January 2006

Please quote our reference when replying.

Dear Mr Simove,

Application No: 2401335 **in Class** 16
For the Mark: THE TRADEMARK OFFICE HAS NO SENSE OF HUMOUR
Applicant: Sheridan Simove

ACCEPTANCE OF TRADE MARK APPLICATION

Thank you for your letter of 19 January 2006.

I note your instructions to amend the wording of the list of goods to read:

Class 16
Printed publications.

I have amended the application accordingly and I am pleased to confirm that the Section 3(6) objection can now be waived.

The requirements for registration appear to be met so the application is accepted. It will now go forward to publication in the Trade Marks Journal as soon as possible. We will advise you of the Journal number and date of publication nearer to the time.

After your mark has been published, there is a three month period in which anybody may oppose its registration. If we receive any such opposition, we will write to tell you and send you guidance notes on "Opposition".

This now meant two things. First, from then on I was the exceptionally proud owner of this phrase and was able to use it with the Registered Trademark symbol, thus:

The Trademark Office Has No Sense Of Humour®

Secondly (and deliciously), by granting me the trademark the Trademark Office had actually proved that the phrase they'd trademarked was factually incorrect – they definitely could see the funny side sometimes and I greatly appreciated that.

There was just one more lovely twist around the corner that I certainly couldn't have foreseen.

A while after I'd been awarded this trademark, I received a brown A4 envelope in the post. I opened it to find a glossy newsletter-style magazine inside. Not recognizing the publication, I thought maybe it had been sent to me by mistake. The title of the magazine, *ITMA Review*, left me none the wiser. The strapline yielded some answers though: it read 'The Institute of Trade Mark Attorneys'. Ah, so this was the trade magazine for trademark experts . . .

The cogs were starting to move in my brain, trying to make connections to why this had been sent to me, but I still couldn't work it out. I checked the brown envelope for a letter, hoping for some explanation, but there was none. So I started to flick through the magazine, turning over the front page. There were no answers on pages 2 or 3 – just big blocks of text topped by rather unexciting headers like 'Registry Practice Working Group'. My eyes scoured the pages for anything relevant to my trademark adventures, but there was nothing. So I turned to the next page.

The answer I'd been looking for was right in front of me. Page 5 contained something wonderful to behold. My eyes were immediately drawn to a box at the bottom of the page, and there it was: my trademark spelt out in big bold letters:

'THE TRADEMARK OFFICE HAS NO SENSE OF HUMOUR'.

The heading above it explained everything: 'Trade Mark of the Month'.

My name and the trademark details were printed alongside the trademark itself and the whole piece was highlighted by a light grey box.

Trade Mark of the Month

2401335

Page 1 of 1

Trade Marks Journal No. 6622 24 February 2006

2401335 30 August 2005 (16)

THE TRADEMARK OFFICE HAS NO SENSE OF HUMOUR

Printed Publications.

Sheridan Simove, 2 Grosvenor House, Hornsey Street, London SW19 0JN.

Now, this wasn't the Nobel Prize, an Academy Award, or even a BAFTA – but still, I was tickled pink to know that the industry paper had thought that my trademark was interesting (or ridiculous) enough to be made 'Trademark of the Month'. It's a small achievement in the grand expanse of the universe that still makes me smile today.

'*Listen carefully: I'll say it once more –*
you're just not funny . . . get it?
You think you're so cool, so rebellious creating a greetings
card that's slightly edgy . . . and you sent your designs to
LOADS of companies to see if they would make them into
real greetings cards . . .
and what a bloody surprise – no one liked them . . .
So it's obvious you're not cut out for this ambition
either . . .
So drop it – just drop it . . .'

IDEA 4

Card Games

Many Unhappy Returns

It's my fervent belief that if you enjoy coming up with ideas, then it is a passion that you can extend across all areas of life and business. The process of turning ideas into reality is really just one of overcoming a succession of challenges. And we all know that, every day without fail, simply being alive throws up myriad challenges, both large and small. It's what keeps life interesting.

Soon after the success of launching my own adult sweet range, my creative energy seemed to surge. The small-scale triumph of creating the Clitoris Allsorts dramatically opened my eyes to the possibility that getting anything made was eminently do-able.

One day, while buying a greetings card for a mate's birthday, I was browsing through all the cards noting the huge range on offer when it struck me that it would be exciting to see if I could come up with a greetings card and get it in the shops. For me, that would be a total thrill – I could tick Dream No. 89 off the list.

And so, over the next month, I began to visit any greetings card or gift shop I could find, looking on the backs of cards I thought were similar to the type I might be able to create and noting down the details of any publishers. On the way home, I would then begin to think of ideas.

As always, the driving forces in my creative processes were transparently selfish and egotistical. So I thought, 'What would I enjoy buying?' and 'What could I make that could be a little bit shocking, so that the card gets noticed?' Hmm.

The grey matter started to bubble. I always find it quite a buzz when you set your mind a challenge and then just let it sink in for a while. It's wonderful to discover that sometimes simply by thinking about the challenge or even sometimes not consciously thinking about it, solutions pop up. However, there's always a point when you have to say to yourself clearly, 'I need to think of X', because only then will the creative process begin.

The starting point for my greetings card ideas was the same starting point as for all my ideas. I'm sure you feel most privileged that I'm now about to share my innermost secrets with you. Quick, make a note of where you are right now and what you're doing, so you'll be sure to mark this memorable occasion.

Any feelings of excitement you may have at the prospect of learning the secrets of creativity will soon be substituted with feelings of disappointment when you find out how simple my process for coming up with ideas is. It's hardly the secret formula for making a working 'water engine' (and before any oil barons read this and plan to assassinate me: no, I haven't invented one), but anyway, here's the system I frequently use when I'm trying to come up with a new concept:

Shed's blueprint for coming up with an idea

1. Take one bad pun
2. Go for something controversial

These two factors seem to permeate a lot of my creative thoughts. First, puns. Now I'm sure you know what a pun is – playing with the sounds of words in a sentence to produce a phrase that sounds similar but has another meaning. The upshot is usually, in my case anyway, a rather poor joke.

Mostly, puns elicit a slight groan from the person reading or hearing them. Some people say sarcasm is the lowest form of wit, but I'm not sure. Maybe puns are. But they've served me exceptionally well when generating new ideas for both businesses and loved ones, so they can't be so bad.

Personally, I think puns are punbelievably good tools for generating ideas. I've built my whole career on bad puns. Perhaps I have a disease where I can't stop creating puns, I'm not sure. Actually, I do feel a bit punder the weather.

I'll stop now.

I previously thought that my love of wordplay and puns had come from working on *The Big Breakfast*. The crazy anarchy of this 'anything goes' programme allowed us the opportunity constantly to come up with ideas for show segments. And because we weren't allowed to be just downright rude or crude, we had to be slightly more creative with our humour and this often involved wordplay that *alluded* to rudeness. For example, one of the interactive games in the show was called 'Get Your Knobbly Nuts Out' and involved blindfolded celebrities swimming in a huge cereal bowl surrounded by giant nuts, while the viewer directed them to scoop the nuts out with a spoon.

A lot of the items on the show seemed to work with a pun title. 'Who Wants to Win a Mini On Air?' was a quiz where the prize was a Mini car; 'The Gran National' was a race with grannies on motorized scooters; and 'Court with Your Pants Down' was a frenetic tennis game where contestants had to play tennis while putting on underwear.

Because these games proved a hit with viewers, we got into a habit of brainstorming that involved puns as a starting point.

I once came up with a game based on a rubber chicken I found one night in the props cupboard at work. It was a floppy, rather comical plastic animal that just tickled me when I looked at it. The way the head flopped around when it was held upright was just tragic. The thought that there was a factory somewhere in the world actually producing rubber chickens made me wonder. What are the board meetings of the Rubber Chicken Company Incorporated like? Does the CEO talk about the new model C156 with the slightly longer beak?

I took the bendy bird back to my desk. Because I thought it was an amusing object, I decided to create a game for the show around it. Blimey, TV production at its most cerebral.

The chicken stared at me with its rubbery eyes, willing me to come up with a half-decent piece of entertainment. I decided to create a pun to go with the chicken. In fact, as soon as I clapped eyes on it, I couldn't stop myself thinking of chicken-related puns. They just came thick and fast: 'Fowl Play', 'The Big Beak-fest', 'Why Don't You Cluck Off', 'Plucking Great', 'Eggs-travaganza', and so on . . . But none of them sparked me into thinking up a fully worked-out game for the show, so I ditched them. Then, it happened. A chicken pun popped into my head that gave me the answer I was looking for. It was a ready-made game and pun all in one. Within thirty seconds I had ideas for the actual game-play sparking off all over the place in my slightly fevered mind. After writing a few notes down, I walked straight into my boss's office and said, 'I've got a new game for you boss!'

He was used to my random pitches back then, so he just smiled wryly and said, 'Go on then Shed.'

And so off I launched into my pitch.

'OK. In this game, our presenter hangs thirty feet up in the air, dangling from a hot-air balloon. He holds a wicker basket in his hands. He is dressed in a fluffy yellow chicken outfit. On the ground is a huge catapult. This catapult fires rubber chickens high into the air – like these,' I held up my new friend from the props cupboard, '– and a celebrity who appears on the show must fire as many rubber chickens into the basket as they can in one minute. Are you with me so far?'

'Yeahh,' my boss said rather warily. I cracked on.

'Three viewers who have called up must predict how many chickens the celebrity will get in the basket and the viewer with the closest prediction wins a prize. That's it!'

I paused for effect before announcing the title, which you've probably guessed by now. 'So, may I present to you our brand-new competition: "Poultry in Motion".'

What happened next still amuses me, amazes me and makes me realize how lucky I was back then. My boss considered for a second, then asked me a couple of questions about the game-play. He then checked if I'd found out that we could indeed get a hot-air balloon. I told him that I knew a company who'd love to supply one. Well, that was that.

'Great Shed – I love it! Go make it happen.'

Now for me that's the first pretty funny part: that my boss actually agreed to this ludicrous notion. Of course, it was exactly my job to come up with this wondrous nonsense and his job to decide if the viewers would find it entertaining, but it still gives me such a kick just how quickly my game from a bad pun got the thumbs up.

But that's not all – the next bit is even better. What then happened is that I visited all the different parts of the television company to speak with loads of different experts in a completely serious manner about making the new game.

First I popped upstairs to see the super-trendy graphics guys to discuss how I wanted a chicken title sequence made. Then I visited the costuming girl to let her know how I needed the outfits to look. And the poor props lady had to build the catapult and get forty rubber chickens ordered.

Next I designed the cue cards (from which the presenter would read the script), giving them a suitable 'Poultry in Motion' logo. I happened to find one among my stuff when I moved flat a while back, and you can see it below.

Lastly I spoke with some musical composers from another company we worked with, asking them to write me a jingle, plus I then briefed the director, the crew and, of course, the presenter. The presenter at the time was Dermot O'Leary, a good-looking, great chap and complete professional who, to his credit, loved the idea of being suspended higher than a house from a hot-air balloon wearing a chicken suit. What a guy!

The next day I rehearsed my new item. Lucky we did, because we discovered that the catapult fired the chickens far too hard.

Concerned I might kill a presenter with a rubber bird, we swiftly adjusted the catapult so it fired with less vigour. One more rehearsal and then the next day it's on air. Get that! Just *two days* after I had the idea, it's on TV! The jingle played with a jaunty melody and chicken noises, the graphics looked swish, the chickens flew effortlessly, and the whole thing was a roaring (or clucking) success. In just forty-eight hours, a completely ephemeral idea had lived and breathed and hopefully entertained millions of people too (or I wasn't doing my job correctly). How cool is that! And that's why for me at that time in my life it was the best job in the world. Only looking back do I realize how lucky I was then. These days it takes at least eighteen months to get a TV idea on air . . .

Apart from the use of puns, the second common theme that seems to occur in many of my ideas is a search for controversy, edginess, raging against the machine – the need to be naughty, to shock. I think this stems directly from the fact that I've always been someone who loves to question everything.

I have a fervent belief that, as humans, we must always question what we do – surely that's the only way we can become good people (whatever 'good' is) and hopefully act as a progressive force for the world. But, blimey, we're straying into the whole 'Why are we here?' issue and that's a bit deep, so let's get back to being naughty.

I think I get my questioning nature from my mum. She's very clever and quite cynical, with a dry sense of humour. Growing up, I would question everyone and everything around me and it was quite infuriating for my parents and teachers. I would ask (and still do) 'Why is it like that?' on a regular basis. If you ask that sort of question enough, you may find yourself quickly railing against common conventions. I caused a huge fuss for my parents and teachers when I was sixteen. Like many teenagers, I questioned the whole education system that I was being pushed through.

'Why do I have to do A-levels?'.

'Why do I have to go to university?'

These questions are still valid. There are countless examples of people who've chosen another route and are both happy and successful. And yet, though it sticks in my throat, there's no denying my degree helped me get my first job. Ah well.

For me, questioning goes hand in hand with creativity. If you question everything and ask 'Why is it like that?', then sometimes you come up with new and more positive solutions.

As you might have cottoned by now, creativity is a subject I'm fiercely passionate about. I believe we are all creative. It's just that some of us haven't been encouraged to come up with ideas and act on them. Every human on this earth is capable of having a thought then acting upon that thought. And that's creativity in a nutshell for me. It's so incredibly empowering to think 'I want to do X' and to find yourself taking steps towards making it happen, then seeing it happen. You do it every day anyway – hundreds of times a day in fact. Even when you think, 'I'll get up now', or 'I'll eat a sandwich now', you're really doing a very simple version of the creative process which is: Think Then Do.

More specifically, the creative process is: Think of an Idea – Work Out How to Make it Happen – Then Act on Those Steps to Make it Happen.

Ideas creation is just a natural extension of Think Then Do. Making a sandwich or getting up may seem automatic processes, but they both contain the core principles of creation. The thought pops into your head 'I want a sandwich'. You then think (maybe unconsciously), 'How can I get that sandwich', and then . . . you get the sandwich!

I see a massive correlation between completing a simple task and succeeding at a more challenging task – the only difference is the number of steps involved. If you break every action down into steps, it becomes easy.

Here's an example: I will compare 'going to the toilet' with 'becoming a pop star and releasing a number-one record'. I think both involve the same processes (given the music industry's reputation, I could make a cheap gag here about both involving a load of crap, but of course I'm far too classy for that). Here's why the processes are similar: both have an end goal – in one the end goal is getting rid of your stomach contents; in the other it's selling more records than anyone else that week.

Both have a 'starting thought': in one it's 'I want to get rid of my waste matter'; the other is, 'I want to be a number-one-selling pop star'. And this is important: both start with a *thought* – that's all! The seemingly flimsy and yet incredibly powerful mental process of *thought*.

Any person who becomes a top-selling pop star doesn't just become a pop star overnight. At some stage in their life they were most certainly not a pop star. One day, they thought, 'I want to be a pop star.'

It's similar to the scenario that happened in your life earlier today. There was a point where you weren't thinking about visiting the toilet, but then at some stage you did think about it. Once you'd thought of it, you made it happen. You performed the following process: the thought of 'I need the loo'; then the decision 'I'll go to the loo now'; then the subconscious planning for how to get to the toilet. Notice that you can get to the toilet by many slightly different routes – you just have to decide on which one and act on that plan. By doing so, you'll reach the toilet, where you finish the job, as it were. Done.

Being a pop star and going to the toilet aren't such different goals.

As for pop stardom, the thought that triggers the whole process towards success is: 'I want to be a pop star'. This then becomes: 'How can I become a pop star?' Once this question has been asked, some answers will be obvious; some will have to be found out. All the answers will help push you towards your goal. So, the question 'How can I become a pop star?' can be answered with, 'I need to sing' (not even essential these days), 'I need a record company', 'I need a record released', 'I need lots of people to buy my record . . .' By focusing on making these steps happen one by one and then doing them, the end goal will definitely be reached.

OK, let's get back to the greetings cards. Now, here was my challenge: I needed some original ideas for some cards that would get a publisher's attention.

So my personal creative systems started up. Off I went. I was thinking puns . . . I was thinking 'naughty' . . . and luckily lots of ideas popped out, spilling from my mind and into my fingers, which were firmly tapping away at the keyboard of my computer. By the time I'd finished working, I'd produced a range of cards I was proud of.

I sent my masterpieces off to nine companies. All of them rejected the ideas point blank. Here are just a couple of the many rejection slips:

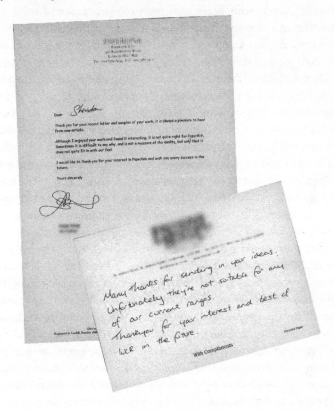

It seemed no one wanted to publish my cards. This blanket rejection hit me hard. Rejection at any time in life is hard to take, especially when someone is saying that something you've done isn't good enough. It's natural to start doubting yourself; everyone does it at some point (and sometimes all the time).

The rejections knocked my confidence so much that I didn't send my greetings card designs out to any more companies. They just sat on my shelf under piles of documents for a long time.

This may be a cliché, but it's always true that if you don't keep trying, you'll never succeed. There's one certainty when you're attempting to reach any goal: you'll definitely fail whenever you quit. And yet I completely understand the urge to give up. Sometimes it's so tiring and hurtful to keep plugging on that stopping just happens naturally. But, at some point, you must risk rejection and try again, otherwise you categorically will not succeed in your goal.

Years after this first stab at breaking into the greetings card business, and having had a few more successes with launching other products (which I'll tell you about soon), a chance discovery inspired me to have another go at getting my own card published. A friend of mine happened to show me a greetings card that she'd just bought for her sister's birthday. It showed an ornately illustrated biblical scene in which a male figure stands resplendent in fine white robes. To his right, a large group of pauper types sit reverentially on the grass gazing up adoringly at the messiah figure. A young boy in the foreground can be clearly seen offering an ornate gold plate, full of food, to the white-robed man, who (via a speech bubble) says, 'Oh, no – mine was the herb-crusted cod with the rocket and parmesan salad . . .'

Not only was this well written but also, because of the religious imagery, it was mildly blasphemous. I immediately thought about how my own contentious card designs were also in this vein. Maybe the team that created the card my friend had bought would appreciate some of my designs. I quickly noted down the name of the company printed on the back of the card: it was called kiss me kwik ltd.

The next morning, I dived on to my computer to use the wondrous swimming pool of knowledge that is the internet, quickly discovering the 'kiss me kwik' website complete with contact details. Isn't that marvellous! I never cease to be thrilled at the ease with which you can find something through the network of computers built by a visionary university lecturer called Tim Berners-Lee.

Pumped with a little shot of adrenalin, I picked up the phone and dialled the number on the screen flickering in front of me. A man answered. I took a punt that he was the 'Simon' detailed on the website as the person to contact. Luckily, he was. I introduced myself and then launched into a frenetic spiel.

'Hi . . . I'm a product designer and saw one of your cards, which I thought was superb – the one with the Jesus figure offering food to the peasants – the herb-crusted cod . . .'

'Ah yes,' Simon said, recognizing his product.

'. . . and I've got some cards that are similar in mood – feeling – and wondered if you'd like to see them perhaps?' I continued.

'OK – yeah, that sounds good,' he replied.

We continued to chat for a few minutes and, as we did, I got a feel for the guy on the other end of the phone. You can always tell so much about someone by speaking to them on the blower. He sounded in his late twenties or early thirties and he had a measured southern England accent – not posh exactly, but I guessed he'd had a middle-class upbringing. I imagined him wearing a crisp white shirt with smart jeans. His voice was bright and friendly, and he spoke with me in a welcoming and encouraging way, so I had a good feeling about Simon.

I put the phone down and immediately fired off an email to him, complete with some card designs I'd scanned in. I wouldn't normally send any work over the internet because I believe it's better to pitch in person and, secondly, I always think that anything you send via computer can be stolen by a fifteen-year-old hacker. But I took a chance.

I sent Simon four designs. Thinking he'd at least consider something religiously contentious (based on the fact that one of his own cards flirted in that area), I sent him two that could be deemed controversial by some people. So, if you're of a sensitive religious nature, please look away now. Otherwise, here are two of them:

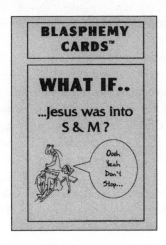

Remarkably, the Jesus card doesn't feature a pun. For me, that's very unusual and quite a welcome change.

The other two cards I emailed over, however, did rely heavily on wordplay. They're both pretty cringeworthy. Here we go:

A few hours after I'd sent these gems off, the icon in the bottom right of my computer screen showed I'd received an email. It was from Simon. It was one line long.

'Shed – thanks for the cards. Love the "Seal" one. Yours, Simon,' it said.

OK. I took the words in. This was a great result. Someone in the business liked one of my designs. Progress at last.

I called Simon up immediately and we arranged to meet two days later so I could show him all my greetings card ideas. At that time, they numbered nine, and I'd already shown him four. Thinking I'd need some more to pitch, I spent the next two nights designing new cards. Spurred on by his positive response to the 'Seal of Approval', I decided to create a whole range of 'Animals You Seldom See', taking advantage of the double meanings of many animal names. In the end I produced sixteen new cards in this range. Here are two:

Ideas Man

The day of the pitch arrived quickly. I drove down to Brighton, my bag bulging with cards printed on very helpful pre-creased greetings-card paper that you can buy from specialist craft stores.

Simon's office was up some stairs in a little warehouse building in a quiet street near Brighton's fashionable shopping district The Lanes. I always love visiting somebody's business – it's so exciting to see what they've built from scratch. Visiting kiss me kwik was no exception. And of course I now had the chance to meet Simon. As he greeted me at the door, I saw a tall, well-toned fellow in his early thirties, with a youthful, smiley face and a shock of short black hair. He wore a printed T-shirt, trendy jeans and designer trainers.

He took me down a short corridor past piles of boxes crammed full of greetings cards ready to be shipped out. His office had a real charm about it. The brickwork on the walls was still showing and this was offset by the requisite Apple Mac in the corner, sitting there like the beautiful computer buddha it is. Dozens of pictures and pieces ripped out of magazines decorated the walls. I immediately recognized it as a richly creative space.

After some polite chat, we got down to business. I slightly nervously brought out my bag of ideas. Ah, the revered bag of ideas!

I trotted out twenty-eight (count them, twenty-eight) lovingly designed cards. Simon was refreshingly candid, although his candour meant that he immediately told me he didn't like a card as soon as he saw it.

I was a bit surprised to realize that, after twenty-seven cards, Simon still only liked one – the Seal joke. All the work on other animal puns had come to nothing. Ah well, I wasn't downhearted. The fact that it looked as if one of the cards would be published was thrilling.

I wearily brought out the twenty-eighth card. This one:

'I like that one,' Simon said. What?! Was I hearing things? I asked him to repeat himself – after twenty-six rejections I had to check I wasn't hearing things.

'Yeah – that's funny,' he confirmed.

Three days later, Simon sent me a contract for the right to publish the two cards. I was happy to read that I'd receive 9 pence for each card that was sold. I wouldn't make my millions from this idea, but I was elated. I was going to get some greetings cards published!

In the end, unfortunately, the Rubbish card never got made. Simon got feedback from his customers that a card with a rubbish bag on the front wouldn't sell, so it was dropped. I wasn't too upset. I'm rather embarrassed to admit that the card doesn't quite work anyway. The double wordplay between 'refuse' meaning 'trash' and 'refuse' meaning 'rebuff or reject' isn't very good because actually these words don't rhyme when you say them out loud. So I wasn't heartbroken to discover that this one had been dropped.

Months later, an envelope dropped through my door. It contained my first-ever published greetings card. And I am very proud to show it to you now:

The seal of approval

Once the Seal card hit the shops, other exciting opportunities started to unfold. I was content with getting a single card on to the shelves, but, just as I've discovered on a number of occasions, once an idea ceases to become just an idea and becomes physically formed, delightful spin-off surprises seem to start happening. And the real bonus is that you don't have to do much more work for this phenomenon to occur.

After the card had been out a few months, I got a call from Simon. He'd already rung once since the card had been released to let me know about a royalty cheque for the first batch sold. Even though

I made just pennies on each card, it all added up to some great extra cash; more than that, I was thrilled by the idea that people had enjoyed the card enough to buy it. When Simon rang again, I instantly thought he was calling to let me know about another cheque.

'Hey, the Seal cards have been selling well you know . . .' he started. Good stuff, I thought. Some people appreciate a bad pun. He continued, '. . . and recently I met this guy who wants to turn some of my cards into video "e-cards" for mobile phones. So how would you feel about your Seal being made into a video card?' he asked.

This was an unexpected bolt from the blue. I'd never thought that an idea for a cardboard card could be turned into something so up to date. But actually once he'd told me about the idea, it seemed a natural progression.

'Yeah, great Sim,' I said excitedly. 'How's it going to work?'

'Well, I'll give them the image from the greetings card plus the joke, then they make a little video clip out of it. People can pay to download it on to their mobile phone – and you'll get a cut of each fee.'

I told Simon I thought it was a great idea and we left it at that. Over the next year, the mobile e-card concept completely left my mind, but I tried to get more cards published with a small amount of success. Simon asked me to write some jokes for pre-existing images from old knitwear catalogues and a few of those got made into greetings cards, and one other card that was based totally on my own design also hit the shelves.

The inspiration for this new card came when I began thinking about how I could capitalize on people buying cards at Christmas. I spooled through all the Christmas associations in my mind and eventually thought of the song 'I'm Dreaming Of A White Christmas', which plays in stores across the world during the festive period. It was only when I made the leap to thinking of the singer of that song – the legendary Bing Crosby – that the answer arrived.

My mind immediately leapt on the similarity between the words 'bing' and 'bling', which at the time had just appeared as a slang word in the media and was becoming more and more common in everyday conversation. The term had come to mean 'showy or ostentatious' and it was frequently used when referring to the huge pieces of jewellery often worn by rap-music stars. The possibilities of mixing the persona of a showy rap star with an old-time classic singer began to stimulate me.

I immediately found an image of Bing Crosby looking suitably sober and conservative, and proceeded to cover his face and smart suit with images of huge pieces of diamond jewellery I'd also tracked down on the net. As an added touch, I changed his eyebrows to look as if he'd shaved them – a style much favoured by the rap community.

After a lot of fiddling, the singer looked like he'd grown up in the Bronx and been on a mad shopping spree at Tiffany's.

And so, Bling Crosby was born. Here's the card that sold that Christmas:

BLING CROSBY

I thought that was the end of my greetings-card adventures, but there was an unexpected twist around the corner.

One day as I was driving to work, I received a text from a friend I hadn't seen for ages. Trying not to crash, I manoeuvred my phone into my palm, pressed a couple of buttons and opened the message. Glancing down, I saw the text was written completely in block capitals, which was the way this particular friend always wrote her texts. It is a curious phenomenon that writing a message in this manner makes it seem as if the words are being shouted. In the unique lyricism of email and texting, the use of capitals to spell words has come to denote emphasis and even force. Thus it always amuses me to get a text written totally in block capitals – as though the person is bellowing the message with a red, angry face, no matter how tame it is. This one read:

> HEY SHERIDAN I WAS IN A
> BAR LAST NIGHT AND
> YOUR GREETINGS CARD
> POPPED UP ON AN AD ON
> MTV, THAT'S FANTASTIC.
> HOPE YOU'RE WELL JO X

Now, as I'm telling you this, it'll be pretty obvious what this was all about. But I didn't make the link at the time. So as soon as I had parked up, I rang Jo to ask her what she'd seen. She explained: 'I looked at the screen and it was your Seal of Approval card on an advert.'

My mind raced. It had been so long since I'd had the conversation about the video e-cards, it took a second or two for the penny to drop.

'Ohhh – I know what it is,' I said. 'Was it for a mobile phone download?'

'Yeah – uhh, I dunno . . . think so,' Jo replied.

Once I was back at my flat, I called Simon and he confirmed that the company he had partnered with had decided to run my card on a TV advert. This was wildly exciting to me and I was desperate to see it. I started recording huge blocks of MTV in the hope that my ad would come on. After a couple of days of random recording, I was speeding through an ad break in the popular show *Pimp My Ride* – and BAM! – there it was. The advert was very colourful and pretty basic. It showed the image of the Seal with light-hearted comedy music over it, then the speech bubble animated on making the Seal say 'You look lovely today', followed by a full-screen punchline page which read 'The seal of approval'. Then some very bad canned laughter kicked in. It was a pretty simple video e-card, but the gag seemed to work perfectly nevertheless.

And so that was how my little greetings card became a (as pretentious media people like to say) 'cross-platform entity'. Not only was the idea a physical card in a high-street shop; it was now a downloadable clip available for people to send to their friends. The same idea was working in two media – paper and video. This further reinforced my belief that if you've got a good idea, then it can often be applied to many business types. So I always try to remind myself that if an idea is ever rejected by one area of business, it may well be welcome in another . . .

'You've been trying to make this kids' craze get off the ground for FOUR years and it's still not happening. Don't you think it's time you gave up? . . .'

IDEA 5

Making Brand-New World-Famous Celebrities

How I tried to create a global phenomenon

The inspiration for the next all-consuming brainwave came from two completely different toy crazes that have performed the incredible feat of capturing the imagination of children across the world in a quite astonishing way. One touched my life more directly than the other.

The idea in question had been bubbling in my subconscious since I was a teenager. It was only after I'd left Planet 24 and been working for a number of years in television that I'd kick-started the exciting process, working on it in the evenings and at weekends.

As a youngster in the 1980s, like many others my age, I got caught up in the 'Cabbage Patch Kid' frenzy. This toy phenomenon was a simple, but clever range of dolls based on the premise that each life-sized, padded-bodied, plastic-faced doll was slightly different from any other doll and therefore marketed as 'unique'. Every single Cabbage Patch Kid doll had vaguely similar cutesy features and a birth certificate. Thus, as a child, you could adopt something that was a one-of-a-kind and it could be yours alone – a highly attractive proposition to a child. News reports even featured spoof Cabbage Patch Kid nurseries that the manufacturer had mocked up, complete with fields of little heads surrounded by cabbage leaves poking out of the ground, as if growing from the soil of a real-life cabbage patch. The dolls sold in their millions around the world.

While this range gobbled up parents' money everywhere, someone at a trading card and sticker company called Topps had the bright idea of releasing a range of collectible stickers that playfully spoofed the Cabbage Patch Kid brand. Topps created a set of characters under the banner Garbage Pail Kids, the joke being that instead of a cabbage patch, all these kids were born from a rubbish bin. The title set the tone for the subversive nature of the stickers. Instead of adorable dolls, each sticker showed a named character with the recognizable chubby features of a Cabbage Patch Kid, but something awful had happened to that doll. One sticker from the first series showed a little doll with his finger on a button and a huge nuclear explosion bursting from his head. His name: ADAM BOMB.

The whole series followed this formula of a punning name linked with a quirky illustration for each odd character. Sometimes the character visualizations were quite grotesque, like FLAT PAT, who was shown lying on the road, stone dead, having been recently run over by a steamroller. ELECTRIC BILL was shown being shocked on an electric chair, his head and body clamped in and his back arching as the voltage flowed through him. And these cards were aimed at youngsters!

The fact that the stickers were fairly graphic in content made them merchandise that teachers and parents wouldn't immediately approve of. In turn, the fact that adults didn't like them made them even more attractive to kids, who swapped them with fervour as they tried to collect the whole set. This sticker craze swept the world and engaged me as a kid too.

It was particularly interesting that the Garbage Pail Kids series appealed to both boys and girls, compared with some other sticker ranges – say soccer-star collections. This meant that the possible market for the series was instantly doubled. Millions upon millions of packets of the cards flew off the shelves in over seventy-two countries. Remarkably, Garbage Pail Kids sticker cards are still selling today, a new series being released every couple of years.

In the late 1990s, when I was much older, another hugely successful collectible card collection also caught my interest. I watched the 'Pokémon' phenomenon with utter fascination and deep admiration. It had begun when a clever chap in Japan created a set of fantasy characters that each had its own distinct personality and special powers. Children around the globe were enraptured with this well-thought-through fantasy world. It spawned a huge industry, with the brand extending to cartoons, a feature-length movie, toys, computer games, lunchboxes, socks and quite possibly a Pokémon-branded colostomy bag.

The success stories of the Garbage Pail Kids sticker collection and the Pokémon trading cards rattled around in my mind for years.

At first, I deeply admired them. Then I analysed them. Then I became obsessed with them. What made them successful? Could I produce something even half as good?

The challenge of creating a collectible craze for kids really got me going. Not least because it was a huge task. Young people (I'm talking about those aged seven to eleven) are difficult to entertain because an idea can't be marketed successfully to them if it isn't inherently interesting to them. In some ways they are the harshest audience – very honest and demanding. They also appreciate layers of meaning.

Once I'd let these sticker and trading-card ranges sink into my brain and teased out some of the reasons for their success, I was ready (and extremely determined) to think up a brand-new range of my own. My internal brainstorm started with identifying the characteristics I believed a trading-card or sticker series needed. Then I addressed those needs. The thoughts came like this:

- I need a set of engaging characters.
- The range must be topical in some way.
- The characters must be colourful and well drawn.
- They must be comical.
- I want the range to look grotesque.
- It would be a bonus if the range was slightly subversive or naughty.

The answer eventually arrived when I tackled the second requirement in the list. I wanted a 'topical' range that referred to something going on in the world that kids would know and care about. I made a list of the media phenomena occurring around the world that were rich enough to be spoofed. It was a short list.

First, I came up with the idea of spoofing Pokémon and calling the new range 'Jokémon', slightly perverting each character in the real series to produce brand-new quirky creatures. So, for example, the original main character Pikachu, a cute yellow mouse-type creature, became Pick & Chew, a cute yellow mouse-like animal bearing an uncanny resemblance to the original, who would be shown picking his nose and eating the gooey green bogey coming out of his nostril. Get it? I was sure that a funny character eating snot would amuse kids and repulse parents in equal measure – exactly the tone I was seeking.

Quite apart from the possible legal copyright infringements of 'Jokémon', however, I felt the idea was pretty weak, plus I was faced with the stark realization that I'd actually missed the boat on the whole Pokémon phenomenon anyway. The global craze for this card range was starting to wane around the time I came up with my idea and that would have greatly weakened the impact of my spoof. So I wrote up a huge list of 'Jokémon' characters and then changed the name of the card collection to 'Pukémon' – a reference to the sickening look I wanted the visuals to have. I spent hours on a proposal, complete with a cool 'Pukémon' logo mimicking the real one.

I ditched this range pretty quickly though. A new card collection just wasn't going to work unless the subject matter it was spoofing was firmly in the public consciousness.

Luckily, the next idea was much better. It took months to arrive in my mind, but thankfully it did. During those weeks, I was kept busy rewriting a game show called *Distraction* for Channel 4, but at the weekends I focused on the second requirement for a successful card collection – topicality. I kept asking myself the same question. What is the current thing a lot of the world is obsessed with?

I needed a subject that kids would know well enough that, when it was spoofed, they'd understand the joke. Then it hit me. The answer was the global (and rather abstract) phenomenon of 'celebrity'. Quite apart from the fact that I worked in the television business, an industry that created and revered celebrities, the concepts of 'fame' and especially famous stars are something many people around the world seem to be very interested in. The emergence of whole racks of magazines devoted solely to the lives of celebrities, the amount of space given over to them in the newspapers, and the fact that these days you can become a celebrity by appearing on a reality show convinced me that this was an area ripe to explore.

Celebrities are worshipped by many people all over the globe as aspirational figures, and their success and fame seem to be something that society deems worthy. It doesn't always matter if a certain famous person has done anything of worth. Being 'famous for being famous' seems to be acceptable, and, in fact, desirable. This bundle of contradictions attracted me greatly. I also felt that the children I was aiming to entertain with my new range were sufficiently immersed in the media world to appreciate the celebrity arena I was going to play with. How many ten-year-olds have a picture of someone famous on their wall?

I set out to poke some fun at the alluring, yet often shallow, world of fame. Immediately I knew what to do. I was going to create a set of brand-new characters that were quirky, odd and sometimes hideously mutated 'stars' that kids would find funny. Each character would have a punning name that referred to the visual predicament they found themselves in. These creatures were 'celebrities from hell', and so I called the range . . . 'HELLEBRITIES'.

I immediately worked on a logo, choosing a suitably fiery typeface for the lettering and then honing the design until it had the impact I was looking for. This is what I came up with:

HELLEBRITIES™

Once I finished the logo, I became even more fired up about the possibilities for this new collectible card collection. There's something wonderful about giving an idea an identity. Once there's something down on paper (or even just on a computer screen), the idea immediately comes to life and a powerful momentum begins.

Hugely enthused, I swiftly drew up a list of characters for the collection, complete with their accompanying traits and detailed imaginings for how they'd look. Then I excitedly dived on the phone to contact a fantastic artist called Bill Greenhead with whom I'd worked on *The Big Breakfast*. Curiously, even though Bill had drawn many fantastic caricatures of football players and other well-known public figures for me over the years, I'd never actually met him. We'd always speak over the phone and he'd either send the drawings by post (before the days of the internet) or more recently by email.

Even though Bill was very busy creating packaging designs for a major supermarket chain, he kindly agreed to illustrate six prototype cards for a rate that was just within my budget. I desperately needed these first characters as fully drawn visuals so I could get on with the business of selling the range.

I'm a demanding and fussy art director, so poor Bill had to put up with many changes from me. Some characters took over sixteen draft drawings before I signed them off. It's lucky then that Bill is a patient and good-natured man, as well as being a super-talented artist. Five months later, these are the first six Hellebrities we produced:

Britney Speared

David Peck'Em

George Cloney

Pee Diddy

I was over the moon with these new characters. They had exactly the look and feel I believed young people might enjoy. I'd compiled a detailed list of over one hundred characters ready to be illustrated, but had no budget to pay for them to be drawn and certainly none to get them printed, shipped and distributed to any outlets. I had to try to find a company who would invest in the idea. Given the high calibre of the first six character visualizations, I thought this would be relatively easy. How wrong I was . . .

Now then, I'm about to do something that feels incredibly odd. Before your very eyes, I will compress a prolonged period of time into just a couple of lines in a book. Here goes:

I went from company to company for *four years* with the Hellebrities range and everyone rejected it.

Oh, woe is me that so many years can be summed up in just one sentence.

Over those four years, I earned a living by working at various television production companies, either producing programmes or trying to create new ones. Even though I loved this stimulating work, I constantly yearned for success in some small way in my own right. And I never lost hope that the Hellebrities range could be an idea that younger people might enjoy.

So every time I had a gap between jobs, I would travel up and down the country with glossy proposals trying to get the Hellebrities off the ground, each time spending hours making documents that were personal to the decision-maker I was meeting. It was excruciatingly frustrating to keep being knocked back. As with all my ideas, I was well aware that I wasn't creating something that was going to push mankind forward in any way, but I deeply believed that the thought processes that had led to the creation of the range meant it was built on a precedent of success. Moreover, I was convinced that its core entertainment value would appeal to young people. So I just kept ploughing on.

My first goal was to sell the idea to Topps, the company who created the original Garbage Pail Kids range in the 1980s. It took numerous phone calls to get anyone to return mine, and when I eventually did make contact, the next step was a meeting at their headquarters in Milton Keynes. As I excitedly pitched the Hellebrities range all those years ago, little did I know that I'd be visiting the Topps offices on numerous occasions in the years to come. Even though Topps kept telling me they loved the range, there was always a sticking point that kept rearing its head. The problem was that Topps had long-standing license agreements linked to celebrities and they worried that launching the Hellebrities range would put these deals at risk.

My dealings with Topps fell into a familiar cycle: every six months I'd contact the head sales guy and we'd meet in Milton Keynes or London and he'd say how he loved the idea. After each meeting I'd chase him up for weeks and get the news that Topps loved the range but weren't quite ready to go with the idea. Then six months later, I'd call up or email him and he'd invite me for another meeting.

I even tried to change my strategy after a couple of years, at one point asking Topps to go halves with me on the start-up (I believed I could raise the money from somewhere) but all the meetings came to nothing. It was all a touch odd and hugely tiring.

What I didn't realise then, was that years later Topps would be involved in a venture that would rock my Hellebrities dreams.

Throughout these four years, I jumped at any possible opportunity to get the trading card series off the ground. One day, an email arrived from a company specializing in children's marketing called Kids Industries. The email had been sent to me because I was a member of PACT – an organization comprising many British television production companies. The email had nothing to do with trading cards; it simply promoted the company as experts in kid-based marketing. Clutching at straws, I thought it might be worth a try to get them on my side.

I contacted the managing director of the company and managed to persuade him to meet me. His diary was so full that he could only pencil me in two months later. On the day of the meeting, I called ahead to confirm he was still all right to meet that afternoon. Lucky I did call. The woman I spoke with told me that the MD had recently left the company. Marvellous.

I envisaged another dead end. But luckily the lady on the phone, who introduced herself as Miranda, said she'd still be willing to see me if I wanted. I eagerly agreed and that afternoon I arrived at the offices of Kids Industries Ltd in Old Street, London. I pressed the button on the door.

'Hi, it's Shed here – here to meet Miranda.'

'Hi Shed, come in. We're downstairs,' a lady's voice replied.

They buzzed me in and I skipped down the cast-iron spiral stairs to a basement office that was more like a toy shop than a corporate workplace. It looked like those cool American internet companies or trendy advertising agencies you see in magazines. The floor was littered with toy cars, action figures and colourful lunchboxes. A high shelf running round the large open-plan room displayed more goodies.

Miranda greeted me with a warm smile and I could tell right away we'd get on. She was in her early thirties, with brown shoulder-length hair, sparkly eyes and a cheeky smile. She bounded around with huge energy and it struck me that, although she greeted me in a professional manner, there was definitely the air of a big kid about her, something I could immediately relate to.

We sat down at a table covered with children's crayons. I spilled out all my product ideas, plucking prototype after prototype out of my bag. I always feel a bit like a travelling salesman when this happens. 'Roll Up! Roll Up! Come see my magnificent marvellous tacky goods!'

Miranda was exceptionally positive about all the ideas I showed her. That was rare enough, but when I brought out the Hellebrities document, complete with the sample cards, she excitedly called her colleagues over to have a look. That was a good sign. She explained to me that, coincidentally and amazingly, Kids Industries were currently working with Panini, one of the biggest distributors of trading-card stickers in the world (and fierce rivals to Topps. Now, I'd been trying to persuade Panini to take the cards for over a year, with no luck. I hoped the clout of a specialized marketing company like Kids Industries could change all that. Miranda said that if her boss, a guy named Gary Pope, liked the range, then their team could put together a business case for why the Hellebrities would be a success. This, of course, would be a crucial step forward.

This step is often crucial in any attempt to launch something new. This is because people who come up with new ideas (me included) often only come up with ideas that they personally enjoy creating and that they *believe* some other people may enjoy buying. I try to have an internal filter that weeds out all the rubbish ideas I have and lets me know when I've thought of something that could have commercial viability. However, it's one thing to think your idea might sell, but it's quite another to have the facts and figures to show why it *will* sell. If you can *prove* to someone you're pitching to that the market is ripe, that the consumers want the idea and that it'll be profitable, then, unsurprisingly, the concept quickly becomes much more attractive to the people whose jobs and money are on the line. So I relished this collaboration.

The meeting ended with Miranda saying she'd ask her boss Gary to call me. I left her toyshop office excited – but not too excited, as I'd been excited and let down lots of times before.

A couple of weeks later I called Gary. He had a strong, slightly gruff voice with the tinge of a South London accent. I imagined him as a sharp-suited wheeler-dealer. We got on straight away. We chatted about ourselves for a bit and Gary told me he loved the Hellebrities range.

'If Panini don't like it, Shed, we'll take it elsewhere,' he said enthusiastically.

Hallelujah. At last, some great people were on my side.

'I'm meeting Panini next week. Send me over all your artwork, we'll prepare a business case and I'll let you know what they think.'

We hammered out a deal that was acceptable to both of us and I put the phone down, delighted that I'd met some experts who were not only fun to work with but also respected in the industry. Maybe this was the key signing I desperately needed to get the product to market. I dearly, dearly hoped so.

Gary called a month later to say that he'd liaised with the UK boss of Panini and had already held a very positive meeting about the Hellebrities range. The boss told Gary that he liked it, but explained he'd have to pitch it to the company directors in Italy the following month before they could move forward with the project.

Knowing that the Italian meeting was pivotal, we decided to prepare fully so we'd have the best chance possible to impress the decision-makers. We went into overdrive, producing huge mock-ups of each trading card, lots of realistic-sized samples and a detailed business presentation describing the reasons why the range would work.

The meeting date came and went. I waited with bated breath for any news. As far as I was concerned, this was my final chance to find a partner willing to manufacture and distribute the collectible card series.

All our work was in vain. Gary sent me an email the next month that he'd forwarded from the Panini guy.

Hurriedly reading it, I learnt that our contact at Panini had discussed the Hellebrities range in detail at their last publishers' meeting and that even though everyone present could see how Hellebrities would hold an attraction for kids, Panini felt they had to pass on the range because it could potentially damage their relationship with current partners and also 'jeopardize possible future agreements'.

Thump. That familiar blow to the stomach. This was extremely disappointing news. My great hope for a partnership that would launch this range had now completely vanished. I felt really low. After years of trying to get these cards off the ground, the last avenue had closed. What was I to do now?

Immediately, a knee-jerk wave of frustration rushed through me. Arggghhh! Yet another setback. I could have given up there and then, but partly because I'd spent so much time on it, I stubbornly refused to quit. My mind raced, searching for a way forward: 'There must be another way to make this work. There *must* be. I just can't give up now . . .'

Over the next few months, I made numerous calls and attended a succession of meetings in the attempt to put together a credible business plan so I could persuade investors to sink their cash into the Hellebrities. I would often daydream that I'd find a partner who'd help me with the business side of things, like Walt Disney's brother Roy helped him build his empire. Walt was the dreamer of the partnership, who believed 'If you create something good enough, the money side of things will take care of itself' (something I believe too). Roy was a brilliant businessman who took care of the less fun, financial side vital for bringing his brother's ideas to fruition, leaving Walt free to think up more great schemes . . .

Because I didn't have a business partner or the budget to launch the whole range of Hellebrities, I tried to formulate another strategy. I racked my brains for other successful crazes that hadn't used trading cards as their medium for bringing the characters to life.

One thought came immediately – Smurfs! Smurfs were a range of cute blue creatures who wore little pointed hats. Created by Pierre Culliford, an illustrator from Brussels who worked under the pseudonym 'Peyo', these characters first became popular in newspaper cartoon strips in the 1950s. Three decades later, some enterprising spark decided to transform the 2-D characters into three dimensions, creating little rubber figurines, each one slightly different from the others.

This series was marketed in an unusually clever way. Instead of flooding the market with the whole range of Smurfs, the release of each character was staggered over time, so that every few months a new blue creature would pop on to the shelves. This created excitement and anticipation about the range. It also performed a couple of neat tricks – first, the collection seemed cheap because the customer bought only one figure at a time; and second, once a customer had started collecting, they felt compelled to keep on collecting, allowing the manufacturer to just keep on releasing Smurf after Smurf, without ever saying how many were actually in the complete set.

A similar ingenious business model was used ten years later, in the late 1990s, when the TY Corporation launched Beanie Babies – little stuffed toy animals in a variety of types and colours. They also drip-fed the collection on to the market in finite numbers, and it was this limited-edition staggered release that created an added excitement around the world and a higher perceived value than 'traditional' toy collections. These little toys sold in their millions.

So, with these two great examples inspiring me, I spent months tracking down companies in the Far East that could make me some three-dimensional Hellebrities figures. My heart sank again and again as the quotes poured in. They were all way over my budget.

A few more months went by and I constantly worried about what to do next. The frustration was compounded by the fact that I couldn't devote more time to the project because I was offered an executive role at Channel 4 looking after the famous (or should that be infamous) reality show *Big Brother*. Working on the programme was incredibly exciting, but all-encompassing too, so I had little time to chase my personal dreams.

The challenge of getting the Hellebrities off the ground was overwhelming, as it seemed as though I was hitting more brick walls than usual, which was both tiring and demoralizing. But, of course, I couldn't give up. Where could I go next?

Then I remembered Gary Pope, the boss of Kids Industries, whom I'd initially contacted over a year before. Even though I hadn't yet met him, I'd got a good feeling about him over the phone and email. He was always so positive and enthusiastic, but also (crucially) knowledgeable about the children's sector too, having worked in it all his life. Maybe Gary was the key to making this range happen.

I hurriedly picked up the phone. 'Gary, it's Shed Simove here – I'm not sure if you remember me . . .'

'Shed! Hi – how are you?' he said cheerfully. 'How's it going?'

I explained that I was healthy (I never take that for granted, as after all it *is* the most important thing in life) but that I'd come to a standstill with the Hellebrities range and desperately needed help.

'Sure Shed, come in and see me. Let's see what we can do,' he said.

A couple of weeks later I hopped on the tube to Kids Industries. I walked down the spiral staircase to their office, and a tall, well-built man bounded towards me, smiling.

'Hello, you must be Shed. I'm Gary. Good to meet you,' he said.

As we exchanged pleasantries, I took a look at the managing director of one of the biggest children's marketing firms in the UK. Gary was dressed in a denim shirt paired with very fashionable yellow-seamed light blue jeans, and matching fluorescent yellow trainers. He had the lean shape of a boxer and, with his short hair and sharp blue eyes, he reminded me a little bit of a well-trained soldier, maybe a commando type, albeit a very trendy one.

Gary firmly shook my hand and led me into the office, where we chatted for an hour, about life, the universe and everything. It seemed that not only did we share a lot of the same thoughts about life, but Gary had also worked with some of the people I'd come across in my TV career. Before the meeting, he had asked their opinion of me and fortunately the report had come back that I was OK. This was an important positive step towards his deciding to work with me to get the Hellebrities off the ground.

Towards the end of the meeting, I steered the conversation round to the matter at hand.

'So do you think you'd want to be involved in this Gary?' I said, motioning to the mock-ups of the trading cards I'd laid out on the table.

'Yeah – yeah, for sure. I think it's got massive potential,' he replied. 'We'd have to come to a deal, but I can help with the strategy ahead. We've got loads of resources here to help "focus group" the range, then we can create a cracking business plan and approach some of my contacts,' he continued.

Wow. It sounded so simple when he said it like that.

We swiftly hammered out a deal that we were both happy with. In return for a significant share in any revenue generated, Gary, Miranda and the team at Kids Industries would plan a strategy to get the range off the ground. At last, after years of trying, this was a huge step forward.

Over the next few months I met with Miranda and Gary to plan the path ahead. I was most impressed with the professional way they approached the challenge. Miranda would often sit down with flowcharts mapping out the steps ahead, or with mood boards for the focus groups. What Gary and Miranda did was provide the business background to the idea and also the credibility of working in the kids' sector, both of which would be crucial when we started approaching investors or partners.

One of the first hurdles Gary helped us leap over was any possible legal obstacle. He put me in touch with the best copyright and image lawyers in the UK. I sat down with these experts to ensure that my range of new characters could be protected and that they wouldn't infringe on anyone else's copyright. The report from the lawyers came back with glowing colours. We were fine to proceed and they'd work with us every step of the way to ensure we did the right thing legally.

Now all we had to do was find an investor for the project and prove to them it would be a success. After a number of meetings, we decided the key to getting powerful decision-makers and investors to back the project was to present them with evidence that would be hard to refute.

It's one thing fiercely believing that your idea will work – and, sure, I could explain the proven foundations that the idea was modelled on – but it's quite another task altogether to answer the question that many people would ask if their money or job were on the line, which is this:

'Just how can you *know* the range will work?'

We decided that the solution was to present our target market, kids aged seven to eleven, with examples of the cards and then film the result.

Gary and Miranda swung into action using their invaluable understanding of how children act. They devised structured interview sessions and carefully planned focus groups to elicit whether kids would actually like the Hellebrities idea. Now, I'm normally sceptical about focus groups, believing that adults who participate often don't express their true feelings because of group dynamics and the artificial nature of the meeting. However, I hoped that the children would be refreshingly honest. Added to this, Kids Industries took elaborate steps to ensure that the children participating didn't feel that they had to like anything that was presented just because it was given to them by an adult. They did this by presenting the children with a wide range of options, then asking the participants to choose their favourite.

The first focus group took place on a Friday and I was to find out the results at a meeting the following Tuesday. The weekend in between was an anxious time. After years of trying to get this idea off the ground because I firmly believed that kids would love the range, my beliefs were now being put to the test in a measurable way.

I almost didn't want the meeting to start.

But it did.

'So, Shed,' Miranda began, 'we did the first focus group – it was four nine-year-olds, five were eight and one seven-year-old – and generally . . .' She paused.

'Yes? Go on . . .' I thought, bracing myself.

'. . . they loved it. They all thought it was great, even the girls.'

Ta-da!

'What? Really?' I asked, seeking reassurance.

Miranda brought out some A4 blow-ups of the six Hellebrities cards showing the characters Britney Speared, Pee Diddy, Mince Charles, David Peck'Em, George Cloney and Saddam Insane.

'Yes, we showed them these and they laughed and loved them. They really liked the gross ones the most.'

This was music to my ears. In fact, it was a full-blown symphony orchestra to my ears. Relief, then delight flooded my body.

Miranda went on to explain that, remarkably, all the children had understood the core gag of the range, which surprised me. For an eight-year-old to comprehend that the punning name referred to the character's appearance was a pretty sophisticated leap. One of the young boys in the groups had remarked, 'You need lots of other people with funny names . . .'

The focus group also unearthed other important feedback. The participants spontaneously suggested other ways the characters could be used. One girl said that she would definitely collect a sticker range, and that she'd also like to wear a T-shirt displaying one of the characters as well.

Miranda also discovered that the kids liked the gorier, more bizarre cards (like Mince Charles). When the group members were asked what their parents and teachers would think of the range, most replied that they believed the adults would disapprove.

'So, would that stop you buying them?' they were questioned.

'No, I just wouldn't show them to my parents,' came the surprising and amusing answer.

I left the Kids Industries office with renewed hope. After being knocked back so many times with this project, it was good to have a boost of positivity to re-energize me. Not only would this news give *me* fresh hope, it meant that Gary and Miranda (who had always believed in the idea anyway) now had solid evidence to show potential partner companies in the future.

More focus groups followed and they all returned results that proved the Hellebrities were a resounding hit with the target audience. And yet, very frustratingly, we still encountered challenge after challenge getting the range off the ground. Many meetings with various merchandise and licensing companies followed, but they all ended with someone saying no. It seemed no one was ready to take it on.

For a long time, it looked likely that I was going to have to end this chapter here, admitting temporary defeat. After all the knockbacks and dead ends, I thought that my only remaining chance of getting the Hellebrities range off the ground would be if someone in a position of power read this book and then helped me to launch the first series.

But as I went back over this chapter, I realized that this was simply not good enough. There was just no way that I could give up.

So I tried yet another strategy. And this time things started to move in the right direction.

I figured that if another company wouldn't produce the trading cards with me, then I'd just have to produce them myself. I knew this goal would be far more challenging and fraught with difficulties than a simple licensing deal involving a partner who would have manufactured and distributed the range, but I had no other options left. I really believed that the Hellebrities would capture people's imagination, so I had to give it my very best shot.

I split up the challenge of launching the series myself into different mini-hurdles, which I wrote down on a piece of paper. In order to get the Hellebrities into the shops, I needed to do the following:

1. Create artwork
2. Manufacture sticker collection
3. Distribute sticker packets

I knew it was pretty easy to get the sticker collection printed in China or Germany. That was one part of the launch that was completely do-able. And I knew I could get a distributor to take the range on a sale-or-return basis, as I'd already researched this part of the business.

The much more difficult challenge was finding the cash to pay my brilliant artist to create the remaining seventy-four characters needed for the first series of eighty. Unfortunately, until I had leapfrogged that hurdle, I couldn't attempt the other two challenges. So I was stuck.

Then, I had a mad thought. Rather than tackling the problem of raising the money to get all the characters created, what if there was a way to get the artwork created much more cheaply . . .

Was it far too cheeky to phone up Bill Greenhead, the talented artist I had worked with, and suggest a different approach?

I nervously called him up.

As always, he greeted me with huge enthusiasm. Bill is one of those people who always makes you feel good after you've spoken with them – a burst of much appreciated positivity.

'Bill, I've hit a brick wall with the Hellebrities,' I started.

'Wow, Shed, you're still going with that?' he asked.

It had been just under four years since he'd created the first six characters and even though I'd phoned him now and again during that time, I hadn't rung him for a long while.

'Yeah, yeah – I believe in it so much Bill,' I replied.

I told him about the numerous companies I'd met, the many meetings I'd attended and the hours spent ringing people and email-ing firms in the hope of securing a partner to launch the range. I told him about how the kids in the focus groups had loved his drawings and how this had made me even more determined to get the cards into the shops.

'Wow – sounds amazing,' Bill said, taking it all in.

I cut to the chase. Deep breath.

'So, Bill, I reckon I can get the Hellebrities printed up and dis-tributed too. The only stumbling block is just getting the first series actually designed.'

I paused, waiting for Bill to say something.

'Oh OK. . . .' he said cheerfully.

I carried on. I had to plunge in. 'So, I was wondering, Bill – I know you're busy, but maybe there's a way we could come to an arrangement – uh . . . perhaps you could think about it – where I could defer payment, or something like that. I dunno . . .'

I was rambling, slightly embarrassed to ask such a talented guy to work for anything less than his full rate.

Then Bill said something that surprised me.

'Well – how about just a royalty, Shed?'

'Well, yeah – great. Would you be OK with that?' I spluttered.

'Yeah. I'll have to fit it in around my other paid work, but I believe in this too. So let's do it!' Bill answered.

'Fantastic!' I said. 'That would be great. Thanks a lot.'

We quickly discussed how we'd move forward, knocked out a deal and I put the phone down.

I sat there, stunned for a second. Wow, what just happened? Had the biggest barrier to getting the Hellebrities launched just fallen down in a flash?

I immediately wished I'd phoned Bill a lot sooner. Perhaps I could have saved years of aggro. But no worries – these challenges are all part of the journey and maybe Bill wouldn't have agreed to such a deal unless he saw how committed I had remained over that time. No matter: the important thing now was that the project was completely possible.

Bill and I immediately started work on some more characters for the Hellebrities first series. Because I'd been working on the range for so long, one of our first six characters had become out of date. In real life, Saddam Hussein had been hanged for his war crimes, therefore our Saddam Insane character didn't work as well any more. How selfish of him to get caught and put to death, eh?

So with only five characters fully drawn, we needed some more. I rattled off some detailed briefs to Bill and five weeks later (after much tweaking and honing), the six masterpieces, below and over the page, were the result:

Having completed these new characters, my enthusiasm peaked once more. Looking at the new cards, I felt certain that this range could be massively successful. I was mentally thoroughly ready to

Bad Pitts

Pope Idle

Rustin Timberlake

Steven Spielburger

tackle the task of creating a full set of eighty and then raising the money to launch the first series of sticker cards.

And then, as sometimes happens, a spanner fell into the works, or rather a whole tool box.

Soon after we'd finished the new characters, my brother Russ came to stay with me in my flat in London. As soon as he stepped through the door, I noticed he looked a bit serious.

'I've got some bad news, Shed.'

Oh no.

When someone says that to me, my brain usually thinks the worst, instantly spewing out thoughts of serious illness or even death. I mean apart from those, anything's pretty much solvable, right?

'Go on, what?' I said, worried.

'Look at this,' he said and he moved towards his briefcase.

My immediate anxiety instantly cooled. I figured Russ would have told me if anything bad had happened to someone we knew.

I watched as Russ pulled out a magazine from his case. As soon as I saw the three red letters on the front I immediately recognized it as a copy of *MAD* magazine, a clever adult comic that my brother and I had enjoyed since we were teenagers.

Russ was leafing through the pages. He stopped at a page headed 'Page-O-Plugs' that showcased some of the latest toys and novelties from around the world. My eyes were immediately drawn to two pictures of gory characters, one of which I instantly recognized as a caricature of the singer Michael Jackson and the other one looked like a horror version of American property multi-millionaire Donald Trump. In the picture, Donald is shown holding his severed leg. Below this drawing were the words 'Donald Stump'. Uh-oh . . .

I quickly scanned the accompanying text next to the pictures.

'Be on the lookout for Topps' new Hollywood Zombies trading cards . . .' it started.

My heart sank. Here was an idea remarkably similar to the Hellebrities range, being released by Topps, the company who I'd been meeting with about Hellebrities for years.

Because my first thought at hearing 'I've got some bad news . . .' was that someone had died, this information didn't hit me as hard as it could, but I was still massively shell-shocked. It was nearly five years since I'd started the Hellebrities range and now to discover that someone else had launched something similar was deeply disappointing.

The next day, I wrote to my contact at Topps to ask him how this had happened. He told me that the Hollywood Zombies idea had originated in America independently to mine, but I couldn't help feeling a bit hard done by. At the very least, it would have been nice to have received an email from Topps to tell me their series was coming out. Apparently, the British arm of Topps hadn't known anything about the planned release of the Hollywood Zombies range.

Now, it's easy to have a knee-jerk reaction in a situation like this and think 'I've been ripped off!', but it's very possible that the same idea can be thought of by two people independently. Also, my contact at Topps had always been a decent guy, so I didn't want to think that my idea had been stolen.

As you can imagine though, it was very unsettling to discover that an idea I'd pitched to a big company had suddenly emerged in a slightly different guise. The whole sequence of events was very disappointing indeed. On the positive side, my contact at Topps informed me that the Hollywood Zombies range wasn't going to be released in the UK, so that left a small glimmer of hope for a successful launch in this country.

I still have huge hopes that the Hellebrities range will get off the ground and be as popular as I think it could be. Perhaps kids around the world will think the Hellebrities characters are funnier, naughtier or more accessible than the Hollywood Zombies, and my range will be propelled to success. So, who knows, but maybe, just maybe, one day the Hellebrities range will turn into a global phenomenon.

I'll certainly give it my best shot.

*'OK So let's get this straight –
first, you've never been to art school . . .
second, you can't draw . . .
and lastly, you don't know anyone in the art business.
And now you're hoping that the world's leading art
collector will buy one of your ridiculous creations?
Ah. Bless you, you deluded fool . . .'*

IDEA 6

Jeanius

But is it Art?

Sometimes an idea is triggered by a completely unrelated source. I got into producing 'art' quite by accident, a few years before I landed the job at Planet 24 that was to train me how to invent and implement new concepts quickly and with a flourish.

It was during my time at university, where I studied for an Experimental Psychology degree, that the first rumblings of mischief came to pass. Although these first ideas were rather crude, they planted the seed of empowerment that was to grow steadily through my life.

I decided to study Experimental Psychology partly because I felt it was my duty to learn about human interaction (it is one of the keys to life is it not?) and partly because I thought it could throw some light on to how screwed up I was (although 'screwed up' is certainly not a term my respected professors would have approved of).

Whenever I attended lectures in the Psychology faculty building, I would marvel at the structure of the sixties-built concrete monolith which housed four floors of scientists trying to bring credibility to a much criticized field.

The Psychology department regularly displayed various artworks throughout the building on huge expanses of white wall. Often the pictures would hang next to a much smaller frame which contained the artist's thoughts and the inspirations behind the artwork. Often these works were produced by students from the university art college. Among them, there seemed to be a high prevalence of abstract contemporary art – that is, most of it didn't look anything like the object it was referring to.

While walking up the stairs one morning to listen to a lecture on why human babies can differentiate a good-looking person from a less attractive person (fascinating), I was particularly bamboozled by a recent addition to the art on a huge wall next to the lecture theatre. There, hanging proudly in the main lobby of the faculty, was a massive canvas, 10 feet high by 5 feet wide. The picture had no frame and was covered in a strange mixture of concrete and black ink, as if both liquids had been sprayed on with a hose. It reminded me of those animal paintings you sometimes see featured on late-night TV clip shows where an animal is given a brush loaded with paint, which it aimlessly swipes at a canvas. The animals shown doing this are most commonly chimpanzees, presumably because they must be the best artists in the animal world. And the huge piece of 'art' that hung resplendent in the Psychology building looked uncannily like one of the chimp pictures.

I looked at it again with a mixture of awe and disbelief. The painting was an enormous mess of grey and black smudges. This mammoth 'work of art' was entitled *Compassion* and had an equally huge price stuck on the wall-tag next to it. I was gobsmacked. Two thoughts ran through my head: first, 'I can't believe this painting is being sold for so much money'; and second, 'I could do that . . .' This second conclusion was easily reached: if I believed a chimpanzee could have painted the canvas then, apart from the hairy knuckles, I felt I had all the requisite skills required. The seeds were sown for a bout of inventive mischief.

I didn't think about art until months later. While I was working with my professor on his thesis about spatial memory, the maps I was using in an experiment suddenly caught my eye and lit my mischief fire.

As part of the thesis, I was testing random subjects to determine whether there was any difference between how people remembered a sequence of steps if they were presented in the real world compared with how they remembered them if they saw them on a map. My apparatus consisted of twelve huge black discs laid out in a specific configuration on the floor of one of the labs. All the black 'spots' were the same size, about the diameter of a dinner plate. There were four different patterns of spots in the study, and the test consisted of a route being tapped out on the discs with a long stick and then the subject retracing that route after a certain time. Quite how this was pushing the boundaries of human understanding forward was slightly beyond me, but as a successful experiment would mean I had completed an important part of my degree, I followed my professor's instructions to the letter.

The spatial test using the black discs was then repeated, with a route being tapped out on a *map* of the spots (which were now penny-sized and printed on a piece of A4 paper). The subject once again had to attempt to repeat the route in the real world by stepping on the large discs on the floor.

It was the maps of twelve randomly arranged black spots that got my creative juices flowing. These were simply four different patterns of twelve black dots on a white background (a bit like a close-up of a very evenly spotted Dalmatian). My mind leaped from these random patterns to the seemingly random aesthetics of the 'art' I'd seen on the walls of the faculty. A plan began to hatch. I wondered what would happen if I framed my 'spot' maps like works of art, gave each one a pretentious title, then told the Psychology department that I was an up-and-coming modern artist and asked them if they'd exhibit my pictures. I decided to find out.

I found a framing shop and nervously parted with some of my student allowance, wondering what the hell I was doing. A week later I went back to the shop to give a title to each picture and add my signature before the final frame was nailed on. I chose suitably pretentious names: *Mid-Life Crisis*, *Scene and not herd* and *Second Honeymoon* were the names of the first three. I wanted the titles to be ridiculously removed from the image, so I could watch to see whether anybody would try to look for a meaning to the picture when in actual fact there wasn't any. For the last picture, I couldn't resist giving it an especially leading title: *The Emperor's New Clothes*.

I wanted to send a clear hint that I knew that modern art can sometimes skate very close to being a con-trick.

A few days later, the pictures were ready. With the stark contrast of the twelve black spots against the white background framed by a jet-black shiny wooden frame, they really did look like some modern work from the seventies. I thought they looked splendid. It's amazing how a decent frame can make any old nonsense look good.

Two of those pictures now hang in my brother's flat. Here they are:

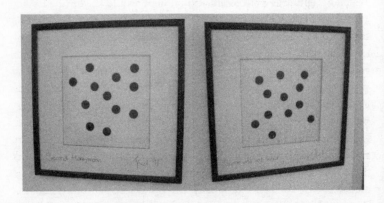

The next challenge was to get the four spot pictures exhibited. I discovered that any artist who wanted to exhibit in the Psychology building had to get permission from a well-respected professor on the third floor. I found the right room with a bright yellow door and knocked.

'Come,' a plummy voice instructed.

I entered a room not much wider than the door frame I'd just walked through. If I'd put my arms out wide, I could have touched both walls, each of which was covered in shelves laden with multi-coloured lever arch files, journals and books. At the far end of the room was a desk, behind which sat a man who was in the middle of what looked like essay-marking. I remember distinctly that he wore half-moon glasses, but I don't recall much else about the professor, apart from the fact that he was around fifty and very friendly.

'Ah, hello,' he said cheerfully.

I introduced myself, apologized for interrupting him, told him I was studying in the department, then quickly got to the point.

'Um . . . I'm an artist and I'd love to exhibit my work in the faculty, please . . .'

'Ah! OK. What sort of art do you do?' Luckily, I was ready for this question.

'Well, mainly very modern pieces – ink on paper,' I bluffed. Well, it was true – the maps were ink on paper, albeit photocopier ink on an A4 sheet.

'Oh, right,' the professor said.

I could tell this man was busy and that he just wanted me out of his office so that he could continue with his life's work. He continued, 'I'm sure that would be fine. Come back and see me next week and when a slot comes free, we'll sort it out for you.'

'Thanks,' I half spluttered, trying not to sound so surprised. 'Thanks a lot.' And that was that.

A fortnight later, my four pictures were up on display. I reacted with a mixture of pride and embarrassment that they'd been given a prestigious place next to the bottom of the stairs on the ground floor – a location passed by virtually everyone coming into the building.

As well as hanging the four spot pictures neatly in a row on the wall, I placed ridiculously high prices on small stickers next to each picture. I hoped the extortionate cost would give the art an inflated status.

I also hung another smaller frame to the left of my artworks. This contained a computer-printed description of the piece, which I'd written in suitably high-brow, flowery language of the sort seen in real modern-art exhibitions. It described how 'the boundaries of art have fallen down recently and now, purely representational forms are making way for a more ethereal visual medium'. It was utter rubbish of course, but it neatly added to the illusion that the four framed pictures of black spots could be deemed 'art'. The Emperor was clearly naked, but would anyone notice?

As it turned out, no they wouldn't. The pictures hung in the Psychology building without much incident. The faculty got no enquiries from anyone wanting to buy them, but I wasn't disappointed. As far as I was concerned, the mere fact that they were displayed and accepted as art was astonishing.

One day, on my way to the lab, I overheard a young man and woman chatting in front of my pictures. I deduced they were academics from their sensible clothing and armfuls of textbooks and files. They both looked slightly puzzled, but intrigued. They were pointing at the picture with the title *Scene and not herd* and I only caught a snippet of their conversation. It went like this:

MAN: Can you see it?

WOMAN: What?

MAN: It's a dog's face. (He moved his finger in a circular motion and pointed at the picture in front of him, which was simply an arrangement of twelve black dots on a white background.)

WOMAN: What?

MAN: Yeah, I think so. They're in the shape of a dog's face – the ears, the nose . . .'

WOMAN: Really?

MAN: Yeah . . . hmm . . . yeah . . .

I couldn't believe it. A dog? Are you kidding? This was a picture of *twelve black spots*.

The pictures stayed up for a couple of weeks. I don't know how many people privately thought they were terrible. Certainly no one objected to them. And nobody noticed that they were the maps from my experiment. I felt that I'd very successfully proved that everyone in the building had reached such a state of acceptance of modern art that they were willing to entertain the fact that pictures of twelve black spots in a pattern were actually real works of art. The really funny thought I had to get my head round was that just maybe they were.

In the end, I sold just one of the pictures. A friend of mine who studied politics was kind enough to show his support by buying one for a price much reduced from the stickered cost. He knew it was all done in jest, and appreciated the ruse. But the fact that someone had bought a picture meant a lot to me.

'One day this'll be worth a lot of money Shed,' he joked. It would be great if he was proved right.

Even though my little project had originally meant to challenge people's acceptance of modern art, I began to be sucked in by the whole art world illusion myself. The process of getting something framed and then seeing it hung with my name was pretty exciting. I also had to admit to myself that my black dot pictures *did* perhaps have a stylized beauty about them.

I began to believe that maybe, just maybe, I could create 'proper' art that had a bit more thought behind it. Then I could be truly proud if people bought the pieces.

Over the next ten years, I rarely created any more artworks. I suppose you could call this my 'desert period' – dry and barren, though without any camels. I can count the number of pictures I made – mostly for people very close to me – on one hand. Then one day I was getting some tools from under the bed to fix a light socket that had blown and I happened to find some of the pictures from years ago. I flipped through them nostalgically. As I did, a notion started to come into my head.

One of the pictures was made out of some jeans I'd cut up. It showed a group of sperm (cut out from denim) swimming towards a round piece of material with frayed edges: the denim egg. The piece displayed the title that inspired it: another play-on-words that mixed genetics with fashion – *It's All In The Jeans.*

Once I'd discovered the stunning punning possibilities of the word 'jeans', it had spurred me on to create more denim-related works. One showed a picture of Einstein which I'd printed on to a pocket cut from some Levi 501s. That one was called *Jeanius*.

The last picture in the group with the same theme was rather more blasphemous. Entitled *Jeansus Christ*, it was a Christ figure cut from denim in the crucifix position, arms outstretched. I cut it out of the material where two seams on the jeans met, forming a cross, thus intensifying the crucifixion imagery.

As I looked at these related pictures, something bubbled inside my brain. A question took hold. Would anyone think they were any good? And if so, was there a way I could sell them?

I tried to sell them on eBay, but no one was interested. I didn't get a single bid. Slightly gutted, I ploughed on with another idea. Perhaps a company making jeans would be interested? I thought that maybe if I created lots more denim works of art, a jeans brand might think they had marketing potential as a collection.

I trawled charity shops for pairs of jeans in preparation to make more denim art. The shop assistants were frequently baffled when I would ask for a certain pair of jeans, but not mind about the size.

'Oh don't worry about that – I'm going to cut them up,' I'd explain. Cue a polite, but slightly puzzled, look.

I swiftly produced three more jeans pictures. *Jeaneology* had my family tree printed on a pocket of some jeans. For *Nothing Seams Right* I cut out different seams from a pair of jeans and then placed them on the right of the picture. And for *Zip Code* I printed a phrase in Morse code on the zipper section of some jeans.

I filmed myself talking about these artworks and sent the tape to the advertising company who ran the Levi's campaign. Unfortunately they weren't interested. Apparently, because the artworks had punning names that were English-specific, I was told that this idea wouldn't work on a global scale. So that avenue blew out too. What else could I do to try to get some result for my art?

Now around this time, something unrelated yet amazing happened in my life. Because I was lucky enough to be working on the UK version of *Big Brother*, I came into contact with someone in the television business whom I'd never really met properly before. I wasn't to know it then, but he was about to have a massive impact on my life.

Throughout my years in TV, I'd always heard about a 'super-agent' called John Noel. He had quite a reputation as one of the toughest talent agents on the block. Northern, fast-talking and fiercely bright, John was renowned throughout the TV industry for 'telling it like it is'. He got great results for the people lucky enough to be represented by him – 'the talent', as they are called in showbiz circles. The financial people at a production company or broadcaster would always look a bit spooked if I ever picked one of the TV presenters on John Noel's books to work on a show. He was well known for striking hard deals for his coterie of television stars, comedians and actors.

What was particularly unusual about John was that he was known for taking certain people on when no one else would believe in them, then he'd stick with them, sometimes for years, trying to convince others about the person he fiercely believed in. He nurtured people's talent and helped them find an outlet for it.

We met for dinner one night in a converted fifties cinema to talk about one of the presenters he had on his books. Once he'd convinced me of the presenter's fierce work ethic, John asked me what I was doing after *Big Brother*.

'Good question,' I mumbled.

I was at a crossroads in my life. At thirty-three, I knew I was incredibly fortunate to have led such an interesting and privileged life, but I still had a nagging feeling that I wasn't fulfilling my potential. Even though I knew I was lucky to have a good career and a decent flat – and, most importantly, I was healthy – I felt I was floundering, stagnating. The phrase 'one time around' had always resonated strongly with me. It emphasized the often easily forgotten belief that we should appreciate every day we're alive and, if possible, live it to the absolute full.

'I just want things to start happening, John,' I explained. 'I seem to be creating stuff – it just hasn't really succeeded much . . .' I continued.

I told him that I currently had lots of ideas for many different business areas but I was finding it hard to get going. I looked at him, hoping he'd have some advice.

He didn't speak for a moment.

'Well, Shed – I've been hearing good things on the grapevine about you lately . . .'

Crikey, that was good news. Did he mean it? Had he really? Was he just saying that because I was in front of him?

'. . . so why don't I take you on? And we'll see what we can do.'

This was a pretty amazing development, although I didn't know exactly what he was going to help me do. At the time I knew I wanted to 'push the envelope' as they say, to try to make the most of the little skills and passions I had, but I certainly didn't want to be a traditional TV presenter or a jobbing actor, which were John's usual areas of expertise.

'What are we going to do though, John?' I asked lamely, meaning 'What are you going to help *me* to do?' Yes, I was slipping nicely into the role of an egocentric talent after only three seconds.

'Whatever you want, Shed!' he answered.

Wow. It was quite hard to take in. I had an agent.

The immediate impact of having somebody who believed in me enough to be associated with me and spend time on me was very powerful. Half of me thought he'd made a mistake; half of me thought 'At last, someone will help me make something of myself.' I felt more than a little bit saved.

The next few months were a revelation. Not only did John help me when I was struggling financially, but he and his team affected me in a profound way simply because they all believed in me. There's nothing quite like it when people other than your friends and family think you're worth bothering with. Significantly, John was someone willing to spend time and money on my progress, to nurture me and help me fulfil whatever potential I had. That had huge significance for me. After so many false starts and rejections, at last there were some other people who could perhaps help me push my big ideas forward.

Even though John continues to support me unconditionally to this day, I continue to be his most difficult client, not because of my outrageous demands ('I said *green* M&M's and *room-temperature* water . . .') but because I don't really fit into a specific role like some of the other people he represents. I'm not the obvious choice to be a TV presenter or an actor, and often I'd explain to John that my wildest dreams were to become a decent public speaker, touring the world with an entertaining show about my adventures and also to become a consultant for huge companies, creating promotions and new products for them. Even though these goals were unusual requests, slightly out of the sphere of his television world, he never wavered in his support.

One day I was having dinner with John and his son Nik, who also worked at his dad's agency, and the ball got set in motion for another artwork.

The first time I had seen Nik in the agency offices, I had thought he was a presenter, or a model of some kind. He was over 6 foot tall, with a footballer's physique and bright blue eyes like his dad's. All the girls I knew who'd met him thought he was very good looking, but he wasn't arrogant with it – the first time we met I was surprised to find he came across as a very friendly, quick-witted guy who was deeply polite to everyone around him.

Over the previous months, I'd got to know Nik well and he'd continued to surprise me each time we'd met. He often recommended interesting books for me to read and was always incredibly supportive when I wittered on about my worries. We got on well, and I began to consider him a friend.

During lunch at a local gastro-pub, I chatted to John and Nik about the progress of this book and told them I needed their help.

'There's one thing I need. The chapter about my art stuff – it needs an end,' I said a little desperately.

'Yeah, I've been thinking about that,' said Nik. Oh great, I thought. I swiftly remembered that I'd already mentioned this challenge over the phone to Nik. 'I reckon we need to get a celebrity involved,' he said, turning to John.

'Go on,' John prompted.

Nik turned back to me. 'Well, say we get some jeans from a big star. Then you can make them into your art, then we can sell them at auction, maybe for charity – and get someone well known to buy them perhaps . . . That'd be a great ending for the chapter, wouldn't it?'

'Yeah! Sounds good,' I said, the doubt leaking through my voice slightly.

'No, really. It's possible, I reckon. I've got some good contacts in the music industry and I'll ask them,' he reassured me.

We all agreed it was a great idea, but I wasn't totally convinced. It wasn't that I didn't have confidence in Nik – he was well known and well liked throughout the media world; I just knew too well how many requests celebrities get each week for anything from autographs to public appearances, and consequently how many have to be refused. I simply put this idea to the back of my mind while I tried to come up with a more reachable goal for the artworks.

As it turned out, I was to eat my thoughts in spectacular style. Just two weeks later, Nik had worked his magic. He called me up.

'Shed! Gotta result for ya!' he said, his voice booming.

'No way Nik! What? Go on,' I mumbled, now getting excited.

'I've got you some jeans – yeah – from . . . Jessica Simpson – you know? This guy I know at BMG has said we can have some of her jeans.'

I took a moment to process this news. As you probably know, Jessica Simpson is a worldfamous, sexy young pop singer who had also just starred in a hit movie, *The Dukes of Hazzard*. She was, as they say, hot with a capital 'H', and the tabloid newspapers and gossip magazines loved her.

'Serious?' I questioned.

'Yeah – all sorted Shed. They should be sending over some jeans in the next few weeks. You can put them into your art, then hopefully we can get them auctioned off.'

Just as he promised, the jeans arrived the very next month. Nik sent me a Jiffy bag which I opened to find a tiny pair of jeans shorts with Jessica Simpson's signature on the front. Apart from being struck by how small the waist was, I was thrilled to receive this great piece of celebrity merchandise.

Now all I needed was an idea for a piece of art that would neatly include the celebrity jeans. I racked my brain for a picture concept suitable for Jessica's denim. The answer came from the fact that the jeans given to me were actually jean *shorts*. As soon as I concentrated on that word 'shorts', I had the answer.

Immediately, I set to work. The concept I had in mind needed some electronic components because I wanted the finished picture to be slightly interactive.

First, I bought a suitably large canvas from an art shop, then I walked round the corner to an electrical store where I bought wires, miniature lightbulbs and a battery casing. The shop assistants were amazingly helpful, especially when I told them about the Jessica Simpson shorts; one of them even agreed to wire the bulbs up on the canvas so that the actual workings of the picture would be hidden.

The hidden wiring completed, I then spent hours intertwining black and red wire for the front of the picture, placed the bulbs where I wanted them and used crocodile clips to attach the wire to the shorts. Once I'd signed the canvas, my picture was ready to be framed. It was a rather rough concoction of wires, lightbulbs and, lastly, the celebrity denim shorts.

My creation was called *Shorts Circuit*.

Once back from the framer, the next mission was to get the artwork auctioned off. On the back of the canvas, I placed a letter of authenticity from the record company to say the shorts were worn by Jessica Simpson herself. This would ensure that both the press and any buyers would be reassured that this piece contained genuine celebrity memorabilia.

I got back in touch with Nik and arranged a meeting to show him the finished artwork. It looked resplendent, surrounded by its newly added ornate silver frame.

The talented guy at the frame shop had done a great job of embedding the button into the bottom right-hand corner of the frame so that it sat flush against it. When pressed, the button caused the electrical circuit to be completed and all the lightbulbs simultaneously illuminated. Appropriately, the shorts now had a bright entourage surrounding them.

All that was left to do was to sell the finished *Shorts Circuit* artwork for a profit. In order to maximize its value, we had to create some hype connected with it.

It seemed we might have a head start creating some excitement about the shorts. While flicking through the latest copy of *Sky* TV magazine, I came across an article about Jessica Simpson – oh, and get this: in the photo accompanying the small interview with her, she was wearing similar shorts to those in the artwork. Not only that, one of the questions was actually about her shorts. The caption beside the photo even mentioned them, saying 'Jessica in *those* shorts.' It seemed that Jessica wearing the little cut-off denim garments had caused quite a sensation . . .

Cheered by the fact that my artwork had a certain celebrity kudos, I pondered what to do next. And like a persistent woodpecker in my head, the one eternal Art question kept coming back to me again and again.

'What is Art?' . . . 'What is Art?' . . . 'What is Art?' . . .

And this question led me to ask myself, 'When is a picture not a picture – when does it become Art?'

Now I'm sure you'll be well aware of certain works by modern artists that go on to sell for fortunes and win an array of awards. But it seems there's a very thin line between what some people consider a genius artistic endeavour and others mere nonsense. This difference in opinion is completely fascinating – and leads to the most important Art question of all:

'*Who* decides when something is Art?'

Is it the people who exhibit art – like my Psychology faculty professor? Or is it the people who buy art? Or does it need an opinion-former – someone respected – to say whether something is Art-worthy or not?

I was on to something.

If I could find someone who could deem my *Shorts Circuit* picture a work of Art, then that would be a curious and interesting outcome. I would be an Artist with a capital A.

But I wouldn't be satisfied with just anyone judging my work. I wanted the top people to see it – and, ideally, buy it.

There was only one choice for the person I would approach first. The man known around the world as an art expert and opinion-former – Charles Saatchi. This hugely successful man had been a patron of the art world for a long time and an avid collector of the best works around. If Charles would deem my piece artworthy and perhaps even buy it, then the honour of having him purchase a 'Shed Original' would catapult me into the realms of the much-feted artists he'd previously championed. It was a very long shot, but, hey, if he'd buy an unmade bed for hundreds of thousands of pounds, maybe he'd see the utter genius lurking in my punning denim masterpiece. Hmm.

So I set out to track the eminent man down.

I rang round my small collection of contacts and was delighted to discover that a person called Philly Adams worked very closely with Charles and that I should try to speak with her. I rang the number for Philly that my contact had furnished and instantly a recorded message came on the line. 'The number that you dialled has been changed to . . .' the female voice started.

I dialled the new number, now doubting all the information I'd been given. If the number had been changed, then would Philly still be working with Charles? I quickly found out.

'Hello, Philly Adams,' a young, well-spoken voice said.

'Oh, hello there. Sorry to bother you. Uh . . . my name is Sheridan Simove, and I'm writing a book about creativity and adventures. And, uh, Art . . . And I was wondering if there was any possibility . . .'

Sheesh. I was doing badly, wittering away. I was thinking 'I must sound like an idiot.' But I ploughed on.

'And one of the chapters is about the question: "What is Art?" – and it'd be my dream to see what Charles Saatchi would think of my latest work . . .'

A slightly awkward pause.

'Oh, right – OK,' Philly said, taking in the garbled request on the phone. If she was irritated by my cold-calling her, she certainly didn't show it. I was amazed at how pleasant she was.

I quickly asked if I could send her a copy of the book and she kindly said yes. So off I went to the printers, printed over four hundred pages and bound the manuscript up. Then I posted it off and hoped . . .

A few days later, I called Philly to check on progress. Understandably, she hadn't yet read any of the huge ream of paper I'd given her, but said she was planning to dive into it imminently. She asked which chapter was relevant to her and Charles and promised to get back to me within a week.

True to her word, five days later Philly rang.

'Well, I read the chapter,' she started.

'Oh, thanks,' I said, grateful to this complete stranger for taking the time out to help me.

'Yes, enjoyed it, and I spoke to Charles,' Philly continued.

Wow. This was an exciting development. I felt surprised and honoured to have reached the great man in such a relatively small number of steps. I hardly dared ask the next question.

'Oh, superb . . . Thanks, Philly. What did he think?'

'Uh, well . . . This isn't something we'd pursue to buy,' she answered.

Oh dear.

'Oh, really,' I said, hoping for more of an explanation.

'Yes . . . No . . . It's not something we'd buy,' she repeated.

As well as feeling initially disappointed, I noticed myself getting a slight kick out of the fact that Philly used the word 'we'. It always fascinates me when people use 'we' in relation to one person. In an instant it summed up that Charles Saatchi was more than just one man; and rather, the figurehead of a huge team or organization that was so much bigger than a solitary man.

'Oh,' I said. 'Did he actually see the picture? Did he like the art?' I asked, hoping for a smidgeon of feedback from the most renowned art collector in the world.

'Yes. I showed him your book,' Philly replied.

'And he enjoyed it?'

I could tell that she was being incredibly polite and positive, and also rather careful with what she was saying. Given that I was going to write about our conversation, I understood that it would be hard for her (or indeed Charles) to go 'on the record' about what they thought.

'But we hope to see more of Shed in the future,' she added.

'Ah, thanks,' I said, trying to process what exactly that meant.

This last piece of feedback was a lovely touch and I wondered whether Philly and Charles said the same to everyone they turned down. It didn't matter. I was happy to have reached the man I was aiming for and thrilled that Philly had allowed me to even register on his radar.

And who knows, maybe one day I'll meet Charles Saatchi himself and perhaps even sell him one of my Butt Plugs. Surely that product deserves a Turner Prize?

I still needed to pin a value on my *Shorts Circuit* artwork. Changing tack, I called Nik, my contact who'd managed to get the shorts from the record company. He told me that he was currently involved in organizing a high-profile charity auction in a few months' time and suggested that perhaps my shorts picture could be auctioned off then.

Nik mentioned that quite a few famous people and many successful types would be attending the auction and that perhaps one of them might take a fancy to my picture and bid on it. It sounded like a good plan.

As the date of the auction approached, I bashed out a simple press release describing the story behind the artwork and included a brief biography of myself, because I fully realized that the people at the auction might well wonder: 'Who the hell is this "Shed" guy and why should we buy his artwork?'

The night of the big do finally arrived. As well as my framed

Jessica Simpson shorts, there were various other lots on offer, ranging from a signed pair of Arsenal-player Thierry Henry's football boots, to an amazing seven-star holiday in Mauritius. So, some good stuff . . . and my picture, basically.

The affair turned out to be a very glamorous party held in a posh hotel in the centre of London's financial district. Dressed in my suit, I walked into the main dining room, which was full of people milling around gorgeously laid tables. I immediately caught sight of my *Shorts Circuit* picture in pride of place at the front and felt a pang of pride mixed with a slight pinch of uneasiness at having placed my effort next to bona fide memorabilia and amazing holidays.

I went over to the picture to check that the lights were working, and an immaculately dressed middle-aged man in a dinner suit came up to me.

'Did you do that?' he asked.

'Um . . . yes, yes, I did,' I said.

'Are you an artist, then?' he countered.

Hmm. I had to think for a second. Aren't labels fascinating? I'm always struck by how humans love to put something they encounter into a box – and then mark the box with what's in it. We have a fierce need to place something in a neat category so that we can easily understand it.

'Well, um, uh . . . not really. I don't know . . . sort of,' I spluttered unimpressively. I still didn't know if my picture was 'art', and was thus not completely sure if I was an 'artist'. I wasn't even sure if the distinction mattered.

Another well-dressed man spied us talking about the picture and sidled up to me. What he said worried me slightly.

'I really like your picture,' he started.

'Oh, thanks a lot,' I said, delighted.

'Yeah, I want to bid on it,' he said.

'Great,' I chimed.

'Yeah. But my wife won't let me,' he chuckled.

'How come?' I asked, intrigued.

'I want to put it above our bed, but the wife said, "There's no way we're having those shorts in my house, reminding me every day of how thin I'm not."'

I laughed. Fair enough. But would this issue hamper the bidding, I wondered?

Before the auction, the crowd sat down to enjoy a delicious meal of mozzarella drizzled with pesto, baked cod on a bed of mash and an incredible-looking orange dessert served in a miniature wine glass. Ah, the food of the middle class. How on earth did we cope ten years ago when we didn't have pesto?

At my table, I was incredibly lucky to be surrounded by some highly stimulating people. The 'super-agent' John Noel, who had championed me for ages, sat opposite me. Next to him was the breathtakingly stunning TV presenter Kirsty Gallacher and her hunky rugby-player boyfriend. I'd only met Kirsty once before and things hadn't gone well, but I hoped she wouldn't remember me.

That first meeting was around eight years ago, during the time I was working at Planet 24 and way before Kirsty became famous. I was in my early twenties and a junior researcher, working on a brand-new sports quiz show that Planet 24 was making for Sky. It was my job to trawl through clips of sporting events to find funny moments for a 'What Happens Next?' round in the quiz.

One day I went over to the Sky offices to collect the tapes. At the time, Kirsty was working as an assistant producer in the Sports department and was completely unknown to me. I was told to look for her so that I could get the footage I needed to sift through. I wandered around the Sports department and asked a guy nearby where Kirsty Gallacher was. He took me round a corner to some desks where a young girl was sitting. She looked up as the guy said, 'Here she is.'

I don't remember much after that because everything just slowed down. There before me was an absolute vision of a woman. With her clear blue eyes and flawless skin, I found myself looking at someone who was both beautiful and powerfully sexy at the same time. Then something happened that I couldn't control. No, not that, but close. I was actually so blown away by this girl's beauty that I flushed and just completely clammed up. I think the bloke introducing us realized I was collapsing into myself, so he tried to fill the gap by saying, 'This is Kirsty.' And I tried to speak once more.

Nothing.

I felt myself blushing like crazy and this in turn made me feel even more panicky. Wow. It was excruciating. I tried to speak again.

Nope.

By now only seconds had passed, but it was obviously a starkly awkward situation, sensed by all.

Remarkably (and much to my relief) Kirsty took it in her stride and I remember thinking that perhaps she had this effect on a lot of men, because she didn't really miss a beat.

'Hello,' she said with a smile.

I must have mumbled something about needing the tapes from her, because she immediately understood and scuttled off to find them.

When she was gone, I cursed myself for being so pathetic. But before I could compose myself, Kirsty was back with a large box of VHS cassettes.

'Here you go. These should do the trick,' she said, looking directly at me. And that did it once more.

Oh no. My skin went hot and I went beetroot red again. I still couldn't speak properly. I can only guess what she must have thought of the excuse of a man in front of her. It's the only time in my life when a woman's beauty has actually left me speechless.

Luckily, around ten years later, I was a bit better. Even though Kirsty still looked phenomenal, there was no flushing this time (for either of us), and we exchanged pleasantries as we sat down to the meal.

During dinner, I sat next to flame-haired comedy genius Leigh Francis and his stunning wife, Jill. Leigh had become famous for his rubber-mask creations that featured in the highly successful show *Bo' Selecta!* Even though we'd never met properly before, we got on like a house on fire and I thanked the seating gods for sitting me next to such an entertaining duo.

At one point, Leigh asked about my product ideas because he'd heard about them from a guy in his production team. I'd brought some of my products with me in case the person who won the picture wanted them, and I showed Leigh various items from my stable of novelty crap. His eyes lit up as I brought each one out and when I placed the Butt Plug on the white tablecloth in front of us he laughed out loud.

He was turning it over in his hand, and I could see he was thinking of something.

'You should auction this, Shed,' he suggested.

'What? No,' I said. 'No one will want a plastic Butt Plug made by a guy they've never heard of. They've got Thierry Henry's football boots to bid for. A rubber arse isn't quite in the same league, is it?'

'Ok, then we need a celebrity to sign it,' Leigh answered. 'Then it'll be a Celebrity Butt Plug.' He sat back, proud of his brainwave.

'Yeah, good idea,' I said, not entirely sure.

Leigh immediately jumped up and said, 'I'm gonna get Kirsty to sign it. Then it'll be Kirsty Gallacher's Butt Plug. That's gotta be worth something.'

Fair point, I thought. But we just left the idea there.

After the guests had finished eating, the auction began. A very posh, tanned Master of Ceremonies with a shock of white hair introduced each lot with a wonderfully rich and booming voice.

'Ladies and gentlemen, the first lot is a solid-silver pen with a gold filigree pattern, one of only twenty-five made. Who'll start the bidding?'

And so the bids started to roll in. The people gathered were astonishingly generous, and the first set of lots all went for huge wads of cash. I was rather nervous that my picture would let the show down.

After a signed Chelsea football shirt was auctioned off for several hundred pounds, it was time for my picture to be sold.

'Ladies and gentlemen,' the auctioneer began, 'quite a special lot now for you.' 'Special'? That's a polite word for 'crap', isn't it? 'Here we have a signed pair of pop singer Jessica Simpson's shorts mounted in a picture. *Shorts Circuit*, it's called. A marvellous thing, and it's made by the artist . . . Shed . . .'

The people sitting on my table gave a cheer.

'Yes, he's over there. Well done, Shed!' the auctioneer boomed. He moved towards the picture now being held up by one of the organizers.

'And look, ladies and gentlemen, when I press this button on the frame it all lights up!' He pressed the button, the lights flicked on and the capacity audience gave a loud collective 'Oooh . . .' I think the wine had made them rather excitable.

'So, who'll start me at . . .'

Oh, please, someone buy it, I hoped.

'One hundred pounds?'

Silence.

Oh no. Come on. Please.

Silence. A cough.

The auctioneer echoed my private thoughts, saying, 'Come on, you lot. This is a great thing. Perfect for your living room . . . or your bedroom.'

Or even your toilet, I thought.

A voice from behind me broke the silence. 'Go on!' a man said.

'One hundred pounds. Thank you, sir! Who'll give me two hundred?'

'Yes!' shrieked a lady at the front.

'Thank you, madam,' the auctioneer replied. 'Two hundred pounds for this unique work of art. Who'll give me three hundred?'

'OK!' a voice shouted from my left.

Wow. Things seemed to be going well. It seemed that quite a few people wanted the picture.

From then on the auctioneer did a sterling job. As the bids climbed, the people on my table winked and smiled at me encouragingly. I was surprised when the bidding tipped five hundred pounds, but, amazingly, it rattled on at a pace. Six hundred, seven hundred . . . And when the bidding reached the princely sum of nine hundred pounds I held my breath.

'Who will give me one thousand pounds for *Shorts Circuit*?' the auctioneer bellowed.

Blimey, that's a lot of cash for a pair of shorts.

'Yep!' a woman's voice cried out from the other side of the room.

'We have one thousand pounds, ladies and gentleman!' the auctioneer said.

The whole room clapped and cheered. It was all rather exciting.

In the end someone agreed to pay £1,200 for the picture. It wasn't the highest sum bid that night, but I was stunned and delighted at the fact that anyone would be so generous, and secretly hoped they enjoyed the picture enough not to regret spending that amount.

After the auction ended, I went to find the person who had bought the picture. The winner, or rather winners, turned out to be a dashing couple in their mid-thirties called Nick and Sarah. I discovered that Nick was a hedge fund manager, which is one of those high-flying City jobs that you hear about in the financial papers (and absolutely nothing to do with gardening, of course).

'We love it, Shed,' said Sarah.

'Yes, love it,' agreed Nick, as he pushed the red button on and off like an excited child, making the lights around the shorts flash.

'We're going to put it in our living room,' said Nick. 'And we think that when you're famous, Shed, it'll be worth even more . . .'

What a result!

Here's Nick and Sarah with the lovely TV presenter and actress Davina McCall, who is one of the patrons of the charity the auction raised money for:

The fun didn't end there. As the evening drew to an end, my dining partner Leigh Francis bounded over to me, triumphant.

'Look at this, Shed!' he said excitedly. He whipped out one of my novelty Butt Plugs and turned it over to reveal a signature on the side. It said 'Kirsty Gallacher'.

'Great job, Leigh!' I said, laughing. So now we had something else to auction. I went over to thank Kirsty and to take a photo of her with the now valuable Butt Plug.

The auction had finished and many guests were leaving, so I put the signed Butt Plug in my pocket and went home, aiming to post it on eBay the next day. It had been a great evening.

The next morning, I hastily typed up a description for the Butt Plug posting on eBay. I wanted the headline description to catch people's attention, so I typed: Kirsty Gallacher's Butt Plug.

Unfortunately, this decision proved to be one that would cause me trouble. After writing a long spiel about how the Butt Plug came to be signed, I pressed the button to post the first ever Celebrity Butt Plug on the site.

Half an hour later an email popped into my inbox. Oh no. eBay Listing Removed, it screamed.

I scanned the rest of the message. It seemed that my posting had fallen foul of one of eBay's posting rules, which states: 'You are not allowed to list erotica or sexually oriented materials on eBay . . .' which included 'any items which, because of their nature or because of the item description, appear to be designed for use in sexual/adult activity'.

I could understand that a strict reading of these rules would mean that eBay had a point. But I'd seen my Butt Plugs on sale on eBay for at least a year, so I thought it was rather unfair that the new celebrity version should now be banned. Incensed at this grave injustice (protest march, anyone?), I immediately fired off dozens of emails to the eBay support team explaining that the Butt Plug in question wasn't the usual type of Butt Plug designed for bedroom activity and found in adult stores. I even phoned eBay headquarters, where, frustratingly, no one could help me. Eventually, a few hours later, someone from the eBay team sent me an email saying that they'd decided to let my posting remain on the site. So that was good news.

Once the posting was up, I rang three tabloid newspapers to tell them about the unique item I was selling, hoping that they'd run the story of the Butt Plug and entice more bidders. Surprisingly, none of the papers was interested in the earth-shattering story of a TV star auctioning off a signed plastic bum.

I should have realized that this apathy was a sign of things to come, but optimistically I ploughed on. I started the bidding on Kirsty's Butt Plug at £20, making sure the auction ended at eight thirty on a Sunday evening (apparently a popular time for browsing and one of the best times to end an eBay auction).

Disappointingly, the auction did not receive one bid and ended without a sale. I immediately relisted the Butt Plug and started the bidding much lower, at £5. This time the auction ended with a sale. The Kirsty Gallacher Celebrity Butt Plug got one bid and sold for the rather poor amount of a fiver to a buyer named Geraint from Buckinghamshire. I was sorry that the celebrity silicone moulded arse didn't raise more, especially since the cost of the two auctions on eBay and posting the Butt Plug by recorded delivery cost me a total of just over six quid. Not the best business deal of the century, I'm sure you'll agree.

All in all, though, my dabbles with Art had resulted in a fulfilling and exciting adventure. They'd culminated in one of my pictures being sold for over £1,000 and a celebrity signing one of my Butt Plugs. So, a good result all round.

My experiences with producing various artworks had also led to compelling questions about the nature of art itself. The answer to the question 'What is Art?' is probably 'Anything'. And that's really rather refreshing, because if we see beauty in most things around us, that allows us to receive a much-needed lift throughout the day.

Wow. I think I'm in danger of disappearing up my own Butt Plug.

So here's the next question for you: if beauty can be found anywhere, would you say that a television show could be classed as Art?

'*You've worked in television for a while – and now you think you can automatically think up new TV shows that will make it to air? What makes you think you're better than all the thousands of other people around the world trying to create new programmes?*

And why do all your ideas aim to shock? You're just showing off again . . . do you really expect any of these ridiculous concepts to get off the ground?'

IDEA 7

Fifty-Seven Channels And Nothing On

Creating a new TV show can be challenging . . .

During my time working in television, I've come up with lots of ideas for new programmes. As my knowledge and contacts grew over the years, so the doors slowly started to open, allowing me to reach the people who made the decisions about which of these shows were actually made. However, even though I was through the door, that didn't mean they always liked my ideas.

Once, I pitched a concept for a new TV show to the BBC. I wonder if you'll like it . . .

So there I was, in a bare meeting room in the BBC television centre, standing awkwardly in front of ten smart executives – a TV jury of sorts – poised to judge me and my idea for a new programme. I kicked off the pitch with a question aimed to get them excited.

'Do you wish you knew exactly what people think of you?' I began boldly.

Ten faces stared back at me and no one said anything. This wasn't unusual in a pitch. Most decision-makers are very busy people and have seen dozens of pitches before so they often have an 'impress me' attitude.

I quickly pressed on: 'Well now you could find out what people actually honestly think of you – by appearing in a brand-new television show . . .' My voice grew louder for the next bit and I hoped my passion would get them going, as I proudly announced: 'Ladies and Gentlemen, may I present my brand-new programme: "Fake Your Own Funeral" . . .'

Now I had everyone's attention.

'In this groundbreaking show,' I continued, 'we take one person, convince all their friends and family that they're *dead*,' I paused at this point, 'and then film the aftermath with hidden cameras, so they get to see exactly how people react and who turns up to see them off.'

I stopped talking and glanced up – one lady in horn-rimmed glasses sniggered and one of the top bosses in the Entertainment Department looked horrified. From the mood of the room, I could easily tell the outcome of my short pitch – it was the old lead-balloon scenario. Oh dear.

I later found out my idea had been officially rejected. No problem. It sounds like a cliché to say this, but I know that rejection is simply part of the journey to success. So I try to force myself to take the attitude that I'll just have to try harder next time, remembering the motto that I came up with while working at *The Big Breakfast*: 'In the Kingdom of the Blind, the One-Idea Man is King'.

In other words, ideas are the key to success in all areas of business.

Another show of mine was a little less contentious than the funeral one and thus ended with a better result. The idea in question was for a travel reality show. It popped into my head after I'd decided to attend a TV festival in Cannes. At the time I was feverishly trying to branch out by myself as a programme developer. In recent years, a number of huge break-out TV shows had emerged, like *Who Wants to Be a Millionaire?*, *Survivor* and, of course, *Big Brother* (which I'd experienced directly, having worked on it for a couple of years by then). These programmes became huge worldwide hits, generating enormous sums of cash and changing the face of television as well. It was an exciting time, and like a lot of other people in TV I found myself caught up in the gold rush that ensued. Everyone was super keen to come up with the next hit series that would blow big. In theory, it was possible to have an idea while sitting at home, write it up and then pitch it to a broadcaster who would give the green light for your programme to hit the airwaves, kick-starting its chance to become the global television phenomenon you hoped. The reality was enormously different . . .

So, I took myself off to Cannes for the annual international television festival MIPCOM. I needed to make some contacts in other countries and see first hand how the buying and selling of TV shows took place.

The festival was an odd affair, full of TV executives flouncing around schmoozing and boozing. I returned from France slightly confused. There seemed to be so much demand for exciting new programmes, but not actually many of them around. Most of the show ideas being touted about were remarkably similar to other shows already on TV. I vowed to try my hand at thinking up something a bit more original that I could offer to the international production companies.

Travelling back on the plane, I pondered how lucky I was to be flying from country to country and just how amazing it was to be alive during a time when you could jump on a huge metal object that could land you in a completely different, stimulating location only hours later. Simultaneously, my mind scanned back through all the last-minute holidays I'd been on when I was younger. They all involved me (and a group of friends) flying to a resort, mostly in Spain, that comprised a collection of nightclubs and chip shops. It was like being in Britain, but in the sun, which was exactly what a huge number of youngsters wanted, and in fact still do.

Something about this phenomenon caught in my mind. I backtracked my thoughts: 'It's like being in Britain, but in the sun . . .' Boom! Here was the trigger for the new show concept. I spent the rest of the flight scribbling the bare bones of the idea in the margins of one of those slightly crumpled in-flight magazines.

Back home at my computer, I furiously typed out the format for the new programme. I knew it had to be fully thought through before I could sell it. It took a few months to get it exactly right, but once I'd finished the first draft, I wondered what I could do next. I knew it would be hard to pitch the idea on my own, both because there was a danger of its being ripped off and also because I just didn't have enough clout to reach or influence companies outside Britain, which is where

I wanted to sell this idea. But fortunately, I knew someone who did.

By chance, four months earlier whilst in France at a TV conference, I'd met a plucky young businessman named Tobi Huthmann. At the time, Tobi was working for a large television distribution company, travelling around the globe selling proven television formats to producers in a wide range of countries. I bumped into him one night at a rather glamorous party on an executive yacht and we immediately hit it off. When we met, Tobi was looking very dapper, dressed in a smart khaki summer suit. A tall, well-built man, he had the look of a European male model. His hair was short, dark brown and lustrous. He had a clear complexion, with rosy cheeks and bright blue eyes that seemed to bulge with energy when he talked. When he did, he spoke immaculate English with just a tinge of a German accent which gave away his Berlin roots.

Months later, Tobi got in touch out of the blue. He said he'd been thinking about selling hand-picked exciting 'paper formats' to his roster of clients in production companies and broadcasting houses across the world. 'Paper format' is the term given to a programme idea that hasn't been made yet, as opposed to one that *has* already been made and aired, and so exists on tape – this is simply called a 'format'. Tobi wanted to try to sell some of my paper formats. Good news. But there was a hitch.

Paper formats are notoriously difficult to sell because they are 'only' an idea and there is no proof that they'll work. This creates a very frustrating business loop, which goes like this:

The TV companies are commercial entities set up to make money. They obtain money from advertisers, who pay to reach the people watching the TV company's programmes. If no one watches, then no money comes in.

Now pretend you're the head of a TV company. (If you really *are* the head of a TV company, don't worry – you can still play along, and please be sure to remember this little exercise if I ever pitch to you in the future . . .). I come in to see you with two ideas for TV shows. One has already been aired and garnered huge numbers of viewers in another country. I have a tape of this programme and a detailed manual to show you how it works and how you can make it for your own country. The other show I pitch to you is a new programme idea on paper, not proven in any way. Even though the paper format might be a far more exciting idea than the previously aired show, your job is to make a profit for the company – so which one do you reckon you'll be more inclined to buy? Of course, most people will probably buy the show with the proven track record.

This process is completely understandable, but unfortunately it doesn't favour 'creativity' because many decision-makers will opt for putting a programme on their channel that has done well elsewhere or in the past, rather than risk their jobs on something new and unproven. That's pretty understandable.

That's why I thank the TV gods that there are broadcasters like the UK's Channel 4 and America's HBO, and even the BBC. These companies aren't *solely* after profit and will take chances with completely new ideas.

Crikey, I seem to have hopped on to my soapbox. A thousand apologies. Back to the TV idea I had . . .

I met Tobi at his posh central London offices, armed with my new format proudly bound into a lovingly typed proposal and nestling in my bag. We sat round a huge, dark brown wooden table, then Tobi kicked things off.

'Come on then, Shed, tell us this big idea you've been working on,' he said, straight to the point.

'OK Tob,' I replied. 'Here we go.'

I brought a bound document out of my bag. The front page bore the name of the show embedded in a logo that I'd designed:

'OK Tob. This is a simple show idea. It's called, "The Great Package Holiday Swindle" and here's what happens.' I paused for effect. 'We pick thirty British people who've never been to Spain before and we tell them that we're going to fly them to a Spanish resort for a two-week holiday and lessons in the native culture. OK?'

'Go on,' Tobi said with a smile.

'Well, when we fly these people to Spain, we'll fly them during the summer – and at night. The plane will circle above the UK for four hours and then we'll touch down in Cornwall, where we've created a Spanish airport. We'll then take the holidaymakers to a fake Spanish resort, complete with real Spaniards and fake British holidaymakers, and see how long it takes them to figure out they haven't really left their own country.'

'Ha ha – no way! That's great!' Tobi laughed.

Good news. He liked it so far. I then went on to explain the logistics of making the show work and how we'd keep the viewers completely gripped episode after episode.

Three weeks later Tobi called me.

'Shed, I think I've got someone interested in the "Holiday Swindle".' Wow, that was an amazingly quick turnaround.

It turned out that Tobi had spoken to a very forward-thinking TV producer who ran a production company in his home country, Germany. Tobi had pitched the show with the main idea altered to appeal to a German audience. Instead of English holidaymakers being taken to a fake Spanish resort, German tourists would fly to 'Spain' instead. It was the same core idea – the German holidaymakers would touch down in southern Germany, where the TV company had created a Spanish resort designed to fool the participants that they were in Spain.

Over the next few months, Tobi worked his magic on the producer from Germany, managing to persuade him to take out an 'option' on the show. This meant the company agreed to pay us a small amount of cash for permission to take the idea to broadcasters who could fund the show. If successful, the company would then make the series and get it broadcast on German television. It was an amazing first step in the process of getting a TV programme made. Unfortunately, things got a bit weird from then on.

I was rather surprised, but overjoyed, when the German company offered to fly us to Germany so they could discuss the idea further. They wanted me to pitch the show to their top guy, Michael. A few months later I found myself in the exciting position of being flown across to Cologne for the meeting.

As ever, I was very nervous about turning up to a meeting without bringing something extra to the proceedings. I was about to meet an experienced television-maker, in another country, and all I had was a simple idea on paper. I needed something more – something that would start to bring the 'fake Spain in the middle of Germany' programme to life.

I hit upon a plan to interview members of the German public about their impressions of Spain. I wanted to create a fast-moving videotape of colourful characters that I could show during the meeting. There were just a few tiny problems with this: I lived in London, I didn't know anything about the culture of Spanish holidays in Germany and, crucially, I didn't speak German.

Luckily, Tobi was on hand to make things happen. He put me in touch with a talented friend of his in Munich who was working his way up the television ladder. After I spoke with him on the phone, wonderfully this guy agreed to go out to film people in the streets talking about what they associated with Spain.

It turned out that there were similarities between English and German holidaymakers visiting Spain. In the same way that many English people jump on a plane to the Costa del Sol for a drink-fuelled 'bender', there was an equivalent area of Spain for German holidaymakers called 'Der Ballermann', which attracted lots of German youngsters.

With Tobi by my side as interpreter and co-producer, I used my computer to edit the footage and proudly labelled up a videotape ready for the big meeting in Germany. We had created a one and a half minute film of a range of great German characters talking about Spain and Spanish resorts. There weren't any big revelations on the tape – most of the people mentioned themes we're all familiar with – 'sun . . . paella . . . San Miguel . . . .drinking . . .' – but the tape was funny, short and, most importantly, gave a few pointers to what we'd have to do to make the con work. It meant I had something to bring to the meeting other than just words.

Soon the big day for the German pitch arrived. We excitedly jumped on a plane, flew to Cologne and then checked in to our hotel. It was the first time I'd been summoned to another country to talk about one of my ideas. This was a big deal.

But the actual meeting was a disaster.

It was one of those rare episodes that you couldn't make up, even if you wanted to. It turned out like a scene from a bad sitcom.

Before I arrived, I had presumed (naively, as it turns out) that because the German company had optioned the 'Holiday Swindle', everyone at the company would think the central premise of the show was good and that this meeting would be about how we'd proceed to making a pilot. After all, the company had not only paid for the option, they'd flown me and Tobi across to talk about it. So I assumed that our contact Michael would welcome us with open arms and would then want to discuss how to move forward. Well, as the old business adage says, 'Don't ASSUME – because when you ASSUME . . . it makes an ASS out of U and ME . . .' And hey, in this situation, I was most certainly the ASS.

The problem seemed to be that, even though Michael was a talented and dynamic TV executive, he'd been given this project to look after despite the fact that he didn't believe in it. Right from the off, he kept asking me to justify how the programme could be made. Rather than looking for solutions, he seemed delighted to point out the many ways the show couldn't be made. It was excruciating and demoralizing to have been flown across the continent to be told that your idea was an unrealistic, ridiculous proposition. There was still a chance though – the tape. Maybe that would help show Michael that it was feasible to convince a group of Germans that they were in Spain when in fact they were in deepest Germany.

I jumped up, popped it in the TV and sat back. It was the longest one and a half minutes I've ever experienced. Michael did not laugh once. When it finished, he didn't make any comment about it. Nothing. He just went back to pointing out the flaws in the format. I was tempted to say 'What did you think of the tape?', but I knew that I was just craving positive feedback in a situation where none was forthcoming. I actually found the situation so bizarre it became funny. I couldn't believe that the company had paid money for this idea, I'd made a tape, prepared a document for the meeting, come to another country and then found out that the guy I was seeing didn't even like the idea. It was upsetting, but tragically hilarious too.

And so there ends the story of 'The Great Package Holiday Swindle'. Tobi and I hightailed it back to the UK, both slightly baffled at the reception we'd received. The show never got off the ground in Germany or indeed anywhere else. My hope is that, even if it's not made as a reality TV show, it could make a great story for a movie.

Little did I know that while I was in Germany, back in Britain a well-known production company was working on a similar, but much better version of this idea. One year later, I got a phone call from a friend at Channel 4 asking me if I'd be interested in working on a new show they were making. It was to be called *Space Cadets* and it was to be the biggest practical joke in television history. I immediately signed up and the show went to air soon afterwards.

This programme turned out to be a groundbreaking and truly amazing piece of television, in which twelve members of the British public were told they were to be flown to Russia, where four of them would then be chosen to be launched into space in a space shuttle. The truth behind this elaborate ruse was that the participants were actually flown to an airbase in the south-east of England, near Ipswich, which had been mocked up to look like a Russian airbase. It was absolutely freezing on the base (I had to wear extra socks to stop my toes going numb), which added to the illusion that the cadets were in Russia. At the end of the training, the chosen 'astronauts' entered the interior of a space shuttle built by Hollywood set designers. Amazingly – and emotionally for all concerned – the cadets believed they were in space and on one occasion when the front shutters were opened, they also believed they were looking at the earth from thousands of miles up. In fact, they were looking at an image of the earth projected on to a state-of-the-art screen 3 metres away.

Now, as you've no doubt noticed, there are some similarities between my 'Great Package Holiday Swindle' idea and this one, although undoubtedly the *Space Cadets* format is a far more ambitious, well-thought-out and exciting idea in many ways. I had the germ of an idea, but hadn't formulated it well enough, whereas the creators of *Space Cadets* had made a wonderful tableau that had a real point to it, with dozens of built-in, exciting televisual moments. Not for the first time, I realized that even though I'd firmly believed in my package-holiday show, in fact I didn't have all the answers. Often if a project is proving hard to get off the ground, it may be because it needs changing to become something slightly different and, dare I say it, better.

Both 'The Great Package Holiday Swindle' and 'Fake Your Own Funeral' are big, rather wild ideas that haven't been made yet. But still, my philosophy is that all ideas have their time. This belief has been proved by things that have happened to me in the past. Some years back I wrote a number of morally questionable formats that involved plastic surgery in 'entertainment' shows. One was a game show where the winner won plastic surgery as the star prize. It was called 'Nip & Tuck', strapline: 'Cutting Edge Television'. All the broadcasters rejected the shows, saying they were simply distasteful. Lo and behold, a few years later many entertainment shows involving cosmetic surgery appeared on our screens including *Extreme Makeover* and *Plastic Surgery Live*. So it demonstrates that ideas aren't 'good' or 'bad', but sometimes there is a right time for a particular idea to flourish. So that's why you should never give up. Sometimes it's just the timing that's important.

Even if my ideas don't get taken on, I'd rather be coming up with concepts that get extreme reactions – and that includes negative ones – than boring old 'bland-o-vision' type shows. There are enough programmes on television that look exactly the same.

Throughout my time in the TV world, I had always wanted to make a show that would be highly original and entertaining, but also thought-provoking and meaningful as well. Before I began seriously developing and pitching television programmes, and way before I came up with the funeral show or before *Space Cadets* aired, one of my early big ideas for a television show actually did get off the ground. I could never have imagined in my wildest dreams – or nightmares – what would happen . . .

'*Yes indeed, you must be one arrogant idiot to even think that you can pull off this TV show – of course you can't! And if you reckon anyone's gonna like this idea, then you're totally mad and stupid too . . .*

Even if you do pull it off, you're gonna hurt a lot of people – decent, valuable members of society, good, non-cynical, un-television people . . .

Only someone very twisted would do this . . .

Oh and who are you anyway? Well, I'll tell you: a dysfunctional, emotionally stunted, selfish, self-serving, hedonistic, exploitative idiot with a completely hazy moral compass . . . So leave those poor people at the channel alone and just drop this idea for a TV show that's all about YOU . . .

I'll say it once again, as you didn't seem to be listening all the other times:
YOU ARE GOING TO HURT A LOT OF GOOD PEOPLE . . .'

I Really, Really Went Back In Time

The idea that landed me on the front pages

I am on the run. It is a sunny day in late March and I'm sitting on the bed in a posh hotel room in Bath town centre.

My brain is swirling. I try to take a mental deep breath, so I can process the ludicrous, mind-boggling fact that I, Shed Simove, aged thirty, am . . . on . . . the . . . run.

One of the people I'm with has just put the phone down and hurriedly says that we should turn on the TV. He switches to ITV and it's showing the local news. I know what's coming up. Oh no.

Then, very soon, the news anchor starts a new story:

'A local school is furious after a thirty-year-old TV producer posed as a sixteen-year-old boy for a Channel 4 documentary. The man, Sheridan Simove, spent nine weeks at the school before revealing his true age.'

The news anchor then throws to a female reporter who is standing outside the school. Time seems to slow. The TV news is talking about me – it's surreal. It wasn't meant to happen like this.

The female reporter then gives an account of the story again. She describes how a TV company told the school they wanted to film a documentary about a new boy joining the sixth form. They then filmed this new boy for nine weeks while he attended the school.

However, at the end of term the television company revealed that in fact the 'young-looking' pupil was not aged sixteen, but was really thirty years old. She goes on to say that pupils and teachers are very upset and that Channel 4 has unreservedly apologized.

I am totally focused on the female news reporter, trying to work out what she makes of the story, which at that time, for me, translated into the question, 'What does she make of my life?'

A most curious contradiction seems to be occurring before my very eyes. Her sentences are loaded with condemning, emotive words: 'duped', 'tricked' 'upset', said in a derogatory fashion, suggesting I've done something terrible, but there is no denying it, her face is telling another story. She seems to have the slightest, but yes, definite, smirk on her face, as if she finds the story amusing. The effect of this is that her report could be interpreted (and indeed certainly is by the people collected in my room) as saying that she thinks this wasn't such a heinous act as her words convey.

The news report ends and I try to take stock of what has happened. In the preceding nine weeks, I've carried out the hardest challenge I've ever had to face in my life, bar nothing, and now my life will never be the same. And all because I had a little idea that grew and grew inside my head until it leaped into reality and became a big idea that will reverberate through my life for years to come.

The seed for the idea had been sown four years previously. One day I was reading the newspaper and a story caught my eye, and then my imagination. It recounted a scandal that had rocked a high school in Glasgow, describing how a thirty-two-year-old man named Brian McKinnon had managed to infiltrate himself into the school as one of the pupils in the sixth form in order to re-sit his Higher examinations (Scotland's equivalent of A-levels). On discovering his true age, the school had expelled the man, but he'd managed to remain undetected for months before being found out. The details of the case blew me away – the man had changed his name (bizarrely, to Brandon Lee – the same name as Bruce Lee's famous actor son who tragically died while filming cult movie *The Crow*), faked his birth certificate and, once he'd been admitted to the school, carried on living as a pupil for months and months.

I think my imagination must have been fired a little too much, though, because I turned this story over and over in my head on numerous occasions for a long time afterwards. Little did I know that one day this unusual tale would lead to my very own scandal.

My scandal arose after a long time working towards making a name for myself in TV. During my years on *The Big Breakfast* at Planet 24, I'd spent ages thinking hard about setting up my own television production company. I yearned to make amazing, powerful and entertaining TV (as I still do), but I knew how hard it was to run as a viable television business, not only because of the huge challenge of getting a broadcaster to commission a show from a new independent production company, but also because, even if you do get one show made, the profits are rarely enough to sustain any period without another commission. But, even though these hurdles lay in front of me, incredibly I got the chance to live my dream when a brand-new digital channel was launched in the UK.

Luckily, a very good friend of mine, Damon Beesley – a talented producer with a permanently sunny disposition and a truly good heart – had been taken on as one of the big-wigs at this new channel, an edgy young sister station for Channel 4 called E4. When the channel boss, an eccentric TV visionary named Andrew Newman, asked if there was anyone who could produce a new show for them, Damon suggested me.

Andrew already knew me as we'd worked together at Planet 24 (it's an industry joke that virtually everyone in light-entertainment television has worked there at one point or another). As well as his super-bright mind, Andrew was also known for his quirky dress sense. He collected vintage clothes and would often turn up to work in a diamond jumper twinned with plus-fours and a floppy hat. I used to sit in meetings with him and he'd come up with the most incredible, outlandish and naughty ideas. Once he created a strand for *The Word* called 'The Revengers' which involved viewers getting their own back on people they knew by setting up elaborate stunts that would shock them.

I remember watching Andrew painting markings on a dead rabbit that he'd bought from a butcher to make it look like a female viewer's pet, which had actually been taken out of its cage that morning by an accomplice who lived in her house. An actor went to the girl's door and proceeded to describe how he'd run over a rabbit and then revealed the mangled furball. The victim was understandably distraught, thinking that her beloved bunny had been squashed under a Michelin tyre. All this was secretly filmed, and made harsh, but gripping, viewing. Of course, the victim was eventually told the scenario was a joke arranged by the person seeking revenge and the whole thing aired the following week, to much consternation from a few complaining (older) viewers. I'll never forget Andrew holding the dead rabbit and saying to me (a lowly 'runner' at the time), 'Does it need more fake blood Shed?'

So there I was, finding myself having to judge the amount of fake blood to put on a dead rabbit in order to scare a poor girl into thinking her pet had been squashed. And to think I could have become an accountant.

Now my old colleagues Damon and Andrew called me into their offices and told me that they wanted to commission a special TV programme to help with the new channel's launch. The show they wanted involved a compilation of all the best bits from the channel's output that week. This 'best bits' programme would air on the main channel – Channel 4 – and would act as a showcase for the new sister channel, E4.

And they wanted me to make it.

They said that if I took the job, I'd need to set up a production company and start making the show as soon as the new digital channel launched, in three weeks' time.

I couldn't believe it. And even though I was scared witless, I said 'Yes' immediately. It was unbelievably exciting. There I was, barely twenty-nine years old and with a commission for a thirteen-part series on the freshest, most cutting-edge channel in the UK.

But I couldn't be excited for too long – I had to get on with it.

My learning curve was steep. I swiftly had to rent an office, hire a production manager, an assistant producer and a production secretary, book edit suites and, lastly, create stationery proudly displaying my egotistical production company name: 'The Talent Shed Ltd'.

We made one show every week that aired on Channel 4. Even though in television terms it was a simple 'top ten best moments' programme, it was the first show produced by my production company to air. It was simply thrilling to watch it go out and then check the ratings to find that over a million people had enjoyed the show.

After that, I had the fortune to be asked to produce another clip-show for Channel 4, this time with the up-and-coming comedian Jimmy Carr looking at the inherent humour in corporate videos. It was a one-off half-hour slot, with an incredibly small budget to boot. This meant I had to make the show out of my flat, which was pure hell. When that was finished and successfully aired, I suddenly found myself going from the boss of a successful production company to being just me on my own – just 'Shed' again. It was very odd.

I needed another show to keep the company going. Ideally, I wanted it to be a big, bold idea that would put The Talent Shed on the map as a producer of daring, entertaining and thought-provoking television. So what programme could I make next?

As I thought of shows I could possibly do, the story of how Brandon Lee posed as a teenager when he was over thirty years old kept coming back to me. Like a persistent, annoying gnat buzzing round my skull, it just wouldn't go away. I was approaching the age of thirty, and for me this was significant. I saw it as a benchmark age and felt I needed to embark on something hugely ambitious very soon.

Perhaps it was the fact that I was having a mini mid-life crisis that spurred me on to pick something that would challenge me so much. I just kept thinking over and over that I'd like to try what Brian McKinnon did and film it as a TV show.

The more I thought about it, the more it seemed to make sense. I yearned to see if I could actually get away with being a sixteen-year-old again, and for months and months this was all I could think about. I also began to think that even though a programme would cover the jeopardy of whether or not I could actually carry off this 'gag', it could also focus on much more than just the transformation. I began to analyse why I was so obsessed with the idea of trying to go back to school again and it became clear that if I was ever allowed to pursue the idea (which was hugely unlikely at this time) maybe the programme could have something interesting to say.

I've always been fascinated with the concept of 'youth' and the related issues surrounding this intriguing topic. Because I looked young for my age while I was growing up, I've thought long and hard about how someone's appearance can affect their life. At the time I was developing this programme, I'd also become captivated with the whole issue of 'age labelling', especially words like 'adult' and 'child', 'mature' and 'immature'.

It's an interesting question to ask what exactly defines an 'adult'. My own frustrations while growing up led me to believe that often in society today, young people aren't listened to enough. This issue of 'adult' and 'child' distinctions was further muddied in my mind when I started working in TV. It seemed to me that a childlike ability to dream and to see no boundaries was a positive benefit when working in a creative industry. I also noticed that many adults behaved like children – at least by my definition of the word. Just because someone is 'older' doesn't mean they automatically act with maturity and wisdom, and vice versa.

On top of all this, I was fascinated to see whether I could live a fantasy many people only think about – that is, to get a shot at experiencing a part of my life over again.

I wanted to make a TV show that would make people go 'Wow!' – that would engage them, but also make them think about some serious issues in their life and in society. Blimey, I wasn't (and I'm still not) trying to cure cancer here; I just wanted to excel in a field I love so much by creating a show that was both hugely entertaining and had a deeper merit too. I thought that maybe this one could do that . . .

Once I'd decided that I actually wanted to try to make such a programme, complete with its risky core idea (which I wasn't actually sure that I could carry off), I then needed a pitch document. In the TV world, this document is called a 'treatment' – a very appropriate word in this case, as a lot of people thought I needed psychiatric care when I told them what I was planning.

I sat down to write the treatment. It had to be both a sales document to get anyone reading it excited, and also a manual of how to make the show, so that it was clear it could be more than just a wild idea. The document needed to present this programme as a well-thought-out, viable business proposition.

As I started to write the first page, I naturally found the need for a title at the top of it. The name for the show came pretty easily.

Growing up I'd often seen a poster in the windows of clothes shops that would appear towards the end of the school summer holidays. This poster always used to strike dread in my heart when I saw it. It read simply: 'Back to School'.

I decided that 'Back to School' was a perfect title for the programme, as it neatly described one of the themes in the show: to discover whether I could pull this idea off; and, if I *could* pull it off, to explore what social status I would have second time round.

The first page of the treatment flowed easily. I wrote down the main idea in a sentence: 'I, Sheridan Simove, aged thirty, will attempt to go back to school, posing as a sixteen-year-old pupil.'

Simple.

At this stage, the finer details of how I would actually logistically pull it off weren't formed. The precise procedures were to come later, in the numerous versions of the treatment I went on to produce.

I placed a photo of myself at the top of the page, underneath the title, figuring that anyone reading the document would need to see how young I looked for my age. The rest of the page described the main points of the programme: how I would attend school as a 'normal' pupil; that I wouldn't put on another persona, but that I'd 'be myself', and *just* lie about my age. I'd attend lessons, interact with the other students and, once I'd completed a whole term at the school, I'd then reveal to the students and teachers that I was in fact thirty years old and that they'd been part of a groundbreaking programme that explored the topic of what it is to be a young adult. That was the plan anyway.

The creation of this front page had a significant effect. It gave the idea a form outside the invisible thoughts in my head. There's something really significant about putting an idea down on paper – it almost doesn't exist before then, although of course it does in your head. Once written down, it does miraculously come to life, and for me it becomes a tangible, touchable product. There's then something real to show to others, and that's what I did – I went to Channel 4, undoubtedly the most forward-thinking and experimental channel at that time. It was the beginning of a very long challenge to persuade the clever people who worked there that I could pull the show off.

'It'll never work.'

I've heard that phrase many times in my life, and every time is one time too many. It's up there in the top three responses that I, and lots of other people who pitch ideas, seem to elicit. Also riding consistently high in the 'Responses You Don't Want to Hear after a Pitch' Chart are 'It's not a good idea' and 'That's outrageous – you can't do that'. I encountered all these comments when I started to describe the school idea to TV colleagues I'd worked with in the past.

To Channel 4's credit, I was welcomed into the initial meetings I asked for. Given that all the decision-makers were exceptionally busy, I was under no illusions about how privileged I was to get this treatment. The challenge I faced at the start was that, even though I could get a meeting with the important big-wigs, many people thought this show would be incredibly difficult to make.

A lot of the television executives worried that even if I could pull the deception off, it was just far too risky a proposition to invest in, given that it was my small production company making the series.

Surprisingly, though, the objection I didn't really encounter was that there was no way I could pass as a sixteen-year-old. This fact spurred me on greatly and I began to formulate a plan to solve the understandable objections that I was encountering.

As time went on, the 'Back to School' treatment document grew and grew. I spent hours researching and planning the structure of the show – what I'd do, when I'd do it and how each stage would work. The detailed plan for the content of the show became much more than just following me on my journey: it encompassed filming many of the young people in the school so that the audience could see what these people had to offer.

I wrote over thirty versions of the proposal, and I've no doubt that this persistence made people realize I was completely serious about undertaking the project, but the real breakthrough came when a handful of amazing people got involved.

The first of these was Damon Beesley, my old *Big Breakfast* partner-in-crime. While I worked on the manic morning show, one day I got told that I was to be paired with Damon, who was going to be my new researcher. I was very worried that Damon would think I was a geeky idiot because he was one of the trendier blokes in the office. Previously, I'd only seen him around the studios and made a snap judgement about him. I thought he was one of the 'cool guys' at Planet 24 who wouldn't give me the time of day. But when we started to work together – writing and producing the segments for two alien puppets called 'Zig and Zag' – I quickly realized that he was a phenomenally gentle, good-natured soul with an amazing passion and talent for making great television. We shared the same views on what made good TV (finding out we were both obsessed with *The Larry Sanders Show* was a particularly bonding moment) and we completely clicked. Wonderfully, our work reflected this. We'd often work long hours, thinking up new strands and ideas for the show, buzzing off each other, not stopping until we were both happy. We worked so well together.

Ever since then, Damon and I have been great friends and he has always believed in me. This was to prove incredibly fortuitous given that he later became very influential at Channel 4. It's always great to have a good friend in a high place, isn't it?

When Damon saw that I needed help in getting my school show off the ground, he talked to all the right people at the channel and gave the project the inside support it vitally needed. One significant leap forward was when he talked with Channel 4's best legal executive, a man named Prash Naik. Amazingly, he got behind the show too. Prash was very influential within Channel 4 at the time, so this was an extremely important development. Every day, Prash would make legal (and moral) decisions about what could be broadcast. A lot of the solutions he came up with for producers allowed them to create groundbreaking, edgy and socially impacting programmes.

Even though he's a heavy hitter in the channel, Prash is a quietly spoken man with a round, gentle face and actually looks very young himself. I often wondered if that was why he bought into the project so much. He was an incredible enabler – he made things happen. Where some lawyers would tell you the myriad reasons why something couldn't be done, Prash looked for ways to make it possible. I think he was a rarity because, rather than being a 'suit' (not that he wore a suit) who acted as a policeman, instead he was virtually a television producer himself: he was passionate about making innovative TV and on the side of the programme-makers. On a number of occasions when I worked with him, I felt he was Channel 4's unsung hero. Prash is not only someone who makes things happen, he's the sort of guy you can rely on when a crisis occurs.

Just as well, as it turned out . . .

There were two key moments that significantly influenced the project being given the green light by the powers-that-be at Channel 4. One was when Prash came up with a clever way of making the show legally (if not morally) feasible. Up until the point when he arrived at the solution, all the versions of the treatment had described how my time at school would be secretly filmed with hidden cameras. Prash pointed out that this wasn't legal, or indeed fair to the people in the school, and suggested that instead we create a cover story for filming me openly.

So, we came up with a very simple plan to approach a school saying that we wanted to film a documentary about a sixteen-year-old who was unsure about whether to continue with his education. We'd place this person in their school so the 'new boy' could decide whether to carry on or drop out and we'd film the whole thing. We would also let the school know that, at the same time as filming the new boy, we'd also film large segments involving the current pupils in the school. Their lives and viewpoints would form another part of the documentary, covering what it's like to be a young person. Of course this last part was completely true.

The other significant turn of events came when a highly respected documentary-maker got involved with the project. During the many months I tried to get the idea off the ground, even though Channel 4 was receptive to my ideas, they still hadn't green-lit the show, and in fact it looked very unlikely that it would be commissioned. I wrote so many treatments and came back from dozens of meetings with different decision-makers who said they thought it just couldn't be made.

I got the feeling that I needed to make the project much more attractive by getting an impressive production team to work with me. I figured that I needed an amazing television storyteller to tell (what I hoped might possibly be) an amazing story. I set about trying to find the best documentary-maker working in the television industry.

There was only one choice. Incredibly, about a year earlier I'd seen a stunning programme called *The Gambler* about a man who'd been given a large lump of money to gamble away as he wished. The show was beautifully shot, with a wonderful musical score. All in all, it was a simply riveting film. I'd thought about that masterpiece for a long time after I'd watched it, and now that I needed to team up with a visual storytelling genius, I thought I'd try to meet the top man in the business and see whether on the off-chance he might be interested. It was a very long shot.

I needed help to track this documentary-maker down. One of my oldest friends and supporters at Channel 4 was a wonderful woman who'd been a bit like a career guardian angel. Her name is Charlotte Black. Charlotte is a glamorous, bohemian blonde with an infectious laugh who knows anyone who's anyone in TV. She immediately told me that the person who made the film was a talented director called 'Paul W.' (I'm going to abbreviate the names of some people involved in this project to protect their privacy – you'll see why as the story pans out.)

So I called Paul. When he answered I thought he had an intelligent, gentle voice. Nervously, I began to pitch my ambitious project to this complete stranger on the end of a phone.

'Hello, my name's Sheridan Simove. Hope you don't mind me calling . . . Um – I'm developing a really exciting documentary for Channel 4, and saw your film *The Gambler* – awesome – and thought maybe you might be interested to meet up?'

And so I continued, inarticulately splurging out my excitement as best I could without revealing the actual idea. I didn't want to tell it to Paul over the telephone as I believed (and still do) that the real impact of a pitch comes face to face, when the person can see the fire in your eyes. It was even more important to meet face to face in this case, so the person I was meeting could see for themselves if they thought I could get away with posing as a sixteen-year-old and also whether I was vaguely interesting enough to appear on screen.

Over the phone, Paul explained he was far too busy to take on any new projects. My heart sank, but I managed to persuade him to meet for a coffee anyway.

We met that afternoon in a Starbucks off Soho Square. Paul was tall, in his mid-thirties, with a handsome face and bright blue twinkling eyes. I thought I detected a bit of a maverick glint in them.

After shaking hands, I quickly pitched the show. Paul laughed after I'd said the first sentence – 'I'm going to go back to school as a sixteen-year-old without telling anyone in the school my true age.' He seemed intrigued at first, then proceeded to ask loads of questions. I suggested that perhaps he'd like to come in and see Channel 4 with me, just to see how far I'd got with the project. He said he would and I left the coffee shop ecstatic. The whole meeting had taken no more than ten minutes.

After meeting with Channel 4 a number of times, Paul had heard enough to decide that he'd come on board as executive producer. This was incredible news. Paul would oversee the project from then on and recommended a talented young team to work with me, led by an up-and-coming director called Kate M. Kate's role was not only planning how the documentary would be shot, but she also took a producer role too, something that had been my sole responsibility up until then. It was such a relief to have amazing people working with me, all trying to make something worthwhile happen.

Kate's first (gargantuan) job was the superhuman goal of finding a school that would agree to us filming the documentary. We wanted one with similarities to the high school I attended when I was a teenager – Cardiff High. This had been (and still is, by all accounts) a good state school with fiercely passionate teachers and interesting, engaging students who could make people sit up and believe in the younger generation.

Right from the start we aimed to find a school that we could highlight in a good way. The programme wasn't meant to be an exposé or undercover mission to showcase anything bad going on in schools; this was a programme intended first to give me another chance at being sixteen and, second, to highlight the importance of good teaching and the potential of young people.

With Paul and the team on board, suddenly the project had an extra credibility that reassured the people at Channel 4 whom we approached to bankroll this risky venture. We filmed a short video where I talked about what I was planning to do and sent it to the top bosses at the channel, hoping it would let them see how I came across on camera and sway them if they had any doubts. By this time the project had been seen by a number of different departments at

Channel 4, but there was still no decision. The problem was that all the decision-makers saw the potential in the idea, but for one reason or another it just wasn't right for them at that time. This was hugely frustrating. Every time I thought I was close to getting the programme off the ground, I'd get a call that started, 'Shed, we love the idea, but . . .'

However, slowly but surely, a curious momentum started to build. Every person that passed on the project also told me to try another department, which of course I did.

Eventually I got a call from a forward-thinking team at Channel 4, headed by a well-spoken, ambitious young commissioner named Iain Morris. Iain had been following my progress from the sidelines for a while. At the time, he and my old pal Damon shared a flat and are still good friends today. Damon would recount to Iain how committed I was in getting the programme made, then, after many months of uncertainty, just as I thought the project was doomed never to go ahead, Iain got his boss – a sharp executive commissioner called Caroline Leddy – interested in the project.

One day, after months of more meetings, I explained to Caroline and Iain that I'd become so obsessed with the idea of going back to school that I'd probably go ahead with the challenge on my own, regardless of whether it was going to be aired on TV. I was soon to turn thirty-one and felt this was my last chance to see if I could pull off this bizarre feat. I think everyone understood I meant what I said.

A few days later, I got a call.

Amazingly, wonderfully – and then frighteningly, Channel 4 agreed to make the show.

I say 'frighteningly' because this was the point when I suddenly became very nervous indeed. The fact that Britain's most cutting-edge broadcaster had now agreed to make the programme would mean they'd be paying me and my company a large amount of money to pull the show off. And oh – I didn't know if I could.

As soon as the commission was confirmed, after a brief feeling of relief rather than elation, numerous worries flooded my mind: 'Can I *really* get away with passing as a sixteen-year-old? If I'm rumbled, will Channel 4 want to work with me ever again?'

But one concern kept surfacing much more than the others. I was consumed with the concern that I just may cause a lot of genuinely good people to be very hurt. I knew I had to lie to decent people even to attempt to make the programme happen. As I tried to get to sleep at night, I tried to convince myself that, because I was intending to tell the people involved the truth at some point, the lies were perhaps acceptable ones. I had a blind optimism that everything would turn out OK, but as soon as the commission was green-lit and the task at hand really hit home, I consistently grappled with whether what I was doing was wrong. Indeed, many of these doubts were captured on the footage we filmed.

And yet, I forged ahead.

My life hurtled on like a rollercoaster ride. There was only one school term during which we could film: the spring term, beginning in January, as it would be less intrusive than the summer term, when all the students would be taking important exams. This meant we had to get on with filming the programme immediately.

Kate, the director, did days upon days of solid work, meticulously researching and visiting schools up and down the country. Meanwhile, I was still writing copious memos detailing Channel 4 meetings, creating plans for each shot and trying to put together the infrastructure and staff of the company who would actually produce the show. It was an intense time – but not as intense as it would get later on.

One day, after visiting a number of schools, Kate excitedly called me to say she thought she'd found the perfect place: a medium-sized comprehensive in a town slap bang in Middle England. The school ticked all the boxes on our wish-list exactly. It was full of bright, interesting young people and teachers who really cared.

The next few weeks were tense while we waited to hear whether they would agree to be part of the programme. Kate travelled up and down to the school. Eventually, in a momentous decision, they agreed to take part in the documentary.

As the project began to gain momentum, I started a video diary capturing my personal thoughts. During this time, we also drew up a detailed schedule for the two months ahead. Time was short. There were only ten days available for my 'preparation' before I was due to meet the deputy headmaster for a standard entrance interview. If all went to plan and the school accepted the 'new pupil', I'd be starting there immediately after that with the plan to stay for the whole nine-week term.

It's a very odd feeling when your dreams start to come true. After so many hours of work on this project, my mind couldn't quite take it in that the programme was going ahead. I look back at that time now and view it as a dream state. It was certainly an altered reality – one that I consciously altered – but what was surprising was that the altered reality started turning into my actual reality, with the most disturbing consequences.

I had never been undercover before. I had never done any 'stunts' on this scale or even near it. I had categorically never done anything like the task ahead. I was absolutely petrified.

Before I entered the school, a police check was carried out on all the members of the production team who'd be working there. This is standard procedure when making a television programme involving any filming in close proximity to minors (people aged under sixteen). The process of the police check involved us filling out a form and ticking lots of boxes to confirm we'd never been in trouble with the law or done anything remotely dodgy.

It's weird, but when I started to write on my form, I became a little paranoid. I had the most bizarre nagging doubt that even though I knew I'd never done anything criminal, for a split second I worried that maybe I *had* been involved with the police at some point and had just forgotten it. A weird sort of global guilt I suppose, which might have been picked up by the next check that I undertook . . .

I was also analysed by a psychologist. He chatted with me on a number of occasions, concluding that I had many of the traditional issues of a modern middle-class man (neurotic, slightly dysfunctional, overly analytical – no bedwetting though, thankfully) but that I was fine to be sent into the school.

My police check came back and confirmed that I'd passed. I wonder what it would say today.

These checks were not only important procedure for Channel 4 and my production company as responsible television-makers, they also meant that Kate and the production team could truthfully assure the school that the 'new pupil' had been thoroughly checked out. On a number of occasions, the headmistress and other senior staff asked for assurances about the new boy and we truthfully told them that indeed all the proper checks had been carried out. We stressed that the teenager was perfectly acceptable to enter the school. I *was* acceptable of course. I just wasn't *sixteen*.

With just one week to go, my 'preparation' began. First off, there was the challenge of my name. I'd decided early on that I couldn't use my own name while in the school. 'Sheridan Simove' was a little too distinctive. Even though I wasn't a well-known TV producer, I'd met many people through my travels and, additionally, when you say your name is Shed, people tend to remember such an odd moniker. So to avoid anyone making a chance connection, I had to be called something else.

I needed a name that I'd be able to remember to respond to. It was no good choosing something that I forgot to react to when someone called my name. That would blow my cover in no time. So I chose my middle name, Howard. Some of the team felt it was a bit posh, but I could remember it easily, so it stuck. My second name was also changed, this time in line with my family history. Originally, my Simove forefathers had come from Lithuania with the surname Shimolovski. The different generations had each chosen to change the name (understandably) to something a bit more anglicized. So one branch of the family was called Shimolove, my grandfather's branch became Simove and yet another family line chose to call themselves Simmonds.

I decided to become Howard Simmonds. Now, I could have simply told everyone in the school that Howard Simmonds was my name and left it at that. But there was an extra twist.

I needed a rather specialized piece of kit for my time posing as a sixteen-year-old. Through my research, I'd discovered that anyone under eighteen years old in the UK was only permitted to obtain a very specific bank card called a Solo card. Since the project began, I'd spent a lot of time thinking about how I could possibly pull off the big lie of being sixteen. I'd always felt I would need as many props as possible to help reinforce my alter ego as a sixteen-year-old. This insecurity meant that I desperately wanted a Solo card. It seemed to me to be the only physical proof of my status as an under-eighteen-year-old that I could realistically carry.

There was only one way I could get a bone fide, functional Solo card with 'Howard Simmonds' printed on it. I needed to change my name by deed poll.

So, off I went to a musky office round the corner from where I lived to meet a solicitor specializing in changing people's names. It was actually a very weird experience. Once I'd signed the official document, I was legally 'Howard Simmonds'. It was the first event among many in this odd journey that was to have me questioning the rather deep notions of 'self' and 'personal identity'. Heavy, eh? Well, it really made me stop and think. Your name is so much about who you are. It *is* you. Mine had just been changed and that felt jarring. But this name change had much bigger implications than just a weird feeling.

To get the Solo card I had to send my bank the deed poll confirming my name change. Immediately, all my cards, my bank account and my chequebooks were transformed into entities bearing my new name. It was wonderfully surreal to receive a chequebook with 'Howard Simmonds' printed on it. This project was suddenly becoming very real.

My name change had another, much more significant effect as well. Because I knew I'd want to revert back to my real name, I made the decision not to change any of my company details with Companies House. And so I found myself in the completely bizarre position of not being legally in charge of my own production company. I couldn't even access the company bank account, which was now much fuller since Channel 4 had given a huge injection of money with which to make the programme. I was incredibly fortunate to have a team that I could trust, so I wasn't concerned about anything underhand happening while I went back to school; it was more about this loss of control being another one of many small events that took me further and further away from my real life and into a deeper state of displacement.

All this was happening so fast and was hugely unsettling. As you can imagine, I wasn't sleeping well around that time. In fact, I didn't have refreshing slumber for a long time afterwards. There wasn't time to dwell on any worries, however. In six days' time I was about to try to pull off the most far-fetched idea I'd ever had.

The main part of my 'training' took place in my home town of Cardiff. As Howard Simmonds, I needed a 'back story' – a pre-planned set of plausible circumstances that would explain why I was now re-entering sixth form. I wanted it to be as close to my real life as possible, both because I didn't think I could remember loads of different new facts and also because I wasn't ever planning to play a character while I attended the school: I was simply going to function as my thirty-year-old self, but with lies and omissions that gave me the age of a much younger person. This last point was vital to ensure the experiment testing which social group I'd end up in was going to be valid. I was trying to relive my youth, but with the benefit of experience – something that I and many others have wished for and which had previously been possible only in science-fiction movies.

The back story we settled on for the 'new me' was as follows: I was born in Cardiff (true) and had attended Cardiff High School until I was sixteen (also true). Six months ago my parents had moved to America, taking me with them and enrolling me into a school in

Florida which I hadn't liked, thus precipitating my return to the UK to live with my uncle in Cardiff and having the wish to attend school again back in Britain (all completely false). We chose Orlando as the place where my parents had taken me, as in reality I'd spent a year there working for Disney, which meant I could talk with real knowledge should I be asked about the place.

In order for me to come across convincingly as a contemporary Cardiff teenager, Kate arranged for me to meet a group of young people aged between fifteen and seventeen from the city. They were chosen to give me a crash course in how to be a real-life sixteen-year-old, but they weren't told the full details of what I was planning.

Confirmation of how out of touch I was came when we went shopping for the clothes I needed to be Howard. I kept choosing garments that I thought were suitable for a sixteen-year-old, but which the Cardiff gang looked at in utter disdain, explaining them as being too 'studenty'. It seemed I was choosing clothes suitable for a modern-day university student, rather than a teenage school kid. Instead, they dressed me in the attire of the moment, which was 'gangster chic'. The influence of American rap stars had permeated global youth culture and now it seemed that many young people were being heavily influenced by the urban 'street' look.

While the cameras rolled, we visited shop after shop in Cardiff city centre, picking me out a whole new wardrobe. Every time I tried something on, I thought I looked ridiculous. All the clothes they chose were deliberately picked to be three sizes too big – apparently the cool way to dress. They put me in baggy 'hoodies' – thick fleece tops with hoods, each one emblazoned with a huge brand name like 'FUBU'. To be 'in' with the 'in crowd', I also had to wear a peaked cap slung casually to the side across my head, so we bought several. They also made me buy a chunky silver chain to wear round my neck, a solid silver ring and some Nike-branded glasses.

Resplendent in my huge flapping tracksuit bottoms, garish trainers, my hoody, shiny jewellery and hat, I had all the style of a black rap star from the Bronx. Which was fine, except in real life I was a geeky thirty-year-old white boy from Cardiff. At least it was a comfy look. I suppose you need to be able to move easily when you're a gangster, in case there's trouble in 'da hood'.

The teenagers also insisted I needed an earring, which was duly punched into my left ear – apparently the right ear would denote I was gay. I was learning a lot.

The next big challenge was my hair. Normally I wore it medium long with a light coating of hair wax. My mentors said it needed a major overhaul. Much fun was had by all as I nervously let them cut my locks with some electric clippers. My hair was then plastered to my head with huge amounts of gel and teased into neat points on my forehead. Once again, I thought I looked hilarious, but if that was what was needed to pull me through this, then I was prepared to be fully committed to my shiny new helmet of hair.

There may have been a large disparity in how I normally dressed compared with the average teenager, but the actual difference between our interests was much less. The young people who coached me were heavily into the wide media world – TV, movies, music and the internet, just like me. And also like me and millions of other people, they enjoyed socializing with friends and meeting new people.

As well as the influence of stateside fashion, American culture permeated the teenagers' lives in other ways. One of my group of young Cardiffians was a sixteen-year-old guy named Gareth. His nickname was 'Chief', a much more 'street' designation. Chief was heavily into Tupac Shakur – an American rap star who was tragically killed because of a gang feud. Chief's bedroom was plastered with posters and photos of the rapper. It wasn't just the 'glamorous' aspirational gangster lifestyle of money, girls, cars and clothes that drew him to this successful pop star. He talked passionately about the beauty and truth he saw in the rapper's lyrics. Details like Chief's passion for his hero helped me greatly. Because I could connect with him and his interests, I felt more confident that I might not stick out so much if I ever did manage to attend school as a sixteen-year-old.

Even though I only spent just over a day with my young Cardiff mentors, they helped me immensely. I had the right clothes, the right walk (apparently I wasn't swaggering enough) and Chief and the rest of the group became incorporated into my back story as the Cardiff friends that I'd grown up with. They gave me plausible characters to talk about if I was ever questioned about my mates 'back home'.

The Cardiff youngsters also provided many other bits of detail that really helped my transformation. One such issue came up when I told them what my name in the school was going to be.

'I'm going to be called Howard,' I said.

The teenagers paused.

'Well?' I prompted.

A couple of sniggers. I could tell they weren't impressed.

'Is it that bad?' I pleaded.

'Well, it's a bit geeky,' Chief piped up. The others murmured in agreement, plainly relieved that someone had had the balls to say out loud what they didn't want to.

'I can't change it, so what can I do?' I asked.

They came up with a great solution: I should take on a much cooler nickname. The first one they came up with was 'H'. But as soon as they discovered my second name was to be Simmonds, they jumped on it like a shot. It was settled. I was to be called 'Simmo' for short.

The Cardiff youngsters immediately helped me transfer a 'Simmo' logo on to the new mobile phone we'd bought for me. Important little touches like this helped bring my alter ego to life.

In actual fact, for the nine weeks I attended school as Howard, I wasn't actually asked much about my home life. One thing I quickly realized was, in general, how focused young people are on the present and, to a much lesser extent, the near future. Because they don't have a huge past, they may not be so interested in other people's. At least, that was my experience.

After the trip to Cardiff, I still felt woefully unprepared for the huge task ahead. I was now constantly anxious. The programme schedule was hurtling forward at breakneck speed and I still didn't have the slightest clue whether I would get away with posing as a sixteen-year-old.

During my time in Cardiff, I also visited my parents. I spent a great deal of time with them, most of it stressing over the moral implications of what I was about to do. I asked them the questions that had been churning in my head ever since we landed the commission for the show: 'Am I doing something fundamentally morally wrong? Will I hurt a lot of people?'

My mum said she thought it would be fine, but I could tell my dad was deeply concerned.

Back in London, the final touch to my teenage makeover was about to occur. I'd asked for a brace to be added to my teeth, the theory being that this would make me look younger because dental braces are visually linked with young people. I'd had braces myself when I was sixteen. If the mouthful of metal wasn't bad enough, the ridiculous headgear I'd had to wear (consisting of a leather hat and jutting metal handlebars that fitted into tiny attachments on my brace) also helped my social stigmatization along nicely. When the metal handlebars of the headgear were slid into the metal fittings on the brace, not only did I look like a cross between a space-age pilot and a patient undergoing some sort of brain scan, but I also had to deal with the way the metal scraped against itself as the fittings attached to each other. This caused a spine-tingling screech to race through the brace, and thus through my teeth and my whole body. Therefore I wasn't exactly thrilled at the prospect of having dental architecture crammed into my mouth once more.

One of Soho's finest orthodontists put the braces on my lower teeth. While the expert fixed the metal to my gnashers, I had to wear huge blue plastic glasses that made me look like Brains, the quirky scientist from *Thunderbirds*.

Once the braces were on, my first proper crisis hit. Outside the dental health centre, I had to stop in my tracks. The cameras rolled while I doubled over. A massive wave of sickness mixed with fear had hit me. Kate asked me what was wrong and I told her (and the now familiar camera) that having the braces attached had seemed like a turning point. Maybe the experience struck me so hard because it was such a big change to my appearance. Or maybe it was because having braces took me back to being young again in a powerful, tangible way. Whatever it was, the brace episode completely knocked me for six and was a very low point.

In just two days' time I was due to meet the deputy headmaster for the entrance interview. All I could think was, 'Is this really happening?'

In my personal life, I wasn't able to tell many people in my circle what I was about to do. In fact, only my immediate family and one friend knew what was actually about to happen. This had a further alienating effect. Fudging the truth to friends and colleagues, saying I was 'going away' for a while, was an uneasy thing to do. I was already beginning to feel the unsettling effects of deliberately lying to people around me in such an exacting manner.

For the next two days, I focused solely on the entrance interview. I had to fill in a form that the school used for new entrants. It asked for my exam results, hobbies and hopes for the future. I carefully filled it in with Kate and the team surrounding me, providing moral support.

We decided that the GCSE results we would write on my 'Howard entrance form' would be the same as the actual O-level results that I achieved first time round. There was a slight flaw though – I couldn't remember them. Well, it had been fourteen years.

A quick call to the Welsh Education Board (plus a few quid) landed us a copy of my exam results. On the form, we transferred the O-level grades into the modern-day GCSE marks. When I was sixteen the first time, any student was delighted to get an A. Since then, the GCSE system had brought in a new (and rather bizarre) grading system in which the highest mark students could be awarded was an A* – pronounced 'A-star'. It seemed to me that adding this extra achievable standard was like adding another grade on the top of all the other grades, thus instantly demoting the ones below it. Because scoring A in an exam was now not the top mark, you could say that it was like getting a B in my day. Most strange.

Anyway, because this was the system in use, we had to add some stars to some of the A grades on the entrance form in order to make them look realistic. Apart from these small additions, though, the grades I wrote on the form were exactly the awards I was lucky to get the first time round in my high school. This was important, because one of the aims of the programme was to compare my first experiences in a sixth form with the second time. What had changed since I was younger? Would I end up in the same social group? Would I end up attaining the same grades in the same subjects?

In order to memorize my GCSE grades just in case I was ever asked them at my new school, I stuck up numerous pages of the 'Howard Grades' on the walls of my flat. I also dictated the list of subjects on to a Dictaphone which I played over and over again, even leaving it running while I fell asleep, hoping it would permeate my subconscious. I knew that GCSE results would be important to a sixteen-year-old and was completely paranoid that I'd blow everything by forgetting mine. So I walked round and round my flat for days reciting the list: 'English Language A, Maths A*, Geography A . . .' The grades became a cyclical mantra. Eventually I could reel them off like machine-gun fire. In the event, it was very lucky I could.

The day of the entrance interview finally arrived.

Even though the orthodontist hadn't fully tightened my brace when he attached it, it still made my teeth ache horribly and blistered my gums badly as well. Blistering is common – the gums have to toughen slightly when they're getting used to the metal edges of the brace. When 'crunch day' arrived and it was time for me to go to meet the deputy headmaster, my mouth was still very swollen. I found it hard to talk, which wasn't the most ideal situation, given the task ahead.

Coupled with a lack of sleep the night before, the significance of the day lay very heavily on me. That afternoon's meeting was the first test of whether I could pull off this whole caper. I worried constantly about all the people I'd let down if I got rumbled. I still wasn't sure if I could pull it off and I'm not convinced my team thought I could either.

I shaved meticulously, trying to eradicate any hint of whisker from my cheeks, then slowly pulled on the smart set of 'Howard clothes' I'd bought with the Cardiff teenagers. My outfit consisted of an oversized 'Ben Sherman' shirt, plain black trousers and some very conventional black shoes bought from the high-street store *Next*. I was attending an interview after all, so it was appropriate to make an effort. I also donned my silver chain and ring to complete my persona. My earring was firmly positioned in my ear, as I couldn't take it out for fear of the tiny hole growing back. A large handful of hair gel helped with the last touch. I flattened my glistening hair, teasing it carefully into a fringe of points on my forehead. I was now Howard.

Director Kate picked me up in our hire car and we set off on the trip to the town where the school was based. The journey was petrifying. All the way to the school, I felt violently ill. My stomach churned like a washing machine, getting worse the nearer we got. A number of times I thought I was going to throw up. Whenever we took another turning or motorway junction, my stomach lurched again. Kate was amazingly patient during my repetitive queries about how long we had before we arrived. I was trying to prepare myself, get in a fit state for the meeting, but I was a mess. I lapsed into a strange, frightened, dream-like state, the adrenalin surging through my body.

As we neared the school, we began to drive through a great deal of picturesque countryside. This was a beautiful part of the world. As we entered the town where the school was situated I saw a collection of Tudor buildings; then, as we penetrated the centre, there were all the usual high-street shops, like Dixons and Marks & Spencer, but with a friendlier, much slower feel than most big-city high streets.

As we rounded the corner and the school came into sight, my mind was swimming. I tried to take it all in. I saw a grey building. I tried to control myself. I was all over the place. For some reason, my attention kept coming back to my mouth, which was dry as a camel's toe and stinging as if there were a thousand tiny tacks under my bottom lip. I cursed the nettles in my mouth, but in a way I was grateful for the painful distraction. It took my mind off the crushing situation at hand.

Our car pulled into the school car park.

'Are you ready Shed?' Kate asked.

It was time.

'Uh . . . wait . . . wait,' I said, trying to slow things down. My heart was racing.

Kate explained that we couldn't wait any longer. We had to go in to meet the deputy head. This was it.

I looked into camera, explained how I was feeling (scared shitless) and then I, Sheridan Simove, a thirty-year-old TV producer, walked into the school as Howard Simmonds, a sixteen-year-old from Cardiff.

This was the first time of many when my mental and physical state seemed to change drastically. My whole body seemed to switch into an odd limbo mode, where I felt not wholly in control of my movements, and my mind felt as if it was on autopilot. From that point on, when I was in the school as Howard, I frequently felt that I was having a kind of out-of-body experience. It was a very detached feeling, one where I knew I was moving my limbs myself, talking through my own mouth, and yet it felt as if it wasn't me.

We walked through the front doors of the school, then Kate left me with the camera crew and went to an office round the corner. I tried to take everything in as I stood in the lobby of the school for the first time – the school photos of kids lined up in rows, the hessian mat on the floor, the trophies in cabinets . . .

Kate was back. 'He's just coming,' she said.

Ten seconds later, someone came round the corner.

A tall, lean man with bright eyes and rosy cheeks greeted me with a smile. He was smartly dressed in a shiny grey suit and carried a black folder.

'Hello, I'm Mr H., deputy headmaster. Welcome, Howard.'

He called me 'Howard' like it was my name, which of course it was to him. How weird.

In my normal life, I might well have greeted him by his first name. Though in this situation of course, being a student, I would never do so. I'd actually thought obsessively about this moment beforehand. So, from that point on, I would either greet him as 'Mr H.' or I'd say . . .

'Hello, sir,' finding it oddly natural to do so.

It was happening. I was doing it. I was actually there.

Mr H. took us to a small office where two low chairs covered in bobbly orange material were facing each other. He motioned for me to sit in one and proceeded to tell me what would happen in the meeting. First, he'd give me a brief introduction to the school and then we'd discuss my past history, exam results and hopes for the future so he could decide whether I was a suitable candidate for his sixth form.

My heart was pumping like an oil drill.

'Keep it together,' I told myself. 'Get a grip.'

Looking at Mr H. as he talked to me, I quickly became fixated on his face. His kind blue eyes seemed to peer into my very soul. I kept thinking, 'He's smiling a lot. He must have guessed straight away that

I'm not really sixteen.' I really thought he knew what was going on. It was a very eerie experience. 'Is this working?' I wondered. 'Should I carry on?'

I did.

Things then took a drastic turn for the worse. Once Mr H. had told me a bit about his school, much of which washed over me in my heightened state, he then asked me a question that completely threw me.

'OK – right, let's have a look at your entrance form so we can discuss your grades and see what subjects you want to study while you're here,' he said cheerfully.

My heart stopped. The form! I didn't have it. I'd left it in the car. A further level of panic overtook me.

'Um . . . I've forgotten it . . .' I said, my voice trailing off.

Oh no. This was not good. The form was the one thing I had to remember and I'd left it in the car. I cursed myself. Like a helpless child, I glanced at Kate for a way out.

'Ah – we must have left it in the car,' she explained.

'Not to worry,' Mr H. said, without missing a beat. 'I've got another one here.' He opened his black folder and pulled out a form covered in boxes.

'Let's go through your GCSEs Howard.' That name again. Odd. Was this really working? I still wasn't sure and believed Mr H.'s eyes were boring through mine, making it easy for him to see the lies inside my brain.

I started to rattle off my exam results.

'Maths A-star, Geography A—'

'Whoa – slow down!' said Mr H.

I paused. Then carried on:

'English Literature A . . .'

Once Mr H. had noted these A grades, I continued on to the Bs. I was beginning to relax just a smidgeon.

'Um, English Literature B—' I started.

'Uh . . .' Mr H. paused.

What now? He checked his form, reading it back to me.

'English Literature: A?' he questioned.

I'd made another mistake. In the confusion, I'd got mixed up and told Mr H. the wrong grade for English Literature. It should have been a B – English Language was an A. I mumbled this, worried. It was a small mistake, but it had a big effect on my mental state. This tiny error was another stressor and had a huge impact.

The oddest thing then started to happen. I began to get so disturbed by the situation that my body triggered the 'fight or flight' response. Adrenalin coursed through my veins. I couldn't physically 'fly' out of the situation, so my mind decided to remove itself by nearly shutting down. I found myself paralysed with fear and on a number of occasions when Mr H. asked me something, I almost couldn't speak. I was aware this was happening, but not really in control of it. It was such a strange sensation to feel myself descend into a catatonic state. It was as if there was a bizarre zombie inhabiting my body, not me. I couldn't control what was happening, but definitely knew it wasn't very helpful to the job at hand, so I kept glancing up to Kate and the camera crew, willing them to hear my thoughts so they might somehow help.

Luckily, my shut-down happened about halfway through the interview, so it wasn't too damaging. Kate was a trouper, interjecting a number of times when I stopped responding to explain, 'He's just nervous.'

But I was furious with myself. I thought I'd blown it and was completely resigned to the fact that it was all over. As the interview progressed, Mr H. kept smiling and carefully looking at me, which I took to mean he had definitely rumbled me. In actual fact, the truth was far simpler: he was just a kind, caring bloke who was conscious of being filmed while he interviewed what he thought was a very nervous youngster.

Mr H. then asked me to decide what subjects I was going to study while I was at the school. I'd already considered this at length. Deciding on the topics I was to study was one bit of the preparation that actually filled me with great joy. It seemed like an exceptionally exciting chance to me – here I was with the incredible opportunity to make real the fantasy of going back to school and doing it all again with the benefit of hindsight. I could try out the 'What if?' scenario that most people never encounter. It was like going back in time to change my decisions to see if anything would be different. It made me focus very carefully on what I'd do differently second time round and what areas of my early life I would change.

The first time I attended sixth form, I'd taken Biology, History and Sociology as A-levels. This time, the first subject I chose was English Language because I now believe mastery of the written word is a wonderful skill to have, and I'd always dreamed about being a proper writer (I'm still dreaming). Next, I chose Business Studies. Running my own company and having a keen interest in the dynamic world of business made this one a top choice. My grapples with morality also made the third choice easy: Philosophy. The irony of choosing this subject wasn't lost on me either. Here I was, about to plunge headlong into an act that was morally questionable and part of it would take me into lessons about human ethics and moral rights. Hmm . . .

Finally, I managed to tell Mr H. that I'd like to study a fourth topic, General Studies, which examined society and the way social groups function. The curriculum encompassed areas like politics, religion and the influence of the media (yeah, nice).

I was worried about overloading my schedule with four A-levels, but I genuinely found all these topics fascinating and relished learning more about them. Plus, all of us on the production team felt that I should make the most of my time in school in order for the programme to have any meaningful comparison with my real school days.

There was also another factor that made General Studies an interesting proposition, laden with just a dash of extra jeopardy: it was taught by the headmistress, Mrs J.

When Mr H. eventually wound down the interview, it was like someone untying a rope wound tight around my chest. He gave me a school timetable and explained that he'd help me fill in my schedule tomorrow.

'Uh? Tomorrow?' I thought. 'But surely you've discovered what's happening here, haven't you, or are you playing with me?' I was in complete denial that this was working.

I left the room in a foggy daze and went back to the car park on my own. Kate and the crew wanted to film Mr H.'s impressions of me after the interview so they stayed behind with him. I couldn't walk out of the school fast enough.

Simon, the assistant producer, was waiting in the car for me. A gentle soul with a round face, he looked older than his twenty-eight years. He had an air of maturity about him, in stark contrast to my air of juvenility. When we first met, this shared looks–age disparity had made us bond right away.

I climbed into the car and slumped into the back seat, desperately distraught. In what was to become a common occurrence, Simon comforted me.

'He knew, he knew . . .' I said.

'What – really? Are you sure?' he asked.

'I made so many mistakes. There's no way he'll believe it,' I continued, rambling.

Simon tried to comfort me by explaining that the interview was done now and that was that – I couldn't change anything. Which was indeed true. We sat in the car waiting for Kate for what seemed like ages. I really believed that Mr H. had found us out and that she was in there with him while he went mad at her.

Kate returned after a while with the crew, who bundled into their mini van. No one in our car said anything until the doors were closed. We were all far too nervous about being overheard in the school car park. Kate shut the door and I searched her face for clues. I thought it was all over right there and then.

A pause. She smiled.

'Well? Well?' I implored through clenched teeth.

Kate said two words:

'You're in.'

Another pause while I let this sink in. Then it did.

Oh shit.

'What? What?' I stuttered. 'No way. He knew didn't he . . .?'

'No, he didn't,' Kate countered firmly. 'You're in – you did it!'

Kate excitedly explained that once the entrance interview had finished and I'd left, Mr H. had enthusiastically reported that he'd liked me a lot and was happy to look after me in the coming months. Remarkably, the induction interview seemed to have gone *well*. Interestingly, the camera crew told me that my shutdowns simply came across as the natural nervous reaction of a sixteen-year-old.

I couldn't quite process all this information. I sat numbly in the back of the car, shaking my head, asking 'Are you sure? Are you sure?' over and over. It was a hard realization to take that Mr H. had actually accepted me as a sixteen-year-old. As further proof that I'd truly managed to gain entry into the school, Kate pulled out a yellow ringbound pad from one of the camera bags. It had the words *'Sixth Form, Believing In Success, Student Organiser 2001/2002'* on the front, and just above this heading was a ClipArt picture of a mortar board.

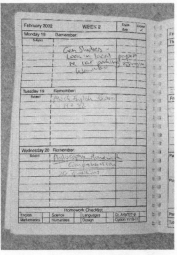

'Mr H. gave you this, Howard,' Kate said. She was really starting to enjoy calling me Howard. 'It's for you to write up which lessons you should be in, so you remember what you've got when,' she continued excitedly, a glint in her eye. I don't think she could quite believe we were pulling this off either.

Mr H. had suggested to Kate that I should meet two prominent sixth-formers who'd give me a tour round the school. Tomorrow.

Then, next week, I'd start lessons. Bloody hell. I couldn't believe this was happening. Were Kate and the crew pulling my leg? Was the joke on me?

We left the school grounds, dizzy with a mixture of success and disbelief. Our destination was a rented house which was only a mile away from the school, our home for the next ten weeks. The plan was that we'd live near the school and other pupils, so that I'd completely immerse myself in this new life. The cover story was that the crew were acting as my legal guardians during this time.

Living so near the school had a number of effects on me during the time we made the programme and they certainly weren't all positive. It meant I had to be constantly vigilant about 'being Howard', which was exhausting. My fellow students could drop in at any time, so I could never let my guard down properly. It added to my sense of paranoia, which grew exponentially as the weeks went on.

When we returned to the house, we filmed my thoughts about the entrance interview. I sat on the floor while a single light lit me from above. It was an appropriately 'other-worldly' scene.

I think I was still rather baffled by the experience: pleased that I'd seemingly got through, yet not quite believing I had; guilty that I was lying to decent people and perhaps just a tiny bit gutted that I hadn't been rumbled so it could all stop.

When I woke the next day, I didn't want to get up. I knew what was planned for that morning and it filled me with dread. I was due to meet the headmistress, my form tutor and get a guided tour of the school from two sixth-formers. It was the next stage of the programme, and of my induction into the school. I'd apparently passed myself off as a sixteen-year-old to one person, but what about a whole school? Surely they'd rumble me? Surely?

I got dressed in my casual Howard gear this time – a baggy hoody and tracksuit bottoms. I then shaved very carefully. In fact, shaving was to become an elaborate ritual every morning. As I was deeply concerned that my stubble would give me away (not that it's that dark or anything), I became fanatical about getting the closest shave possible. This was slightly ironic, given that during my real teenage years I'd always wished for stubble, watching with envy as the faster-developing boys proudly displayed their whiskers. But, just like my father when he was a lad, I started shaving very late compared with my peers.

The 'Howard shaving ritual' went like this: a very hot shower first, during which I pushed my face under for as long as I could bear. Next, I'd jump out of the shower and apply copious drops of shaving oil liberally to my beard area. Then I'd shave with a new razor, jump back into the shower and then back to the basin for another going over with the razor, plus more oil. (On some mornings, I even experimented with heating the oil by placing the little glass bottle in a basin of hot water, desperate to try anything that might help achieve a smoother look.) The last stage of the ritual involved covering my face in shaving foam and pressing the blade firmly to my flesh for a last try.

During my time at the school, I also kept an eye on my stubble every time I visited the toilet. I even took a disposable razor with me. Sometimes I shaved three times in one day.

After the shaving, I forged on with getting ready to go into school. My jewellery was slung on, then I gelled my hair down with 'half a tub of gel', as Kate would often say. I teased my shiny hair into neat points, making sure that my receding hairline was covered as much as possible.

After a little breakfast (I couldn't get much down), I grabbed my schoolbag containing the timetable book given to me by Mr H. and we set off for school. On the way there, I saw many kids in uniform, pupils from the lower part walking to school. My stomach heaved. This was it.

I was really, *really*, going back to school.

We arrived just after nine in the morning. Deputy head Mr H. was standing at the front entrance, ready to greet us. Behind him were two sixth-form pupils, a girl with an English Rose complexion and a tall guy with glasses dressed all in black.

'Morning Howard!' boomed a cheery Mr H.

'Hello!' I said, trying to appear upbeat. Once again, my mental state seemed to fog, as if all the neurons in my brain were trying to process the situation I was in, but couldn't.

Mr H. then introduced me to the sixth-formers now at his side, who smiled welcomingly. I looked at their faces, at the same time as trying not to act oddly. 'Are they noticing? Have they noticed?' I kept thinking.

'They'll show you around today,' Mr H. said.

Just then, another figure entered the foyer. A smart woman in her forties, with a cheerful face and brisk walk, thrust her hand out.

'Ah – you must be Howard. Hello!'

I guessed who she was right away.

'I'm Mrs J. Welcome.'

It was the headmistress.

I remember finding it rather odd and very kind that she'd intro-duced herself to me with her first name – after all, she believed I was a sixteen-year-old pupil. I discovered that this behaviour was just one small part of how Mrs J.'s attitude towards her pupils surfaced. She treated the young people in her care with respect and spoke with them as equals. This made her respected in turn and popular with the pupils.

Kate had met Mrs J. a number of times before, so the two of them exchanged greetings and chatted briefly, while I stood next to them nervously. The headmistress left soon afterwards, wishing me all the best, and the two sixth-formers led the way for the grand tour with me and the camera crew in tow.

My guides took me round classrooms, up and down stairs, but it was a lot to take in. I couldn't quite manage it. The pupils chatted away to me, mostly about the school. They were incredibly friendly, asking very few questions about me or my life, which was a great relief. My head spun. I just couldn't believe they were accepting me as a teenager.

On our tour round the school, sometimes we'd be stopped by an adult who would introduce themselves as one of the teachers. They would then welcome me to their school. Everyone I met greeted me with a warm smile and it definitely seemed that there was quite a buzz about the documentary being filmed in the school. People were eager to see who this new boy was; plus it appeared that most of the students and teachers were excited that their school and their lives were to be showcased. But certainly not all the teachers were happy for the film crew to be invading their territory – in fact a couple of them declined to be filmed.

The idea that most people at the school wanted to appear on television in a successful programme was one of the facts I tried to hang on to throughout the nine weeks I was there. Right at the end of my stint as a pupil, I filmed 'exit interviews' with all the young people I'd bonded with. During this filming, I was the only person to know that shortly I would reveal all about my true age.

I started each interview by asking the person what their hopes for the documentary were. A large number expressed similar sentiments: that it would put the school on the map, make them famous and get adults to listen to young people a bit more. I played these comments over and over in my mind, trying to reassure myself that everything would be fine because these aims were exactly the same aims that we had on the production side. 'Surely it'll be fine,' I reassured myself.

The tour ended at the classroom that was to be my base. I was introduced to my form teacher, a rugged, well-built fellow in his mid-thirties with the look of a super-fit, tanned landscape gardener. I'll call him Mr R. The pupils informed me that everyone called him 'R' for short.

'Does he mind?' I asked.

'No way – R's really cool,' came the reply.

As it turned out, they were right. R was one of those rare teachers who had a presence about him that garnered both respect and friendship from the pupils. Every morning I'd go to my form room where he would call out our names. He taught Geography, so the room was plastered with maps and filled with globes and various brightly coloured papier-mâché volcanoes that were the result of a recent class project.

Through my time here, I had a chance to see how deeply R cared for his pupils. He certainly treated them as equals, yet he could also lay down the law when it was called for. He had that fine balancing act off to a 'T' – to let the young people he looked after make their own decisions but also to steer them in the right direction.

As I walked through the corridors, I kept catching glimpses of other sixth-formers either chatting together in alcoves or sitting in classrooms. I stared at the boys to see whether they looked younger than me. The global worry about getting found out was still huge in my mind. My heart would soar whenever I saw an older-looking guy – a 'fast developer' who had started to shave and had an older face. Remarkably, I concluded pretty quickly that I didn't look so different from some of the real sixth-formers.

My concerns about being rumbled because of my appearance actually disappeared quite rapidly – within a week or so in fact. They were fast replaced with many other much bigger anxieties, such as the worry about lying to people I was bonding with; the worry of bumping into someone in the town high street who might have met me in my real life; and also the ever-present nagging doubt of making a mistake that would possibly give my true identity away. One such mistake happened on my very first proper day, the next Monday.

After a very uneasy weekend holed up in our rented house, not quite believing the whole charade was actually working, I started school for real – as Howard.

I went to registration with my fellow sixth-formers and dutifully replied 'Sir!' when my name was called. My brain was whirring away at a million miles an hour, on high alert that day (and indeed for the first few weeks), filtering everything I did and said. It was exhausting. After a while, this state of heightened concentration did wane a little as it became clear that just 'being myself' wouldn't automatically reveal my true age. But it was still always extremely draining keeping up the double life.

I pulled the little yellow ring-bound student organizer given to me by Mr H. out of my bag. It contained my timetable for the term, and I wanted to see which classroom I had to go to after registration was over.

My first lesson was Business Studies, taught by deputy head Mr H. That was when I made my first big mistake. Even before I got to the lesson, my form tutor Mr R. had checked with me to see if I knew how to get to the room where the lesson was held. I said I didn't, nervous about making my way through the maze of unfamiliar corridors. Luckily the camera crew knew where the correct classroom was located and we set off. When I arrived, and pushed through the heavy school door into the room, I was late. The classroom was filled with brown plastic tables in a U shape. Students sat round the tables, quite a few with laptops in front of them. 'That didn't happen in my day,' I thought to myself, feeling old.

Mr H. greeted me excitedly. 'Everyone, this is Howard.'

Everyone mumbled 'Hi Howard,' then after a tiny pause we all laughed nervously.

'Sit over there,' said Mr H., pointing to a spare chair next to a young lad with long hair and a skater look about him. I sat down and the skater guy said 'Hi.' I was to get to know him well in the coming weeks. A lovely, thoughtful, smart chap.

I looked round the room, having another out-of-body experience. I was sitting with all the other students in a classroom, wondering what the heck was happening to me. Was this a dream? No, it definitely wasn't. I was awake, and extremely delighted to see that two of my fellow students had braces on their teeth just like me. Not for the last time, I kept stealing glances at the boys' faces to see how different they were to mine. Every time I spotted someone with the smallest amount of whisker I was elated. Much to my pleasure, the guy I was sitting next to had a strong, mature face which I didn't think was a million miles away from looking like mine. But was I persuading myself that everything was all right, when in fact it wasn't?

My stream of neuroses was interrupted as Mr H. started the lesson. He explained that our assignment for this term was to complete a structured business analysis on a specific product, either an already existing one in the shops or (much more excitingly) a product we could make up ourselves. As you can imagine, the task of creating a new product immediately lit my fire.

Every minute that went by weighed on me. I just couldn't get over the clear fact that I was back at school again and now being set an assignment. But I also relished the practical approach to the learning of using theory to create a thorough business plan. It was my first lesson back at school and already I was inspired. Superb.

Mr H. instructed the class to go to the school library so we could begin researching our products. The library was an L-shaped configuration of maroon-coloured rooms, one full of books, one full of computer terminals. The skater guy took me under his wing and we sat in front of one of a bank of computer screens together. I was fascinated to see some of the students checking their emails and some others visiting music websites so they could listen to tunes while getting on with work. This was normal behaviour to them, but very different to my eighties low-tech Cardiff High School library, which was filled with rows of books and nothing else.

Then the error happened. I asked my study partner what product he was going to use for his business assignment case study.

'Crisps,' he replied.

'Oh . . . yeah?' I replied. Then, trying to help, I made a mistake. 'Have you contacted Smiths?' I asked.

Now, I don't know why I mentioned the company Smiths. Smiths Crisps had been around when I was a kid but hadn't been a well-known brand for at least ten years now. My stomach did a backward double somersault.

'Uh?' the skater boy said.

I panicked a bit, my whole face flushing, but I quickly got my composure, continuing as if I hadn't blurted my first utterance.

'Have you contacted Walkers?' I replied. I looked at his face for any glimpse of recognition that anything was wrong.

'No – hmmm, good idea,' he shrugged.

It was all over in seconds. To me this tiny mistake was a big upset, but no one else even flinched.

Over the nine weeks I attended this school, I forged some very real friendships. Looking back, maybe that was one of the reasons I caused so much upset at the end. Even though I set out to be very cautious about making friends, because the people I met were decent, interesting and fun, bonds naturally formed.

The constant attention of the cameras certainly gave me a head start socially, at least at the beginning of term. Everyone at the school believed I was the main focus of the documentary being filmed, which consequently made me more appealing than normal. Also, some of the sixth-formers (understandably) wanted to get on the telly and the easiest way to do so was to be near the new boy. But as time went on, many people got bored with the cameras or were satisfied they'd been filmed, so I found myself with friendships that were meaningful. You'll have to ask the people I bonded with how meaningful they felt the friendships were to them . . .

On a number of occasions I was asked by my fellow pupils why the production team had picked me for the documentary. I took the fact that this question was being asked to mean that I was coming across as a pretty unremarkable teenager, which was a good indicator that I was assimilating well.

'I dunno,' I'd answer, in the appropriate manner.

Among the ever-present feelings of 'unreality' and anxiety that arose from my going back to school, a number of events stand out in particular.

One of these arose quite by accident in my Philosophy class. Mrs J., the headmistress, taught this engaging and challenging subject. I thoroughly enjoyed many of the modules we studied, both revelling in the interesting topics we covered and at the same time squirming at the irony that some of the modules dealt with morality and media manipulation.

Halfway into term, Mrs J. said she was putting together a new presentation for the morning assemblies given to the lower school – pupils aged eleven to fifteen – and that she was going to need volunteers. I saw some of the students shrink down into their seats.

'The new assembly is going to be about how we should accept others,' she went on. 'It's to show the younger members of the school that no matter how different we all are, it shouldn't really matter. It'll be really simple and quick and I need eight of you to help me please. Anyone interested?' Mrs J. looked round the room expectantly. She was a huge presence at the school – people knew that if she asked for something, it was going to get done.

A pause.

'Go on then, miss,' one of the boys said, treading the fine line between being a good student and not too much of an 'arse-kisser'. She was the headmistress after all; but more than that, Mrs J. was a fine leader who didn't patronize the students. Thus she gained real respect from the majority of the sixth form, something quite unusual these days.

'Thank you,' Mrs J. replied.

A couple of others also agreed. And then she turned to me.

Oh no.

'Howard, would you like to be involved?' she asked.

What could I say? I absolutely didn't want to be part of the assembly, especially as it was presenting to younger parts of the school. It's one thing being a liar to numerous over-sixteen-year-olds, but standing up in front of kids aged eleven to fifteen as something I wasn't made me feel yet another notch more uneasy.

But I couldn't say no.

'Ah . . . yes, miss.'

'Excellent. Anyone else? Come on!'

Once Mrs J. had filled up all the places for her presentation, she handed out a script she'd written. A typewritten photocopied A4 sheet was passed to me.

At the top was the title of the assembly. My heart sank. It was so mind-blowingly relevant that I had a sudden (and now increasingly frequent) pang of paranoid suspicion that my production team had engineered the situation. The title read:

'The Right To Be Different'

And so that's how I found myself standing with seven good-natured sixteen- and seventeen-year-olds in front of a packed assembly full of even younger people, taking part in a sketch about 'being different'. Wild, eh?

The assembly skit was very simple, hammering home the central message in an easily understandable way. The eight of us stood in a line and each person would hold up a prop.

The first person in the line held up a piece of fruit and would say: 'I like bananas.'

The second person would hold up their yellow fruit and repeat: 'I too like bananas.'

And so it went on down the line until the last person had their turn. This last person held up a different fruit and proudly proclaimed, 'I like apples.'

At that point, the rest of the group all cried in unison: 'What? You like apples?!' The group then turned on the apple-lover. 'We can't be friends with you! You like apples – that's stupid!'

And then the group would play-act bullying the 'apple person' into leaving. 'You can't be friends with us – you like apples! How ridiculous. Please leave!' And the last person would then leave the line.

This basic structure was then repeated with the remaining sixth-formers playing out another similar scenario, the fruits being replaced with hats, colour preferences and so on.

The idea, of course, was to show that disliking someone on the basis of their fruit choice or style of headgear was as ludicrous as disliking them for any arbitrary difference – their skin colour, sexual preference, religion or lifestyle. It was an effective little skit that engaged the younger kids well and brought the issue of discrimin-ation to life in a beautifully clear way. Mrs J. created presentations like this a lot. She fervently cared about making the people in her school into decent human beings.

For me the assembly took on an extra ludicrous form. As I stood there taking part in a 'Right To Be Different' presentation time after time, I desperately wanted to break out of being Howard and start shouting at the top of my lungs: 'Hello everyone. You might have noticed how we're talking about the "right to be different" today. WELL, EVERYBODY – CHECK OUT THIS LINE-UP. ONE OF US SIXTH-FORMERS IS *REALLY* DIFFERENT. YES, ONE OF US IS A THIRTY-YEAR-OLD GUY – AND THAT'S ME. IS THAT OK??!! IS IT OK FOR *ME* TO BE DIFFERENT? NOW? HERE? LIKE THIS?!!'

I didn't shout out of course. I just stood there cradling my banana, if you'll pardon the expression.

Another uncomfortable occasion arose when I was chosen to represent the sixth-form with some other students at a Business Seminar day trip attended by youngsters from a number of schools in the local area. Once again, I felt incredibly nervous, worrying that the more new people I came into contact with as Howard, the more chance there was of my being found out. But once again I seemed to blend in.

During this away day, each school group was given a business assignment to crack. I had to bite my lip when the business 'guru' assigned to help our group wouldn't listen to my marketing ideas. He treated me as if I was a stupid kid when I suggested creating a pub-licity stunt to raise awareness for our case-study business. I told the group that I thought it would be a good idea to create a gimmicky poster for our brand and encourage our target consumers to place it somewhere it could be seen by lots of people, then photograph where they managed to place the poster. The consumers who made the best efforts would win a prize.

'No, no, that'll never work.' Our supervisor dismissed me with a wave of his hand. A classic example of an adult shouting down a young person.

That really got my goat. I wanted to tell this negative man how once while working on a youth magazine show I'd made posters for viewers to hold up during Wimbledon matches. The posters successfully appeared in the background of many shots during the tennis games and won a lot of press attention. As the man poured scorn on my suggestion, I felt like saying, 'Well, excuse me, actually I did something similar while I was working on a high-profile TV show a few years back and the stunt landed us on Sky news . . . So maybe we should discuss the idea,' but of course I couldn't.

The strangeness of the school experience was heightened when I attended certain lessons. While I was in school, there was always an adult from the production team with me, usually with a hand-held video camera to record any action. The rules of responsible filming with sixteen- and seventeen-year-olds meant that I had to be in the presence of someone over eighteen at all times.

The constant presence of at least one production-team member served as a reminder that I was 'Shed'. It was a powerful mental anchor that comforted me. Sometimes though, I was left on my own, and that's when it got very weird.

On occasion, the person accompanying me from the production team would wait outside the door of my classroom or in the playground until my lesson ended. This meant I was left 'alone' with a classroom of pupils and a teacher. This still ticked the boxes of responsible filming because there was an adult present with me – the teacher taking the class (even though they were unaware of my real identity of course). In these situations, all links to the television show we were making, and indeed to my real life, had been severed. It was just me, a thirty-year-old guy, sitting in the middle of a classroom of young people and a teacher (who was often much younger than me), all of whom thought I was a normal teenager. It was a powerfully disorientating feeling. On such occasions I felt completely detached from the real world and I'd catch myself being momentarily terrified that I was in fact back at school and that the team had left me. It was intense.

During the nine weeks of term, I attended numerous lessons just like a normal student and worked diligently to complete any schoolwork. I always did my own homework, which was hard going when all I wanted to do was decompress, watch TV, and forget about being Howard. I always put maximum effort into any homework and the only concession to disguising my true age was that now and again

I'd stop myself writing a long word, replacing it with a shorter one.

I gave the schoolwork my 'all' for many reasons. I actually did enjoy learning again – it was exciting and stimulating. Plus, I felt it was my duty to dive in and embrace the experience completely. Sure, I could have hired someone to do my homework (and believe me, I did think about it many times) but it didn't feel the right thing to do. The whole concept of the show was for me to experience being back at school as purely as possible, so it would have been wrong for me to have stinted in participating fully. By engaging in the school experience a second time round, it was possible to film me making direct comparisons about the difficulty of work and the pressure on young people today versus when I went to school when I actually was sixteen.

I also believed that if I performed well in my schoolwork it would clearly demonstrate to the viewers watching the show just how good these teachers were. Oh, and lastly, I also wanted to do well for my personal pride.

That's why I was rather peeved when, one day near the end of term, I received a terrible mark for my Business Studies coursework.

For a long time before I embarked on the film, I'd been thinking about a new 'homeware' product for the dinner table. I thought that perhaps I could use the Business Studies coursework assignment (of preparing a marketing plan for a new or existing product) as a chance to explore this idea more fully.

The inspiration for the new product I was about to develop came from a fascination I've always had with ice sculptures. From an early age, these beautiful, fleeting works of art have mesmerized me. Often seen at weddings or corporate parties, ice sculptures come in various shapes and sizes, including the ever-popular swan design, the slightly less common dolphin or even a bespoke company logo also made from frozen water.

I've always wanted to commission an ice sculpture myself, but they're pretty expensive to get made, as each one has to be hand-sculpted from a block of ice. I began to wonder if I could make my own.

This thought process led me to the idea for personal ice sculptures. Could I create a product that would allow anyone to make their very own ice sculpture in their home? My mind ticked over, dreaming of hundreds of dinner tables with mini ice objects proudly displayed in the centre.

The business assignment that Mr H. had set me as part of my A-level course gave me the impetus to find out whether the idea was workable. I started to write down my plan for a possible ice-sculpture kit to be sold in high-street shops. My basic idea was that each kit would contain a plastic mould that could be filled with water and frozen in a home freezer. The mould would then be carefully broken open to reveal a mini ice sculpture. I envisaged selling them in many different shapes – mini swans (of course), initials, flowers and even a bowl-shaped mould which would produce an 'ice bowl', perfect to serve dessert in. I decided to call these products the 'Ice One Cyril' range.

But that wasn't enough. As usual, I wanted proof that my idea could fly. I decided to take the concept one step further.

When I'd originally thought about a range of mini ice-sculpture moulds, years before I embarked on making the 'Back to School' programme, I'd approached a number of companies involved in injection moulding to see whether it was possible to create a mould that would produce a frozen ice figure. I spoke to a number of experts in the field, all of whom gave me a long list of reasons why it would be impossible to make the simple prototype I wanted. Hurdles of negativity sprang up all over the place, so I decided to leave the project alone for a bit.

Now I was back at school, with scant resources at my disposal, could I do any better? A startling demonstration of how the right attitude and some simple support can get things done was about to take place.

I asked Mr H. whether there was anyone at school who could help me make a mock-up of an ice mould. I garbled out my basic idea for the range and after Mr H. had taken it in, he glanced, surprised, at Kate (who was holding the camera), then said to me, 'Wow, Howard – that's . . . different. Very original!' I was slightly concerned that this concept would alert Mr H. to the fact that I wasn't a sixteen-year-old, but by then the whole school knew that I had a sense of fun, plus some of the other students had ideas that were equally creative, so I thought my idea would be accepted as another concept among the many. It was.

'Why don't you try Mr D. in Design and Tech.,' Mr H. suggested helpfully.

That evening after my last lesson I rushed down to the school's Design department and quickly found Mr D. amid the rows of wooden worktables, each with its own metal vice bolted to the side. He was a stocky man with a weathered face framed by square black plastic glasses. Like all Design teachers I'd ever known, he wore a dirty brown protective coat.

'Hi Mr D. – I'm Howard. Sorry to bother you. Mr H. said to come and see you,' I said from the door.

'Come in! Come in!' he bellowed, beckoning us towards him. Kate interjected.

'Mr D., would it be OK to film? Howard's got an idea he'd love your help with.'

'Oh, sounds interesting. Not sure I'll be able to help, but sure – no problem.'

Kate fired up the camera. I explained to Mr D. that I wanted to make a mould for an ice sculpture.

'Hmm . . . OK,' Mr D. ruffled his hair. 'Well we've got this,' he said, walking towards a large rectangular metal box about the size of a traditional filing cabinet. It had a hinged lid on the top, which Mr D. opened.

'This is a vacuform machine,' he continued. 'We can put something in here and make a plastic mould of it – let me show you.'

This was wonderful news.

Mr D. placed a small block of wood into the belly of the machine and picked up a thick yellow plastic sheet that was leaning against a wall nearby. He slotted the sheet into a small gap at the top of the contraption, so it ended up centred over the wood. Then he flicked a switch on the side of the machine and it whirred into life. The press of a red button then started to blast the sheet with heat, making it melt. Mr D. prodded the plastic with the end of a pencil to check its elasticity and, once he was satisfied, pushed an orange button. The insides of the machine jolted into action. A noisy fan sprang into life and sucked the air out underneath the plastic. This had the effect of pulling the malleable plastic over the wood. The plastic moulded itself beautifully over the wooden block and took its form perfectly. The whole process was a delight to watch. Mr D. switched the machine off and the sheet cooled down in a matter of seconds. When he removed the plastic, it had retained the form of the wooden block and was completely rigid. It was now an exact mould for the block of wood.

'Cool! That's brilliant!' I said.

'Well, you just need to give me something to make a mould from and we'll pop it in,' Mr D. instructed.

My brain started whirring. What shape did I want my first ice sculpture to be? This development was so exciting.

'The only thing is, you've got to make sure that your shape isn't wider at the top than it is at the bottom, or you won't be able to take the object out of the mould,' Mr D. added. That made sense.

I had an inkling what I needed for the first mould. I wanted to make something that would show I was proud to be part of the school.

'Um, sir, could I do a sort of sign with the school's name on it?' I asked.

'Well, I suppose so. You could use a block of wood and then make some letters to stick on top, then mould that,' he replied.

I had another solution. 'Well, sir, could I buy the letters instead?' I said.

'Yes, sure, if you can find some the right size,' he replied.

The next weekend, I bought a packet of large plastic letters from a children's toy shop in the local town centre and stuck them on to a rectangular block of wood I'd found in Mr D.'s workshop.

I went back to see him a few days later and we vacuformed the completed block. It was a great moment to see the yellow plastic forming around the letters.

I thanked Mr D. profusely and took the completed mould to the school canteen, as I needed to use a big freezer to house the large plastic trough. I got quite a few baffled looks from students who saw me lugging the bright yellow mould and chatting with the dinner ladies. Excitedly, I filled the mould with water, and after the dinner ladies made some room in the large industrial-type freezer (by taking out huge bags of chips), we carefully laid the mould inside.

The next day, we opened the top of the freezer to check the mould. The water had frozen solid. It was looking good so far. The next challenge was to separate the ice block from the plastic. I reckoned I knew a way, but I couldn't just blurt it out. I always had to be a little careful when I suggested ideas to people in the school. I didn't want to come across as unnaturally precocious for a sixteen-year-old (or even just pushy), so I waited for the assembled throng to suggest ways to remove the ice stuck fast in the mould.

'Maybe run some hot water over the top of the mould,' said one dinner lady.

Great – just what I'd been thinking.

We did as she suggested, slowly dribbling hot water over the top of the mould, wary of melting the ice inside too much and damaging its form. I gently pushed and flexed the rigid yellow plastic, trying to unleash the block inside.

There was an audible 'Ooohh' as the frozen block finally slid out of the mould. It had worked brilliantly. There in front of us, resplendent, was a large block of ice bearing the name of the school clearly displayed on the front. The piece of ice had a white band running through it, even though I'd used distilled water bought from a chemist, which is free of the impurities found in tapwater that cause the centre of ice cubes to go white. I think the white marks may have been to do with the speed at which I froze the mould, but even with these slight imperfections, I was delighted with the results.

I incorporated a report of this successful prototype into the marketing plan I was writing for my Business Studies assignment. I was pretty confident I'd get a great mark for the work – after all, not only had I thought up a new product, created a business plan for its launch and researched the homewares sector, I'd also made a working prototype of the new idea. Surely that showed some business entrepreneurship, meaning I'd get a good mark?

Uh, actually, no . . .

I proudly handed in my neatly printed assignment to Mr H. and a couple of weeks later he announced that he had marked our work. By this time, I'd been at the school for over a month and already had some feedback on the essays and assignments I'd completed for other subjects (I'd done fairly well but not brilliantly by any stretch).

However, this was my first big project for Mr H., the deputy head, and I was eager to impress him. As I'd got to know Mr H., I'd realized that the similarities between us were uncanny. Although he sometimes let the students take the mickey out of him, he was fiercely passionate about what he did. He was a powerful teacher because he keenly wanted to help his students reach their potential and, even though he strived to make lessons entertaining, when it mattered most he wouldn't stand any nonsense or be deviated from his teaching goals.

Plastered all over the walls in the rooms he taught in were 'Go for it' slogans and messages designed to inspire and motivate his students. (I have similar quotes and phrases stuck to my computer screen.) In fact, I noticed that both he and Mrs J. tried to drum into the pupils that anything was possible, and that tolerance and learning were the keys to being a better person. It was a wonderfully nurturing environment, one which I don't think the pupils realized how lucky they were to be studying within. Having spent time in the world at large, I appreciated this forward-thinking place of study, where the existence of unconditional positivity and belief in 'the self' were actively encouraged.

'Here you go Howard,' Mr H. said cheerfully as he passed me back my Ice One Cyril Ltd assignment. 'He's happy – that must be a good sign,' I thought.

Feverishly flipping to the back of the folder, I did a double take. There had to be a mistake. There, clear as day, was a large letter written in blue biro. It read 'E'. An E! Surely not?

Alongside the mocking letter were a few comments from Mr H. 'Good idea, but more work needed on structure and marketing plan,' he said.

Outside the classroom, I spoke on camera about how disappointed I was with the result. Not only was my personal pride a little dented, but I was also concerned that I'd let Mr H. down too.

It was an amusing outcome though – one which I knew would make good television. The bare facts stared me in the face: I was running a television company turning over a lot of money and I'd just dismally failed at a simple Business Studies assignment. Great.

Overall, I thoroughly enjoyed studying again at this school and found that the 'continuous assessment' modular structure of the A-levels gave me a much more thorough learning experience than when I had crammed for one clump of exams the first time round. This continuous assessment approach was also much more difficult to excel in. It meant that I couldn't coast in lessons all term and then force everything into my short-term memory for a big exam at the end (as I did when I was sixteen the first time round). With the new modular structure of the A-levels, it was vital for students to understand clearly what they were studying, because a lot of the practical coursework needed that knowledge to complete a module successfully.

I also felt it was a much fairer system to grade pupils as they went along, allowing them to accumulate marks that added towards their final score, rather than setting a few exams for each subject at the end of two years, with the final mark dependent solely on those. In my day, you could madly revise for just those two exams and you'd be fine, but if you were ill or feeling sluggish on one of the exam days, then your final mark could be hugely damaged. The new continuous assessment method was much fairer and more effective all round, measuring knowledge and the application of that knowledge in a series of tests rather than one big splurge at the end.

Studying was most certainly harder for me the second time round, because this system meant you had to concentrate in lessons all the time. I felt that I learned much more with the new system – and surely that's the whole point, isn't it?

As well as coping with the usual schoolwork anxieties a normal teenager would have, I also encountered extra problems being Howard. Outside the confines of school, my stress levels were sometimes raised even higher than the average state of paranoia and exhaustion that I constantly felt.

When I ventured out, I was particularly concerned that I would bump into someone from my previous life and they'd blow my cover. When I visited the local Sainsbury's supermarket, where many of the sixth-formers worked on the tills, I used to be petrified that I'd get to the checkout and there'd be somebody queuing up there who knew me as Shed.

Once, when a gang of us from school went to a local shopping mall, I thought I saw someone I recognized. It happened while I was running to the toilet. As I whizzed past the shoppers, my eyes furiously scanned their faces. Then it happened. I locked eyes with a middle-aged woman carrying shopping bags. Shazam! I knew her face. I couldn't work out where I'd seen her before, but I was sure I knew her. I panicked completely.

Even though I was running fast, my heart leapt and a sharp burst of adrenalin fired into my system. My momentum carried me forward to the men's toilets, which weren't that far away. As I stood in front of the urinal, heart beating fast, I tried to calm myself down and collect my thoughts. Where did I know the woman from? Was it from my *Big Breakfast* years? What should I do? Would she be outside waiting for me? Should I go back out? No, of course not. But my friends were waiting for me so I needed to . . .

In the end, I stayed in the toilet for a good five minutes. When I returned to the shopping mall, I tried to shrink physically into myself. I must have looked very suspicious, furtively darting around, looking from side to side. Luckily, the woman was nowhere to be seen, and that was that.

Another stand-out, highly stressful event was my seventeenth birthday party as Howard. This happened towards the end of term and was quite an occasion. I'd purposely given Howard a specific date of birth so that I could ensure I'd be able to hold a birthday party during the making of the film. Not only would it be a light-hearted incident that would provide a change of pace for the documentary, it would also make it very easy for the production team to ask specific 'age' questions about my alter ego without raising any suspicions.

Unfortunately, the birthday party was to cause unforeseen problems. By pure coincidence, one of the students I got close to also had a birthday near that date. The birthday celebration therefore became a joint party. This would have powerful emotional ramifications later on.

In the event, my second seventeenth birthday party was quite a bash. We held it in our rented house – a big, detached four-bedroomed townhouse. We hired dozens of disco lights and a smoke machine and cleared a large space in the living room for a dance floor.

As a production team, we were extremely careful about the consumption of alcohol by anyone under eighteen at the party. We held long discussions about how to manage the gathering without coming across as party poopers. As some of the sixth-formers were over eighteen, they could legally drink, but it was common knowledge that some of the students under that age also drank socially. We were aware that some students might bring their own drink to the house party, so the decision was made to monitor the situation closely and act accordingly. I of course, as Howard, seventeen years of age, wasn't allowed to drink. I used the TV cameras as an excuse not to have any alcohol, but secretly, as Shed, I was relieved that I had a cast-iron excuse not to drink . . .

First, I only drink when I'm comfortable with a situation, happy in myself. When I was being Howard, I was definitely neither of these. Plus, I needed all my wits about me every second I was Howard. I decided to wait until the documentary was over to have a drink. I hoped I'd be sharing champagne with the teachers at some point, celebrating the making of a groundbreaking TV show. How wrong I was.

The party was a huge success, but it triggered a scary moment before it had even started. While handing out the invites, one of the students inadvertently sent me into a deep spiral of anxiety that would last for days.

The incident happened while I was loitering in the corridor outside the sixth-form common room. I was talking with one of 'The Populars', the term given to the social group of cool people who loved sport and who were often more conventionally good-looking than most. We were chatting away and then I said to this guy, 'Are you coming to my party?'

'What party?' he queried.

'For my birthday – next Friday,' I replied. 'Here's an invite.'

'Oh cheers,' he said as he took the photocopied square of paper. He started to leave. Then he turned and the question came.

'How old you gonna be?'

'Seventeen,' I said, like water off a duck's back.

And then, out of his mouth came the words that would cause me so much distress.

'Seventeen! . . .' He paused and looked at me sideways.

'. . . you look about twenty-three!'

I was stunned, but just giggled nervously, then shrugged. It was the first time in my life anyone had ever told me I looked older than my age.

The episode seemed to be of much more significance to me than him.

'Yeah cool – sounds good . . .' he trailed off as he left.

Blimey.

I would later rue one particular decision that I made about what to wear at the party. I wanted the birthday bash to be a colourful, fun celebration, so I decided on a fancy-dress affair. I spent days deliberating about whether to dress as Peter Pan, the first outfit I'd thought of when I knew we were all dressing up. Eventually I did decide to go as Peter Pan, buying white shorts from a sports shop in the town high street and dying them green in a large bucket. My outfit also consisted of green tights, a green top, a green felt hat with a feather in it, a plastic brown belt and a wooden knife.

With hindsight, it was a bad decision. When the truth about my real age finally came out, the decision to go to my party as Peter Pan looked as though I was ridiculing everyone there by flaunting the gag of 'The Boy Who Never Grew Up' in front of their faces without them knowing the true meaning behind it. When everyone at the school eventually found out about the central secret of the documentary, I'm sure it was just another piece of evidence that led them to conclude that I was mocking them. But I didn't choose the character in a sneering way. It was just meant to be a funny, relevant reference and a costume that would look quite comical on screen. I thought everyone would appreciate the joke because it wasn't carried out with malicious intent – just like the whole project, in fact.

The party was a resounding success. The turnout was great and everyone threw themselves into the fancy-dress theme. We had a fantastic disco with the lights that we hired, everyone danced their hearts out and we had even made goody bags for the guests to take home with them. I was given dozens of cards and thoughtful presents, which I felt very guilty about receiving. I always planned to return these presents, but I still have many of them today, surrounded by their original ripped wrapping.

As the term went on, the answer to one question I'd wanted answering right from the beginning eventually arrived. At school the first time round, I definitely wasn't one of the popular set. I always wondered what social group I'd end up with if I had the chance to go back to school with the knowledge and experience of a thirty-year-old. What I found out was a small epiphany for me.

Very soon after arriving at my new school it was clear that the sixth form was divided into neat social groups which the students even had names for. As mentioned before, 'The Populars' were good-looking, sporty types. They were the superficially trendy, cool ones – a sort of equivalent to the 'jock/cheerleader' group found in American schools. The different social groups even had specific places where they sat in the common room. It was amazing – The Populars always sat in the left corner and 'The Skaters' always sat on the right near the pool table. Of course, certain individuals could straddle two or more groups, and indeed some students may have felt they weren't part of any group, but as a whole a strong, fascinating grouping was definitely taking place.

When I went to school the first time round, I wasn't even in a group. I felt slightly marginalized and didn't really belong to any gang. I certainly wasn't cool, even though I yearned to be.

It was much better second time round, thank goodness. I ended up in 'The Mid-Populars'. I found myself gravitating to these people the most. Although it wasn't the coolest gang around, after a few weeks I realized it was the one I wanted to be part of. It's dangerous to generalize wildly, because every person at the school had their own strong personality, but I certainly saw some common threads running through the members of the social groups. The Mid-Populars were a group of welcoming, warm souls, who were keen on getting their schoolwork done to their best ability, but they'd also throw themselves into both bettering themselves outside school and, vitally, having fun too. These people were 'the do-ers' within the sixth form. They organized parties, they ran the school magazine and they set up a business in the school selling children's textbooks. They were exciting and fun to be around. They possessed many qualities that I admired. They embraced life full on and were not scared of its challenges. I wish I'd been like that when I was seventeen.

It was satisfying to discover what social group I ended up in, but even after spending two months here I still couldn't quite process how I got away with it and certain events compounded this.

I remember an incident in one Philosophy lesson towards the very end of term, when we were getting out our pencil cases and my heart jumped. I stared at the hands of the student next to me, awestruck. The realization suddenly hit me that, even though he had hair growing on his face, his fingers were completely smooth. My fingers, in contrast, had tiny little hairs growing out of them near the knuckle. Now, these hairs on my hand are blond and virtually imperceptible, but it gives you an insight into how consistently paranoid I was that this difference then bothered me for the rest of the lesson. From that moment on, I kept checking people's fingers to see if they were hairy. I found myself panicking, thinking, 'I should have shaved my knuckles.' Yes, it was a very odd time.

During the project I noticed another curious (and deeply troubling) side-effect of my transformation. When I managed to return to London at half-term for a much-needed break, I attempted to oversee how the production was going by popping into my company offices and Channel 4 too. What I soon found out was that some of the people I'd known beforehand seemed to be treating me differently. Whereas before I'd garnered respect and been listened to in meetings, I was now frequently brushed aside when I tried to speak. On many occasions, it seemed that I was being treated like someone unconnected with the project, someone who couldn't completely understand what was going on. Remarkably, it appeared that I was being treated as Howard the teenager rather than Shed. I can tell you that this was greatly upsetting. I already felt disjointed while immersed in the project; the last thing I needed was my real life to start unravelling as well. The fact that my company was still legally out of my control because my name was changed by deed poll did not help calm my fears, leading me to grow even more paranoid and agitated than I already was.

Back at school for the second half of term, the experience of reliving my teenage years took on an especially poignant turn one afternoon towards the end of my time there. Every day I attended school was akin to stepping into the 'Twilight Zone' for me, but this episode took the surreality to an even greater level. I found myself in a scene that mirrored the first time I was at school in a most uncanny way.

It happened while I was having a 'catch-up' meeting arranged by Mr R., my Form Tutor. Mr R. had become increasingly caring throughout the term. I saw him every day for registration and he'd always enquire how things were going with my schoolwork and how I was generally. I regularly saw him act this way with other students too – he seemed to know everything about everyone's progress across all their subjects. He'd suddenly look up, pick someone out of the class and say, 'I hear you've been missing Maths classes – wanna talk with me about it?', or he'd encourage someone else, saying, 'Well done in your Biology assignment. Good job – keep it up.'

He was nurturing to me as Howard too. As far as he was concerned, my parents were in America, so I think he felt even more protective towards me because of that. He was an interesting man, because even though he cared about his pupils, he was no pushover by any means, often getting quite stern with the class members who looked like they were veering off the rails. The welfare of his pupils was his prime concern and he treated them with respect. They respected him back too. It seems a trite cliché, but he really was a model teacher.

One morning Mr R. said he needed to see me during my free period to go through what I was going to do next in my life. He wanted to talk with me about my university and career decisions. I was dreading this moment, because it meant I would have to lie even more pointedly than I normally did, looking this guy straight in the eye.

I'd already attended two careers lessons a week for the past eight weeks, and I was getting weary of faking my future as well as my present and past. At first, attending the careers lesson had been a fun exercise, as it allowed me to reconsider my life. The whole class sat staring at computers, spending hours filling in questionnaires designed to see what sort of vocational direction we were heading. We also had to write reports about our plans for the future. This process was created to help the students think about a career path, or at the very least what degree course they wanted to pursue should they decide to attend university, and it worked.

It was quite liberating for me actually to fill in the questionnaires with my truthful present-day feelings to see what career direction they took me. It really allowed me to think hard about the choices I'd made so far in life. It was like having a second chance at choosing a route for my future. I felt both delighted and very lucky to discover that I would probably follow the same route again – a career that involved being creative.

The computer programs into which I inputted my data confirmed I should go into something that was related to media, art or creativity. The software was obviously way more sophisticated than the programs back in my day. I remember the laughable results of one such electronic questionnaire my careers officer made me do when I was in school the first time round. The results described how I should be either an interior designer or a religious leader. Interior designer? Well, maybe – just possibly (although pelmets and wall hangings don't really turn me on). But religious leader? I mean, please! That's way off. Anyone want to join the 'Cult of Shed'? Get a free packet of Clitoris Allsorts when you sign up . . .

So when I sat down with Mr R. to talk about my (Howard's) future, I got ready to lie about how I'd planned to study something design-related at uni. But he wanted to talk more specifically about which direction my studies were headed after the end of term.

'Had any more thoughts about staying on with us, Howard?'

'Um . . . you know, sir . . .' I squirmed.

I'd been asked this question many times before, by various students and teachers. Everyone wanted to know whether I was enjoying my time at their school and whether I'd stay on at the end of term for the summer term and then another year. After all, they'd been told this was one of the objectives of the documentary.

'I really love it here, and everyone's been great – but I haven't decided yet,' I said.

Kate had already primed all the teachers that I wouldn't 'decide' about staying on until right at the end of term. This was a tactic to avoid actively talking about something we knew wasn't going to happen. When the term was over, we'd reveal that instead of carrying on at school or going back to America, I'd be returning to my thirty-year-old life.

'OK, OK. What about uni? Think you'll go?'

Mr R. leant down and removed my school file from his bag.

'Um – yeah, I'd like to,' I replied.

He flicked through the file and removed a large brown piece of card covered with an intricate grid.

'Right. Let's have a look then.'

Mr R. continued flicking through the file until he found my blue entrance form displaying the list of my GCSE results. He placed it on the table, his eyes flicking from the blue form to the manila card. The card was one of those predictor indexes that allowed teachers to plot grades on an axis and it would tell them what A-level results a student would get and thus what level of university they could then apply for. Because Mr R. had been given the same results that I had actually achieved when I was sixteen in Cardiff High, I was very curious to see how this exercise would pan out.

Mr R. checked my exam results and then one by one he made a mark on the brown form. When he finished marking the sheet, he drew a couple of lines between a pair of the marks.

His face seemed to relax.

'OK then . . .'

He seemed to have come to a conclusion.

'Three Bs',' he said with confidence.

Whoa! This utterance catapulted me back thirteen years. The weird 'life-mirror' moment was starting to happen.

Three B grades was exactly the A-level results I'd been predicted at this stage at Cardiff High School. Therefore, you could say that I shouldn't have been all that surprised with the result. The predictor form probably hadn't changed much in fourteen years. But as I sat there in front of Mr R., I found I was feeling the same way I felt the first time round: a large measure of sharp frustration at being pigeonholed at this early stage.

It always irks me when anybody is told what they can or can't expect to achieve, solely based on their past performance. People have such amazing capacities to change and grow. If you tell someone they are capable of X, then often they will only achieve X – or worse, perhaps even less. But as the saying goes, if you tell someone to shoot for the moon, then they may only reach the stars, but they'll get much further than if they'd just been aiming for the stars in the first place.

What bothered me then was exactly what bothered me when I was seventeen. This predicting process has been going on all over the country for years, with students being told they can expect certain results. I find this subtle form of labelling very dangerous and constraining, especially as it could have a drastic outcome on the way someone's life could turn out, as was about to be demonstrated.

'Your grades certainly mean you can get in to one of the good unis,' Mr R. continued, sensing my mild irritation.

'OK, good stuff,' I mumbled, thinking, 'That's what they said last time.'

Then Kate ran with the ball. I'd already told her how the same talk had gone the first time and she too noticed the similarities.

'How about Oxbridge?' she said from behind the camera. I'd also asked the same question at Cardiff High when I was sixteen.

'Could Howard try for the top unis?' Kate pressed.

Mr R. looked down at the form again, tracing his finger over the lines to check he'd calculated right.

'Um . . . well . . . your predicted marks are good . . . but this says that you're just a bit off trying for Oxford or Cambridge. They look for the three-A students really . . .'

I challenged Mr R., annoyed but trying to seem casual.

'But sir, say I worked hard, who knows – maybe I could make it?'

Mr R. made a face as if to say 'Fair enough'. He was certainly someone who believed in pushing his students to fulfil their potential.

'Let's check,' he said.

He drew another line across the form. It was about a quarter of an inch above mine. The line seemed to seal my fate.

'You could certainly try – it's just I think you're just a bit too far off,' Mr R. concluded. I could tell he didn't want to close any doors, but the form in front of him was an industry standard.

'There are loads of good unis – it's just that it's so difficult to get in to Oxbridge,' he said.

Now the full déjà-vu episode was complete. This is exactly what had happened when I'd sat with one of my teachers in Cardiff High. I think it's probably a common occurrence in comprehensive schools.

The only difference to that first assessment meeting was that when I was being told I was not quite good enough to try for the 'top' universities then, I got pretty annoyed and demanded I be allowed to try for Oxford. Even though the teacher didn't want to put me through, an inspiring History tutor named Dr Davies believed in me and allowed me to sit in on his Oxbridge preparation classes to get me ready for the Oxford entrance exam. With his help, I embraced the topics I had to study, eventually becoming so fuelled by his tutelage that I carried index cards full of quotes and vital facts everywhere I went.

I took the entrance exam when I was seventeen and, after an entrance interview, was given a place at Oxford University.

As term went on, the whole task began to affect me deeply on a daily basis. Many times after returning from a day at school I'd feel like my head was going to explode. Often, Simon the assistant producer would notice my state and say, 'Come on, let's go for a drive,' and we'd jump into our hire car. Simon would head for a motorway or an A road and drive me around, sometimes for hours on end. Sometimes I'd curl up on the back seat for the whole journey, other times I'd talk endlessly about how worried I was and how stressed I felt. Simon would always listen calmly and help me through, saying, 'Come on, Bud, it'll be OK . . .' He must have felt like a psychiatrist on wheels.

Throughout the term, I longed for my last day to come. We'd scheduled the final day at school to land the week before term actually ended, so that I could finish on the Friday of that week and then we'd have another week to reveal and explain the whole story about the programme before everyone went on holiday.

Conveniently, it was also the day that the school reports were given out. It therefore seemed even more poignant for me to finish after being given a piece of official feedback about my time at school.

I awoke on that last Friday with a mixture of emotions. I was delighted that very soon I wouldn't have to lie to decent people I was fond of. I was also very nervous about the imminent disclosure of my real age. But my overwhelming feeling was one of relief, that the stressful challenge was about to be over. Little did I know it wouldn't be that simple.

No one at the school knew it was my last day, but the knowledge that the end was in sight affected me greatly. There was most certainly a spring in my step. I spent much of the last day filming 'exit interviews' with my schoolmates. This involved me sitting opposite one of my friends and asking them for their thoughts on the whole documentary experience.

I used these filmed chats to reassure myself in a number of ways. First, even though I'd spent nine weeks as a sixteen- and seventeen-year-old, I still couldn't shake off the feeling that maybe I hadn't got away with it. So I asked each person a question that would clearly reveal just how far I'd managed to pull the deception off.

'How typical a teenager am I?'

The responses were varied and fascinating. Most of my classmates responded that I was pretty typical, which made my heart soar. But an even better response came from one of the girls, a particularly candid speaker.

'I think you're a bit immature for a seventeen-year-old really,' she said. Wow! To me, this was the ultimate accolade as it marked the experiment as a huge success, but afterwards it also made me worry slightly. The person she'd met was me, my thirty-year-old self. Was I really that childish?!

I also asked each person whether they'd enjoyed the filming process and what they hoped the outcome of the programme would be. All the interviewees told me, on camera, that they'd enjoyed having the crew around the school and that it had been exciting making the show. Good news. Their hopes for the programme gave me even more cause for optimism. One guy from my tutor class said, 'Hopefully people will see what people our age are all about and that teenagers should be listened to a lot more.'

Yes, I thought, that's my aim too.

Another student was frank about the glamorous side of being on TV. She said, 'I'd love this documentary to be huge, with loads of people watching us, and our school would be famous and we'd be famous.' Then she paused before adding, 'But who's going to be interested in us lot?'

With the nine weeks' footage I knew we'd filmed, coupled with the main hook of the show – a thirty-year-old man posing as a sixteen-year-old – I really believed we could make both a highly entertaining and unusually thought-provoking programme that would satisfy all these wishes.

At the end of my last Friday, we were given our school reports. Mine was handed to me in a manila envelope with 'Howard Simmonds' written on it. I received it with a great sense of expectation. Being given the report was hugely significant. It was written proof that I'd spent a second time in school (because the experience had often felt like an odd dream), plus it was concrete feedback on how I'd performed and integrated as Howard.

I wanted to have done well and I needn't have worried. I ripped open the envelope to find lots of loose, coloured sheets of A4 and a piece of card on top of them, printed with a mortar board and rosette, carrying the school's motto; five of the sheets contained my report. Within boxes on these sheets, my teachers had written what they thought of me. They were all extremely positive.

As I read these comments, I felt awful. Here were all these people saying genuinely complimentary things about me and I'd deceived them.

Waking up the morning after my last day was a wonderful change. There was a clear physical difference in my body – I felt loosened; my shoulders, my neck and my head all felt as if an object weighing them down had been removed. I didn't have to lie any more – at least that's what I thought at the time; the reality would turn out slightly differently. I believed my days of being Howard and deceiving decent people were over. And the truth was about to come out.

The next day, Sunday, was the big day: finally time to let the cat out of the bag and reveal the whole truth to the people we'd been deceiving all along.

We arranged for the executive producer and the director, Paul and Kate, to meet the headmistress and the deputy head for lunch on Sunday. Again, more lies and half-truths were told to set up this meeting. We told Mrs J. and Mr H. that this was a 'wrap-up discussion' – a 'where do we go next?', 'thank you' meeting, to be held over a meal. Mrs J. and Mr H. naturally thought that this meeting would let them find out what Howard would do next – would he stay at their school after a successful term or would he return to Cardiff to stay with his uncle, or even fly back to the States to join his parents?

I didn't attend this lunch, because we reasoned that it would be far too distracting for me to be there, effectively metamorphosing from a seventeen-year-old pupil into a thirty-year-old TV producer in front of their eyes like some kind of alien in *Star Trek*. So while Paul and Kate went to the meeting I waited anxiously at our home base in the town. With me was Simon, the assistant producer, and a number of Channel 4 executives. Every curtain was drawn in the house, not only to hide the Channel 4 people, but also because I no longer needed to dress as Howard (which was a welcome change), and so I couldn't risk being seen by anyone from school. Gone were the baggy clothes, the jewellery and (hallelujah) the stiff helmet of gel on my head.

At the meeting, Paul and Kate thanked the headmistress and the deputy head for their hospitality and for letting the cameras into their lives. They explained how the documentary had been a great success: Howard had flourished in the nurturing environment of the school and the closeness of the team had allowed them to film a real insight into the lives of young people.

Then they slowly explained that there was one aspect of the documentary that they had omitted to tell everyone about.

Rather than being a seventeen-year-old wanting to go back to school, Howard was in fact a thirty-year-old television producer called Sheridan Simove. They explained that the film was his idea, born out of a deep-seated interest in the concept of adulthood and a belief that the purest way he could get the experience of being a teenager again was to lie to everyone about his true age.

After hours of excruciating waiting, Kate and Paul returned to our rented house. I accosted them in the hall.

'Well?' I said hurriedly. 'Were they OK?'

'Um . . . they were shocked . . .' Kate began.

'It was a lot to take in,' Paul added. He explained that Mrs J. and Mr H. were completely stunned by the news and that they needed to let it sink in.

'Were they angry?' I asked.

'No. More . . . disappointed really,' Kate said.

Oh dear.

'But did they understand why we did it?'

'Not really . . . They need time,' Paul answered.

He went on to explain that he'd told Mrs J. that both he and Kate would be coming into school tomorrow morning with some representatives from Channel 4 to discuss the way forward and to work out how to tell the teachers and pupils without undermining anyone involved.

Everyone at our base seemed to be putting on a brave face that the meeting had gone well. But there was a clear feeling of great anxiety among us all.

Then Kate added something that really knocked me for six. 'There's something else Shed . . .'

Uh-oh. This didn't sound good.

'They want you to go into school tomorrow . . .'

'What? To talk with the sixth form?'

'No, they want you in as Howard, as normal. Just so they can decide when to tell the other teachers and the students.'

'Oh no – you're kidding.'

'No, we're not.'

It was a measure of how disorientating the news must have been to the headmistress that she'd made this request. Just as I thought the stress of 'being Howard' was finally over, the production team and the two head teachers now wanted me to walk back into the school as Howard, and as if nothing had happened since I left on Friday. I'd have to do this with the knowledge that at least two people in the school knew I was in fact a thirty-year-old impostor.

It took the 'bizarre scale' to another level.

The next day was horrific. It was the day when it all went wrong. What I didn't know was that it would get even worse two days later.

Monday morning, I awoke knowing I had to dress as Howard again and go into school as requested by Mrs J. So far I'd tried to grapple with the surreality of the whole experience, but walking into school that day knowing that some people knew who I really was (and that most of the people still didn't) was incredibly overwhelming. I got the familiar sick feeling in my stomach, but it was much fiercer that day. In the event, my time as Howard was about to come to a very final end pretty quickly.

My first lesson was with Mr H. and I sat down to class extremely worried about seeing him. I kept saying to the crew, 'Stay with me, stay with me . . .' I was petrified of the production team leaving, images of an angry lynch mob playing through my mind.

So there I was, sitting at the back of the classroom, surrounded by the other sixth-formers. Mr H. wasn't there yet and I hadn't seen him that day. As each second passed, I wondered who in the school was being told the truth at that moment. When Mr H. entered, I could hardly look at him. His normally jovial demeanour was gone. His face was puffy and he looked exhausted.

He spoke quickly.

'Class, you'll have to excuse me – I've got some stuff to sort out . . . Carry on with your coursework. I'll be back soon.' Then he left.

None of the students really batted an eyelid. I knew that 'the stuff' he referred to was the meeting with Channel 4, which I hoped would go well. Seeing Mr H. raised my doubts though.

'Oh no – he looks awful,' I whispered to assistant producer Simon when no one was looking. I'd asked Simon to stick close by that day.

It was even more uncomfortable than usual to sit with my fellow students, some of whom were by now good friends, knowing that I was still lying to them while some people in the school knew the truth. I desperately wanted to say something, but I just sat there, squirming inside.

A very short while later, Mr H. burst through the door.

'Hi sir, how's it going?' one of the students asked.

He ignored them and looked at me with steely eyes. My heart froze.

'Howard, you need to leave now. Right now!' he barked.

I looked at the crew, uncertain what to do. Like a zombie I got up and headed for the door, all the time checking that Simon was nearby.

I got outside the door, Simon and the camera team with me, and shut it behind me.

'Shit . . . What's happening?' I asked. I was starting to panic. What was going on? Where should I go now?

I quickly became very scared. As we walked down the steps from the Business Studies classroom to the lower floor, our footsteps echoing in the empty stairwell, I stopped a number of times, worried that there would be a gang of furious people at the bottom to meet us.

'Keep going Howard,' Simon reassured me, professional to the last. 'I'm with you Bud.'

'Simon . . . Jesus. What . . . the hell?' It was all a bit much for me.

Of course, there was no gang at the bottom of the stairs and we eventually ended up outside the school in the yard. We turned the corner into the car park to find all the Channel 4 executives and the rest of the team standing by their cars.

Kate instructed the cameraman to turn the cameras off. I didn't realize it at the time, but it was to be the final footage we would film for the programme. No cameras recorded anything that happened from this point on.

'So?' I asked.

'It didn't go well. They're very annoyed,' one of the executives said.

I was then given the whole story. Apparently Mrs J. and Mr H. hadn't slept a wink last night. Today, they felt deeply hurt and angry. The meeting that morning had been with some of the school's Board of Governors, who had also expressed how appalled they were at what had transpired. No amount of explanation would placate them. The school board seemed united in the feeling that they'd been maliciously tricked and humiliated. Worst of all, they wanted assurances that the footage wouldn't be shown without their consent. Oh no.

This was exceptionally bad news.

We all stood there stunned for a second. Everything was starting to unravel.

I asked more questions.

'Who knows now then?'

'Just the governors and a few teachers.'

'When are they going to tell the sixth form?'

'In their own time. They might want you to tell them – they haven't decided yet.'

'What do we do now then?' I asked tiredly.

One of the Channel 4 executives had a plan. 'Let's get out of the town to discuss what to do next.' There was a palpable sense of shell-shock about our little group. Everyone was surprised and disturbed by the events that morning.

As we sped away to an ancient hotel outside the town, despite the evidence that the situation was deteriorating rapidly I still found myself hoping that everything would turn out OK. I hung on to the belief that the sixth-formers would turn everything around. Surely they'd understand why I'd done what I had?

At the hotel an hour later, it was crisis-management time. There was definitely a feeling that the project had gone very wrong and there wasn't a huge amount of confidence that we could put it right. The head teachers and the school board, quite understandably, were now refusing to talk with any of the production team or with Channel 4. So we were left with very few options.

I found myself with a mess of mixed emotions. On the one hand, I was relieved to be out of the school, safe and 'non-Howard', but at the same time I was hugely anxious about both the outcome of this whole project and the effect it was having on the people we'd told. I hadn't talked with anyone who'd been informed yet; I only got to see Mr H. briefly and he looked pretty distraught. This was not good.

The following morning, we heard from the school. They wanted me, Kate and Simon to go in the next day, Wednesday. This was to be the first time I entered the school in my true identity. I anxiously asked Kate whom we were scheduled to meet in the school, but there was no more information. Thoughts raced through my head. Would I just be meeting Mrs J.? The Board of Governors? Would Mr H. be there? Would I see the teachers? The sixth-formers even?

I didn't know what to expect, but I was desperate for a chance to talk with the sixth-formers and explain my intentions.

I hope I'm not being too melodramatic when I say that the next day at the school was one of the worst days (and certainly the most traumatic) of my life.

Kate, Simon and I walked in, all of us very edgy. We knew we were about to face the people we'd deceived. I still held a deep feeling that the sixth-formers would understand why we'd done what we had.

The first person we saw was Mrs J.'s secretary. She greeted us politely, but curtly, then went away round a corner, came back and led us into an office.

Mrs J. was standing up. I looked her straight in the eye.

'Hello,' was the best I could do.

'Hello,' she replied politely. Her face looked drawn and tired. The atmosphere was predictably cold.

'Sit down please,' she said.

A man I'd never seen before was already sitting at the table. He was in his fifties, distinguished looking. He eyed me warily. Mrs J. introduced him as one of the school governors, but my brain didn't take in his name as I was focusing on her. She looked agitated and upset, and was speaking as if she was on autopilot. It struck me that I'd seen this type of look and behaviour before: at funerals. That may sound ridiculous to you, but this event impacted everyone in a huge way.

My heart was in my mouth. Then the man spoke.

'OK. As you know, we're all just trying to come to terms with this and I'd like to hear from you what you think about the situation.'

Even though I'd gone over what I was going to say to Mrs J. and the pupils a million times, my mind went completely blank. So I spoke from the heart.

'Um . . . First off I'd like to apologize for everything,' I began. I looked at Mrs J., hoping she could see I meant what I was saying. I looked back at the man.

'I never, never wanted this upset. But you've just met me for the first time and you know I lied, so you probably think I'm lying now . . .' I blurted.

The governor didn't say anything, partially confirming my conclusion. I continued anyway.

'I've always had an issue about looking young. I wanted to make a TV show that explored youth, adulthood, maturity – issues like that. I wanted to relive my teenage years again because it wasn't brilliant first time for me – it wasn't terrible, but it wasn't brilliant – and I also wanted to celebrate seventeen-year-olds and what it means to be a young person – perhaps give them a voice if that's what they wanted and make people appreciate their potential . . .'

The man didn't look angry, but I got the distinct impression he didn't believe what I was saying. Which was fair enough, of course. My words felt like worthless bits of nothingness, turning straight into a meaningless stream of noise as soon as they left my mouth.

'We always knew we were going to tell you the truth, and I thought, I hoped, everyone would understand. But I was wrong,' I continued.

The governor snorted.

'Excuse me,' Mrs J. said. Then she left the room.

I was very confused about what was going on.

The governor continued. 'Well, you're going to have a chance to speak to everyone now,' he remarked.

'The sixth-formers?' I asked.

'And the teachers.'

Alarm bells started to ring in my head.

Well, this was it, what I'd wanted. At least I would have a chance to try to explain why we'd done what we had. My mind went back to the teachers, specifically Mr R., my form teacher and a man I'd become close to.

'How's Mr R.?' I queried.

I was thrown by what the governor said next.

He cleared his throat. 'Well, he's not happy – not at all. He wants to knock your head off . . .'

With hindsight, I can see how that would be a natural reaction, but at the time it simply sent another wave of fear through me. Jesus. What was going to happen when I saw everyone? Would I be strung up and lynched?

About ten minutes later, after the governor had listened to Kate's and Simon's thoughts, the door opened once more. I thought it would be Mrs J., but it was one of the school secretaries who'd come to get us.

'They're ready for you now. Can you follow me please?' she said flatly, her voice devoid of emotion.

We followed her through the deathly quiet corridors. It seemed no one was around in the sixth-form block. The reason would soon be evident – everyone was in the room we were about to enter.

We stopped at the door of the sports hall, but the lady said, 'You can go in.'

I paused, momentarily paralysed.

It was just me, Kate and Simon about to walk into an intense, pivotal situation. No camera crew, no Channel 4 executives, just the three of us. I felt naked, vulnerable. I sucked some air into my lungs and led the way, pushing the door open.

I remember the next few moments like flash frames.

I enter. Kate and Simon follow me in. The huge hall is completely packed, with row upon row of students sitting in tiers – it's the whole sixth form, around 150 people. Everyone turns to me as I walk in, but my mind is racing and I glance around erratically. I notice many things in a few seconds: a large group of teachers standing to the right. The teachers glare at me. I see Mrs J. at the front of the hall in a position where she has already been addressing the assembled group. The room is bursting with a low buzz.

Then, a complete shock when Mrs J. comes into clear view. I can tell immediately that she has very recently finished crying. Her eyes are ringed red and her face is crumpled. She says something that I can't quite make out, something like 'and here they are now,' but her voice is cracking.

This is a disaster. The sight of the ever-strong Mrs J. breaking down would be hugely distressing to everyone witnessing it.

It seems natural to walk towards her and take my place at the front of the hall, centre stage as it were. I feel my legs shudder.

Then the low buzz gets broken.

'Liar!' someone shouts.

'Shhhhh,' someone else hisses.

Oh no. Oh no.

As I near Mrs J. at the front of the sports hall, the faces of some of the students come into view. Something like an electric shock hits me as I catch sight of the friends I've made while at the school, a group of around ten students who have helped me through my time there. They are all bunched in one row, directly in my eye line. Every single one looks profoundly upset. Their eyes are red, some are still sobbing, even many of the boys' faces are contorted.

This is a very disturbing sight and in that instant it burns indelibly into my memory.

I try to steady myself, knowing that I now have an opportunity to make them all realize that the documentary could be positive for everyone involved. But even though only twenty seconds have elapsed since I stepped into the room, I fear that it's already hopeless.

I stand in front of everyone ready to be judged, relieved I can tell the truth but desperately eager to get out of what seems to be a highly emotional and volatile situation. This isn't going well at all.

Kate and Simon stand either side of me. I can't look at them. Instead, my eyes dart around like a waterhose on the loose. Even though I try not too, I keep feeling compelled to look at the sobbing row of friends in front of me.

I start, my voice shaky and low.

'First off, I've got to accept complete responsibility for what's happened. It was my idea in the first place – my company. Kate and Simon are just working, doing their jobs. All this was my idea. So please don't blame them.'

Dozens of angry, upset faces in front of me. I glimpse one guy (who'd been a great friend to me) wiping tears away from behind his glasses.

I plough on breathlessly.

'I didn't want it to turn out like this. I thought you'd see that I didn't mean this to be about . . . tricking you. I just thought that was the only way I was going to have a chance at going to school again. I was always going to tell you and it was so hard sometimes . . .

'I've always had issues with how I look young and always thought that people make assumptions about other people just because they look young. So I wanted to make a programme that would show that young people have something to offer and make people think about how it shouldn't matter what you look like or what age you are. It should maybe matter about what you do . . .'

'Are you lying now?' someone shouts angrily.

'Yeah,' someone agrees.

My eyes dart around trying to see who's making these comments, but there are nearly two hundred people in the room so the voices seem to come from nowhere.

'Let him speak,' one of the teachers says.

'No, I'm not lying now. But yeah – fair enough – of course anything I say now you'll think I am . . . am,' I shrug, frustrated and increasingly upset. 'I can only tell you that I was me. The person you got to know was *me*. The main difference was that I just didn't talk about my past life – but everything else, it was real. I connected with you. You were so good to me. It was so hard to lie every day.'

'He's lying,' a different voice says.

I sigh.

One girl then shouted from the back. I could see her face. She was angry and upset.

'You're thirty, you're meant to be responsible. We're young – and you're teaching us that the way to get ahead in life is to lie and mess with people's emotions. We're going to remember this for the rest of our lives. Did you enjoy messing with us? Are you twisted?' she sobbed.

The situation was starting to overwhelm me.

'Well, maybe I am . . . fucked up. I'm not sure. I didn't mean to hurt you. I didn't want to hurt you. Many times at the start of this I was so concerned about hurting people . . .'

'Huh – you couldn't have been that concerned,' someone interrupted.

'Yeah, you're right. I put my own ambitions on the line and I knew there was a chance that people would be hurt, but I thought it would turn out OK – I really did. Quite a few people said to me that they wanted this documentary to put their school on the map and perhaps make people listen to you. That's what I wanted as well.'

'Lying again,' someone shouted.

I could see that I was fighting a losing battle.

And so this disjointed dialogue went on for the next forty minutes. I kept trying to explain myself, but I'd always be heckled by someone saying I was a liar, with which I couldn't argue.

After a long while, Mrs J. wound down proceedings and the teachers left. Some of the sixth-formers left too and I was very perturbed that all my closest friends walked out of the sports hall, some in each other's arms. I felt I needed to talk with them – at least to apologize to them personally. As the gathering broke up, I asked a number of students to try to persuade my close friends to come back and talk with me.

Some of the remaining students wanted to hear about my real life, so I sat on a chair while they huddled around me sitting on the floor on sports mats. I kept being asked what about 'Howard's' life was true in terms of my own real life – I suppose they were trying to get their heads round who the person in front of them was. It must have been an incredibly difficult experience to see me instantly change from one person to another.

'Your hair's different,' was all one shy girl could manage.

I repeated that I *was* from Cardiff, and that no, my parents weren't in America. I explained that my real life had been virtually identical to Howard's life, and once again I stressed that I had always been myself with regards to how I reacted to the events in school and how I felt about the people I'd bonded with during my time there.

'I laughed when I found things funny. I was really friends with my friends,' I remember saying lamely.

Once I'd explained my career in television, I got a few questions about celebrities I'd worked with and quite a few students seemed very interested in my personal wealth.

'Are you really rich then?' one said.

'No, not at all. I'm a lucky boy and I can't complain. I have my own flat and car, but I'm not rich,' I replied.

On the outskirts of the group, Kate and Simon tried to explain their point of view to a number of sixth-formers. The atmosphere was better for a while. But then that gathering broke up and I gravitated towards Kate and Simon, suggesting we move into the playground.

But things went bad out there. Three girls came up to me screaming, tears streaming down their faces.

'How dare you do this? We trusted you. You're so fucked up. You've done so much damage,' one cried.

I just stood there, nearly breaking down myself.

'We're young – we're at a critical stage in our lives. We trusted you – you betrayed us, you freak,' another raged, an inch from my face.

Only two people during the whole episode, one lad and one girl, came up to me with a positive view on what had happened.

'It must have been really hard. You've done an amazing thing,' one of the popular guys said.

'I don't think you meant to hurt people,' the girl said.

'Well I didn't want to, but I knew it was a possibility, so what kind of person does that make me?' I replied.

She just shrugged.

One final incident also bothers me to this day. Right at the end of the main sports hall debacle, one of the students said something very pertinent.

'You come here, play around with our lives and now you'll just go back to London and forget all about us. We were just a project to you,' she said.

'No, that's not how it'll be. I won't just go back to London . . .'

And you know what really cuts me up today? That's exactly what I did. Everything spiralled out of control and I just went back to my flat in the East End, completely dazed. (A couple of years later, I did attempt to get in touch with the people I was very close to, but apart from a few emails, it didn't go much further than that.)

Eventually I told Kate and Simon that I felt it was time to leave. Things got a bit scary from then on. The three of us were wandering around in a school full of very upset and angry people. By now, the entire school had been told the truth, with every child in each year receiving a letter to take home to show their guardians. The letter related the deception that been carried out and reassured parents that all proper checks had been administered on the production team and that there was never any danger to anyone in the school.

We eventually found ourselves in the hallway at the front of the school, with no one escorting us and the huge desire to get out. It was very strange. I was momentarily frozen, not wanting to stay but at the same time not wanting to leave in case there was anyone waiting for me outside the gates.

We frantically called one of the Channel 4 executives to come and get us, but they couldn't get to us for at least half an hour, so the decision was made that we should start walking back to our rented house a mile away. It was to result in yet another disturbing episode.

We left through the front doors. It was to be the last time I was ever to set foot in that school.

As we started to walk home, it coincided with the end of the school day. Hundreds of pupils streamed out of the school and as soon as they recognized us they shouted various forms of abuse. A small group of kids followed us for a long time, all the way down the road. Given the disturbed state I was already in, their relentless shouts of 'Liar', 'Freak' and (more bizarrely) 'Thirty' hit me like little stones.

Eventually, the Channel 4 car pulled up and we piled into it, relieved.

The whole experience that afternoon was simply horrendous. It haunts me to this day.

That evening the story broke to the media. I was whisked off to a hotel while all hell started to break loose. News camera crews descended on the school, I started getting calls on my mobile from tabloid journalists and local television news ran the story.

The next day it hit the newspapers. It was a slow news day, so the story made the front pages of a couple of the papers – the *Sun* and the *Daily Telegraph*. The front pages. What the hell? The papers universally condemned what I'd done.

| Ideas Man

4 FAKE TV SCANDAL 4

CHANNEL FRAUD

String of phoneys shame our telly

By PAUL THOMPSON

Head fury at 'spotty nerd' scam

By JAMIE PYATT

A LIVID headmistress told yesterday how her school was duped by a Channel 4 show maker who pretended to be a nerdy sixth-former.

Howard's way . . . the pupil, really TV man Sheridan Simove, is pushed in trolley by pals during the school's rag week

SHOCKING CON FROM

Dressing for the Oscars
Nicole Kidman's secrets. Style Page 22

The Daily Telegraph means business
Our robust City pages are edited by Neil Collins. 'Someone you turn to first every single day,' said the British Press Awards judges, naming him Financial Journalist of the Year. City comment Page 30

The Daily Telegraph

www.telegraph.co.uk — Britain's biggest-selling quality daily — Thursday, March 21, 2002 50p

UK warns Saddam of nuclear retaliation

School conned by Channel 4 producer who posed as pupil

While this was all happening, I couldn't really get my head around the small whirlwind that was blowing. Since I'd left the school, I'd been whisked out of the area and was staying in a 'safe house' with one of the Channel 4 executives. I had no contact with the press at all. So how did they obtain photos of me for the front pages? Well, I'd had brushes with the press in the past . . .

The photo gracing the front page of the *Daily Telegraph* had been taken a few years earlier, on one of the rare occasions in my life I'd worn a suit. The picture was taken for a free local newspaper called *The Wharf* which covered the Docklands area of east London. *The Wharf* had been delivered to my workplace, Planet 24, every week and I'd perused it for years, during the time I worked on *The Big Breakfast* and other shows. It was a much higher-quality local newspaper than some, as its catchment area covered the whole of the Canary Wharf financial district. There were no feeble 'MRS SMITH'S CAT STUCK UP TREE' stories of the type sometimes seen in lesser publications; this was a slickly produced, relevant and meaty read. Thus, when I finally decided to leave Planet 24 and I needed publicity to raise money for various internet schemes, it was one of the first places I targeted. I managed to pester the editor of *The Wharf* into meeting with me and eventually he agreed to run a column charting my adventures during the dot.com goldrush that was happening at the time. For eighteen weeks *The Wharf* ran my column entitled 'Diary of a dot.com Entrepreneur'.

It was a huge thrill to be published in this way. Even though I wasn't being paid for the articles, the exposure in the paper to many wealthy people meant I got to meet a dozen or so fascinating characters who were willing to invest money in my web-based ideas. The dot.com bubble burst soon afterwards – fortunately before I'd taken anyone's money from them – but the whole experience had given me confidence in my ability to meet people and raise investment if I ever came up with an idea I thought was a safe bet.

The *Sun* also put the school story on their front page. Next to the big black letters of the headline, 'FAKE TV SCANDAL', was a small photo of my face. This photo had been taken three years earlier and must have been meticulously collated so that when the school story broke and a researcher typed in my name to an image database, the picture neatly popped up.

The photo was originally taken to accompany another (rather odd) story I was involved in at that time. While I was working on *The Big Breakfast*, one of my responsibilities was to find a replacement female host when our regular presenter decided to leave the programme. It was a big responsibility, as the morning show was the favourite watch for millions of viewers. The search for a new 'talent' involved my viewing hundreds of showreels and screen-testing over fifty potential candidates. It was actually a nerve-racking task. I was fiercely passionate and protective of the show, so I wanted to discover a new presenter our viewers would be excited to watch.

One day during the search, I returned to my office (which was packed to the ceiling with VHS tapes) to find the red light of my answer machine blinking away. I sat down and pressed the message-recall button as I had many times before.

The electronic system clicked in. 'You have one message,' the digital voice said. 'Beep.'

'Hi Shed! How are yoooo!' a female voice shrieked happily. I recognized the slightly American drawl straight way.

'It's Caprice.'

It was Caprice. As in Caprice, the beautiful blonde supermodel. Now, before you get the impression that my life was all showbiz parties and celebrity friends (it most certainly wasn't), there was a logical reason why Caprice had called. I'd been the first producer to create a feature about her that appeared on British television. She and her agent had always been grateful to me for that, and so now I was about to get a most unexpected and rare invite.

'I'm having a party this Saturday, sweetie, and I was wondering if you'd like to come.'

How kind! Now, unfortunately, I'd already arranged to go out with some friends I hadn't seen for a while that weekend, so I just couldn't make Caprice's bash. It was a pity, as I'm sure her celebration would have been a great night, but I couldn't let my mates down. I called Caprice's agent to thank her for the invite and then politely explained why I couldn't attend.

I put the phone down. Then I made a mistake.

Because it was exciting for me to get a personal invite to Caprice's party, I foolishly boasted to one of the guys in the office about it and how I couldn't take her up on her kind offer.

It just so happened that the same night, the guy I told in the office attended a press event where he got chatting to a journalist, casually mentioning my phone call from Caprice. Then all it took was a bit of background research and a photographer who snapped me outside my office and 'Hey presto!', four days later an article appeared in a national newspaper.

I was leafing through the *Sun* and, much to my surprise, as I turned the page I was confronted with a large picture of myself next to the headline 'Q: WHY IS CAPRICE BEGGING THIS NERD FOR A DATE? A: HE PICKS THE NEXT BIG BREAKFAST STAR'.

First, it was most odd looking at my face in print, almost as if it was a joke that somebody had played. I couldn't believe it was real. What was even more hilarious, though, was the story next to the picture. It chronicled how Caprice had been 'begging' me for a date despite my being 'nerdy', only because I had the power to pick the next presenter for *The Big Breakfast*. Not only did this tenuous reflection of the truth make me chuckle, the article also printed my full name wrongly as 'Sheldon Simove'.

During the time immediately after the school incident, there was one other source of photos that the newspapers used too: the students who'd mixed with me. One such image taken by a fellow sixth-former appeared with an extremely unusual article about the 'Back to School' documentary in the biggest-selling tabloid Sunday paper on the weekend after the story broke. The headline of the article screamed accusingly: 'SECRET DRUG SHAME OF C4'S PETER PAN FAKER'. Drug shame? I myself was fascinated to find out what my drug shame was.

The article was accompanied by a (very well-composed) full-length photo of me in my Peter Pan outfit that one of the students had taken at my (Howard's) seventeenth birthday party. I wonder if one of the pupils got a lot of money for the snap? If so, good on them.

The *News of the World* article was very loosely based on a conversation I'd had while I was Howard. The main body of the text described how my 'secret drug shame' was that once, as Howard, I'd told some of the students that I thought smoking marijuana was OK. I actually remember the conversation in question very well. It took place in a pub around a small table packed with sixth-formers and Kate was there too. A few of the sixth-formers were talking about smoking pot. One said to me, 'Howard, do you smoke weed?'

'Uh . . . no,' I replied truthfully. From a young age I've had asthma, so smoking has always been out for me. I explained this and then added, 'I think it's fine though . . .'

And that was that. The conversation swiftly moved on to another topic.

The article was another eye-opener into the workings of the media. It was fascinating to see how a small conversation about how I thought smoking pot was acceptable could be blown into such a misleading headline about me having a 'secret drug shame'. But I had no real gripes with the press. I'd committed a very public act, and would have welcomed publicity had the programme gone to plan, so I couldn't really complain now I was being criticized or demonized. All my friends and family knew I didn't have a drugs shame. Yes, I have lots of other demons and issues maybe, but (as yet) recreational drugs have never played a part in my life – apart from alcohol on a night out of course – so the write-up didn't bother me at all. The Peter Pan article was just another surreal straw on the top of the totally surreal camel that I'd been riding over the last few months.

Because large numbers of the press had camped outside my flat soon after the story broke, I was forced to go into hiding for almost two weeks. After spending a couple of days in a hotel, I was moved again. I stayed with one of the Channel 4 commissioning editors for the next week, in a perpetual state of disorientation and mild panic. The calls kept coming from the press, on my mobile (which I turned off) and to my friends and colleagues. My parents had a television crew turn up outside their house in Cardiff, which my mum thought was most exciting.

One journalist even managed to get inside the gated complex where I lived at the time, but luckily I wasn't there. I know the journalist got in because my brother heard the bangs on the front door of my flat, which he was looking after for me while I was on the run. For a week or so after the story appeared in the press, I didn't even venture outside for fear of being hounded or pilloried. It was all exceptionally bizarre.

Even after the circus of the preceding few days, I still had hopes that the documentary would be made and shown. There was one last chance: the rough-cut tape.

My production team had put together a rough-cut of the first programme in the series of three. This one-hour episode was to focus on me, my motives and what happened when I had a second chance at being sixteen. The second show was to focus mainly on the young people in the school and the third was to explore how everyone felt after the revelation and to draw conclusions from what had been learned by all.

I was very concerned about showing the rough-cut tape to the people at the school so soon after I'd left there, for a number of reasons. First, it was the one programme that focused mainly on me. I believe it would have been much better to showcase the second programme, as it would have proved that the documentary wasn't out to stitch anyone up – on the contrary, it was designed as an examination of maturity and a celebration of young people. But unfortunately at that time the first show was all that was even barely cut. Second, the rough-cut had been edited in a hurry while I was still in the school, so I hadn't been able to oversee it. All the footage shot before I entered the school, when I agonized over the morality of this project, had been cut out to save time. I was deeply unhappy about this. I felt it was vitally important for everyone to see that before entering school as Howard I was concerned about the risks of hurting people – especially because it turned out to be exactly what happened. I figured that at least the school would see that I hadn't just taken on the whole project as one big gag.

Instead, though, the tape unfortunately reinforced the impression that the project was a bit of a laugh and that I'd just waltzed in like a professional TV prankster to dupe decent people with no compunction or care for their feelings. That just wasn't the case.

The call came a few days after we'd sent the rough-cut to the school. The teachers hated it. Even more damning, the sixth-formers hated it. Everyone thought it was mocking, patronizing and flippant.

One comment that came back was that the sixth-formers had felt that the footage in the rough-cut conveyed that I was laughing at the people in the school. This interpretation bothered me greatly because it was far from the reality. When I laughed while speaking to camera, I wasn't sneering at the people who accepted me; in fact I was frequently hysterical at the entirely ludicrous situation I found myself in. I was completely incredulous at what was happening. I, a thirty-year-old, was managing to get away with posing as a sixteen-year-old and attending school. I mean, that's pretty ridiculous.

Contrary to what the sixth-formers and teachers believed, I didn't view the people in the town who welcomed me into their lives as inferior in any way. Quite the opposite; not only did I get both to deeply like and to respect the teachers and the young people I met, but I also quickly began to think that *I* was the person with the deficiency. The teachers and students I met were moral, contributing members of society, whereas to a large extent I was an ambitious, fame-seeking TV producer ready to risk hurting some innocents to make a name for myself in my chosen career. Hmm . . .

But the sixth-formers and the teachers remained convinced I was mocking them. A specific incident on the tape reinforced their belief that I was being derisive. It neatly highlights how an event can be interpreted in a number of ways.

The clip in question showed me getting my English homework back after being marked. Now, as I've mentioned, I put absolutely genuine effort into all my schoolwork, only ever holding back in the rare situation when I needed to omit tiny details that might betray my age. So, I was very keen to see how I'd got on in my studies. The

English homework I completed had been to write an analysis of a number of conversations that our teacher, Ms P. – an inspiring, lively lady in her late twenties (yes, younger than me) – had given us. She'd been teaching us about the intricacies of syntax and language, studying phenomena such as 'Discourse Markers', 'Idiolects' and 'Adjacency Triplets'. This was all new to me and utterly fascinating. It was like finding out valuable secrets of writing that not many people knew. By totally deconstructing sentences, Ms P. made us aware of the power of words, structure and pacing. The work was complicated, requiring me to read conversations word by word to recognize the linguistic markers Ms P. had taught us.

At the beginning of one lesson, our teacher announced that she had marked our homework. She cradled a large pile of lined A4 sheets, some handwritten, some (like mine) written on computer. She called out the names on the homework sheets one by one. I was nervous and excited to get my work back. I genuinely wanted to do well – for my personal pride, of course, but for the school too, to show them and the viewers that I was thriving under their mentorship.

'Howard?'

'Miss.'

'Well done,' she said, almost under her breath, trying to encourage me while at the same time not single me out too much just because I was the new boy.

Ms P. handed me my neatly typed sheets, now covered in lots of pencilled comments. I discreetly turned over the front pages to look at the bottom of the last page to see the mark I'd been awarded. All at once I saw a small postage-stamp-sized gold sparkly with a croissant printed on it, stuck next to a handwritten symbol for the mark 'A minus'. Immediately my fellow pupils asked how I'd done. I tried to keep it low key, showing the girl who sat next to me the croissant sticker and grade.

'A minus – nice one Howard!'

I was pleased too.

After class had finished, I filmed a reaction piece when no one was around. 'A minus!' I chuckled, feeling pleased with myself. Then I tempered my excitement, not wanting to make out I'd performed brain surgery: 'Well, I should be able to do well – I'm thirty years old after all!' I said this worried that my excitement over the grade might look foolish. I certainly didn't intend to denigrate the completed task, which was actually really tough.

However, the people at the school took this brief clip to mean that I was laughing at how easy the homework was and that my reaction signalled that I believed I'd just flippantly waltzed in and got a decent mark. They thought I was insinuating that schoolwork was easy, demeaning their achievements. What they didn't see was the hours of careful effort it took me to get that mark.

Anyway, the damage was done. The rough-cut tape was the final nail in the final coffin. The majority of people at the school hated it. There was nothing more we could do then.

Even Mark Thompson, the brand-new chief executive of Channel 4, got involved in the rapidly escalating situation surrounding the documentary, having arrived in the job just days earlier. He immediately found himself embroiled in this very public scandal involving his new channel. He phoned the headmistress to apologize for the hurt caused and to explain the good intentions behind the piece, but it was no use. The school just saw Channel 4 as the 'other side', which of course they were.

Eventually, after a week and a half, I nervously returned to my flat in east London. My quiet home with no one else there. No cameras, no production team, no Channel 4 people, just me. My flat was so far away from the gorgeous town I'd been living in and from anything TV-related that it seemed eerily as if the whole school event had never happened. I slipped into a profound state of shock. I didn't know what to do next. In the next few weeks I took care of admin chores like changing my name back to 'Sheridan Simove' and signing off the television production budget. The team came off the payroll and went back to their lives.

Among other things, I felt like a failure. I wrote letters to the headmistress, my form tutor and to the young people I'd become closest to, apologizing for the upset I'd caused them. It was all rather traumatic to say the least. Apart from these few momentary distractions, I didn't know what to do with myself. My head spun.

Two weeks later I got called in to Channel 4 to speak with the legal team. They had some incredibly bad news. The school was still furious. Then the bombshell came. The programme would not be aired. I was completely devastated.

For me, the 'Back to School' documentary we filmed is the best work I've ever done. It has all the traits of a film worth showing – jeopardy, engaging characters in the school, poignant stories, many funny moments and, ultimately, may well be thought-provoking. So will it ever be shown? I dearly hope so. My dream is that one day the school's Board of Governors and the people whom we filmed will give their consent for the footage to be shown and will get involved in the project. I think we could make an even more interesting programme now all this time has passed, because the storylines of the young people in the school will have moved on so much. When we shot 'Back to School' we followed a number of the sixth-formers (and teachers) in detail, charting their worries at the time and their hopes for the future too. It would be fascinating to see how their lives have changed and whether they followed the paths they predicted. Ultimately, though, for any footage we shot to be made into a programme or feature-length documentary, it would be up to the people whom I disrupted.

So why did this project go so wrong? I'll try to explain.

Maybe I'm blowing it out of proportion, and perhaps I need a long course of therapy, but to me this was a very significant and traumatic event in my life. It wasn't my goal to make so many people upset and angry. I've thought about what I did every day since it happened, trying to work out how it turned out like it did.

Here's my conclusion, for what it's worth. The whole problem was that the project messed with a fundamental human social phenomenon – quite simply, the betrayal of a relationship. Nine weeks may not seem a long time on the face of it, but the period I spent at school was a very intense time. Perhaps it was the presence of the cameras, perhaps it was because the people in the school were such open-hearted souls, perhaps it was even because the whole situation was about bonding and acceptance.

Whatever the reason, Kate, Simon and I formed a deep connection and friendship with many people we met at the school.

These friendships were, of course, built upon quite a few huge lies on our side, but from my point of view at least, these relationships were also built on a huge number of truths. The truths came from everyone at the school who allowed us to get to know their personalities, but also from a large number of truths given by me and the team – that is: our genuine emotional reactions and engagement with all of them.

I'm well aware, though, that this logic doesn't quite pan out. It's too simplistic to ask someone you've betrayed in one way to trust you in all other respects. That's the problem with lying. It's a rigidly black-and-white thing. Once you've told *some* lies, or even just one lie, then you throw doubt on everything you've ever said and done. It's the whole 'if you lied about that, well you must have lied about this' syndrome. And before long, the whole relationship falls down like a pack of cards.

From my side, the connections we forged with the teachers and young people at the school were real. When I was Howard, I still felt that I was being myself – Shed – as I bonded with each person. I believe that that's *why* we bonded. That's why I valued the relationships I formed. When I was Howard, my core values, beliefs and sensibilities came from the same heart I've always had. Therefore, from my point of view, everyone bonded with Shed, the real person. The problem was that conversely, everyone at the school thought the whole relationship was a falsehood, a sham, a trick. And even though the overall premise was a trick, the bonds made were not.

At the risk of over-thinking this whole thing (well, I have been churning it over in my mind for years), the ability to form meaningful relationships – the ability to form bonds and empathize with each other – is what makes us civilized beings. Relationships are about trust and cannot exist without it. A bond will be easily broken if lies get involved. And that's what happened.

Needless to say, the 'Back to School' experience has had a profound effect on my life.

Among other things, these days I try very hard never to lie.

'*Oh no – this girl will think you're an idiot.*
Giving her silly little presents that you made yourself?
Uh . . . no, she'll think you're 'cheap' . . . and desperate.'

How Wooing A Girl
Produced A Product Range

Romance isn't dead, maybe it's just in a coma . . .

The next idea I'd like to tell you about was born in a most unusual way. Its birth is a clear reminder that sometimes day-to-day circumstances can trigger an adventure linked to an original concept, even when you're not actively trying to fulfil a challenge. This one happened when I least expected it: while I was trying to woo someone.

It had been four years since the whole 'Back to School' episode had rocked my world and even though it was still never far from my mind, life was getting back to normal. I'd been working at Channel 4 and the BBC on and off for years, and I was slowly starting to get more confident about trying to make ideas happen outside the TV world.

It was summer and I'd recently met a girl at a party and had been entirely entranced by her – she was smart, funny and totally gorgeous, with bright green eyes and dark hair. I was over the moon that she'd agreed to go out for dinner with me. It was our first date and I was greatly looking forward to the night.

I booked one of the best restaurants I knew, wanting to make the evening a bit special. The posh eatery was on the forty-second floor of a huge skyscraper in the centre of London's financial district and offered stunning views over the city. With its soft blue underlighting and clean metal lines, it was a swish place, a common haunt of rich banker types. It was a bit pretentious I suppose, but hey, I was showing off. The four-week waiting list reflected the restaurant's popularity, so I'd booked ahead and now I was at the bottom of the building, about to go up in the private elevator that was dedicated solely to the restaurant. I handed in my driver's licence to the security guard at reception, then walked through the metal detector. The security there had been tight ever since September 11th, and all these procedures also had the effect of making the place seem even more exclusive. I didn't set off the metal detector, so I went up in the lift and waited slightly nervously at the table next to a window through which I took in a phenomenal cityscape.

My dining partner arrived soon after I did, and we began to feast on a delicious meal of beautifully prepared beef tortillas and grilled vegetables. After the main course, I shuffled nervously in my seat and said I had a small gift to give her. I'd made something to hand over during the meal – a small token that would hopefully make her laugh but also make her realize that I was delighted to be with her.

I dug into the pocket of my jacket to bring out a little package wrapped with green and gold paper.

'Here it is!' I said, somewhat embarrassed (as I knew what was inside).

'No way! What is it?' she said, her eyes widening.

I suddenly wondered if I'd built it up too much and that now she'd be disappointed with the tacky offering cocooned within the giftwrap.

'Open it,' I suggested. 'It's just something small.' (Please insert your own joke here.)

She unwrapped the tiny package, took the contents out and placed them on the table. Her furrowed brow showed she was puzzled by what she found. On the table was a piece of white card about the size of a matchbox with two objects stuck to it: a slightly squashed piece of brown fruit – a date – and a single wooden match with a bright orange head. Neatly printed underneath the date and the match were the following words, which she read aloud:

THE SHED 'HOT DATE'

Instructions:

For hot date, light match and heat date . . .

Yes, it was a groan-inducing gag, but my dining partner seemed to like it anyway. She laughed, thanked me and gave me a kiss. It seemed to have gone down well.

About ten minutes later, something happened that made me smile. On her return from the ladies' room, my date had a mysterious smile on her face. At first I hoped she was smiling at me, but then I got suspicious.

'What?' I said.

'Oh nothing, just something I noticed . . .'

'Go on,' I encouraged.

'Well . . .' she began, 'I do love my "Hot Date", Shed, but look over there.' She gestured to the table next to us.

I glanced over and saw a couple deep in chat. The girl was beaming at the guy. On the table was a light blue box with silver writing emblazoned on the top. In the girl's hand was a chunky shiny bracelet.

I laughed as I understood what was happening on our respective tables. Like my dining companion, I too appreciated the contrast of the situation at one table where the guy was giving his girl a gift of a silver Tiffany bracelet and on the next table the bloke was giving a slightly squashed date on a piece of card.

Over the next few weeks, I tried to think of ever more unusual ways to make my dinner date smile and my bad jokes became a sort of personal running gag between us. On one occasion, I created a very simple website especially for her and then emailed her the link so she could view it at work. The front page of the website proudly displayed my message to her. It proclaimed: 'I think you look gorgeous – tell your parents "well done".'

On another occasion I gave her a miniature bottle topped with a small cork stopper. The tiny label on the bottle described the contents inside as 'Sunshine in a bottle' and another label explained that: 'This bottle has been corked outside on a sunny day to trap real sunshine.' A note next to the bottle explained my feelings. It said, 'You're like bottled sunshine to me.' Blimey, I must have been in a trance back then.

As you can see, the ideas were always pretty cheesy, but also (I hoped) quite fun and thoughtful.

Time went on and one afternoon I was racking my brains thinking of the next gesture when it suddenly hit me that this whole 'romantic gift' wooing process was something that other people might possibly like to try with the special person in their life. I thought that the ideas would make a great 'Little Book' – you know, those tiny square books you buy as stocking fillers or receive for Christmas and then they end up in the toilet.

Fired with this concept, I switched on my computer and started to type out 'The Little Book of Romantic Gestures – fifty ways to show someone you care'. I worked solidly through the night, designing the front and back covers, writing the gestures out and then illustrating each one with a drawing that I scanned into my computer. Here are a couple of examples.

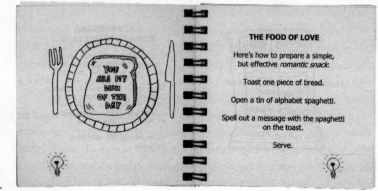

THE FOOD OF LOVE

Here's how to prepare a simple, but effective *romantic snack*:

Toast one piece of bread.

Open a tin of alphabet spaghetti.

Spell out a message with the spaghetti on the toast.

Serve.

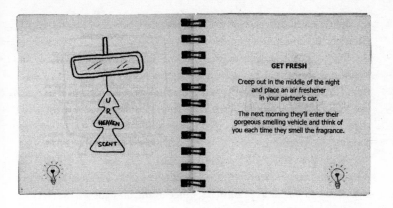

GET FRESH

Creep out in the middle of the night
and place an air freshener
in your partner's car.

The next morning they'll enter their
gorgeous smelling vehicle and think of
you each time they smell the fragrance.

A couple of days later, I took the finished book down to a print shop a couple of miles away and got them to print out a 'life-size' mock-up.

I then sent this mock-up to six publishers. I didn't just send it in a normal envelope, as I felt I needed a gimmick to get my package noticed amongst the pile of submissions that land on every publisher's desk each day. So I created packaging that related to the original inspiration for the book. To get each person's attention, I sent them a packet of dates clearly displayed in a large plastic envelope next to their address and a one-line message personally directed at them. For example, I sent one publisher (whose first name was Wendy) a package with the words 'Fancy a date Wendy?' emblazoned on the front, above the packet of dates that was also clearly visible through the transparent envelope.

These packages were all sent in one recorded-delivery mailshot. When the woman at the post office saw all the envelopes, each with the same packet of dates showing through the plastic envelope and the same slogan printed across the front, but each with a different name – 'Fancy a date Michael?', 'Fancy a date Sarah?' – she gave me a very quizzical look.

A month later, I'd received replies from four of them – all rejections. I never heard from the other two. So I sent out another five books to different publishers. Once again, all I got was a rejection or no reply.

Some weeks later, I was talking with a friend of mine who works in TV called John Gough, telling him how I was finding it hard to get anyone interested in the idea. John is a charming fellow, a dapper ex-teacher who came up with a great idea for a TV show (involving cameras that can see in the dark) that eventually sold round the world. He gave up everything to slog his guts out for years because he believed in his show. I admired him hugely and when we met we forged an instant friendship.

John suggested I meet a colleague of his who designed his own furniture and had an entrepreneurial spirit, thinking this guy might have some advice about how to get the book published.

When I took the book to the furniture entrepreneur, his comments were swift and very incisive.

'This is great Shed . . .'

It's always a relief when someone understands the potential of an idea you're passionate about. But he hadn't finished.

'. . . but you've got a product range here, Shed, not just a book.'

'What do you mean?' I asked, trying to get a handle on his thoughts. Then I got it.

'Ah . . . so I make each idea into a little package – the idea ready to buy,' I said.

'Exactly,' he answered.

What the guy had actually suggested was that I go back to the beginning when the gestures were physical in form and not just ideas in a book.

I bought some neat little plastic bags, printed up some labels and spent the evenings of the next few weeks working on the 'Romantic Gestures' range', a ready-made range of products for people to buy for their loved ones. Here are a few of the prototypes I made, including the one that started the range off:

I pitched the Romantic Gestures range to over a dozen companies during the next year and a half. Nobody was interested in releasing it. No one at all. I went to many demoralizing meetings. Sometimes the person I met liked the concept (and my hopes briefly soared); sometimes they'd just say it wouldn't sell. But every time I'd encounter some small objection that meant the person didn't want to go ahead.

This continual run of knock-backs was especially gut-wrenching. I'd often go to a meeting feeling great, get a rejection, have the sick feeling in the pit of my stomach and then become very frustrated, wondering when I'd be able to launch the product to market. But I'd surprise myself by quickly bouncing back. I strongly believed in the range and the core idea, which meant I just kept carrying on, trying to get the book published and the range off the ground.

A year went by, during which I continued working at Channel 4, being involved with making *Big Brother*. Plus, any spare time I had was taken up with travelling to companies all over the country, always carrying my thick folder of visualizations for product ideas I'd come up with.

I was having very little success, so I decided to have another try at getting the 'Little Book' published.

I was about to print up and send out another batch of mock-ups to different publishers when a coincidence occurred that would lead to a surge of success with getting new products off the ground, and it happened along a path I didn't expect.

One day, a prettily decorated envelope dropped through my letterbox. It was covered in tasteful pink flowers and had an ornate pink border. I didn't recognize any markings on the outside of the letter, but opened it along with the other envelopes that arrived that day, thinking it was yet another piece of junk mail. Inside was a fold-out leaflet covered in glossy pictures and details of interesting Valentine's gifts. It was a mini catalogue of products sent by a company called Worldwide Co, the wholesaler who manufactured them. To this day, I still don't know how it got sent to me, but I'm glad it did, given what subsequently happened.

The range in the catalogue included 'Kiss It Better' plasters and a 'Passion Pen' for measuring how passionate you are. Really neat ideas. Zing! The thought hit me . . .

Maybe, just maybe, the people running this company might be interested in my romantic product range. I spent the next few weeks trying to get through to the managing director, a guy called Michael Sweeney. Once I reached him on the phone, I found him to be charming and receptive, but very busy – a not unusual state of affairs.

'Can I send you a confidentiality agreement?' I asked.

Michael agreed. 'Email it over. I'll take a look.'

I did as he asked and he emailed me right back to say it looked fine. Superb. Now all I had to do was get a meeting with him.

Up until then, my attempts at finding a manufacturer had been following a disappointing pattern. I would track down the boss, take a while to get to him, persuade him to meet, then ages later we'd eventually meet, at which point soon after I'd get a polite 'no thanks.' But when I arrived at Michael's office I felt something different was about to happen.

I finally arranged a meeting when I called him out of the blue, as I was due to be travelling in his area that day. I thought it would be worth a shot to see if he had some time to spare. Amazingly, he said he had half an hour he could spare that afternoon. It must have been the keenness in my voice that persuaded him. I raced back home from a meeting about a new TV show I was working on, hastily printed out the Romantic Gestures proposal I'd written and grabbed my prototypes, before jumping into my car to drive to his office in the west of London.

The print-out of directions I'd got from the internet brought me to my destination with a couple of minutes to spare. I turned up outside a large white factory building, parked in front of some brown folding industrial doors, then hopped out and pressed the front door buzzer.

'Hi there, it's Sheridan Simove here, to see Michael,' I announced.

It always feels odd calling myself the long version of my first name. I often don't call myself 'Shed' straight away in case people think I'm some sort of wacky idiot with a stupid nickname. Umm . . .

Someone buzzed me in and Michael came down to collect me. He was a youthful, fit-looking man in his late thirties with a strong jawline, dressed casually in a trendy shirt and jeans. He was very welcoming, greeting me with a big smile, but I thought he had the air that most successful businessmen have – a slight toughness about him that indicated he'd overcome a lot of challenges. He then led me upstairs to his offices. That's where I got the feeling.

'Come in Shed,' Michael said as he pushed through a heavy metal door.

I entered to see a most wonderful sight. The room was very large, open plan, with small, square factory windows on each side which allowed light to flood in. In the middle of the room were lines of simple, modern metal tables and on them I saw a display that got me very excited.

On the tables were rows upon rows of carefully arranged printed packets and containers. I focused more closely to see numerous different novelty gifts neatly laid out. At the sides of the room stood dozens of shelving units, also covered with quirky product ideas such as 'The Jesus Action Figure' and 'Stick-On Moustaches for all Occasions'. Not only was it my heaven in terms of browsing, it was the first time I'd been to a company making ideas that I aspired to create. In a weird way I felt as though I'd found both my spiritual and my business home.

I gasped like a little kid. 'Wow – cool,' I blurted, very professionally.

Michael grinned and guided me towards a small room off the main room and overlooking it through a glass wall.

'Let's talk in here,' he suggested, as my mind spun.

Then something weird happened.

As you know, for a long time I'd dreamed of creating a product that would eventually go to the shops. But I had an even more specific (and even less attainable) dream to get something into Urban Outfitters, a worldwide chain of cool stores selling hip clothes and inspirational novelty goods. So when Michael led me into the adjoining room and said, 'Sorry about the mess – I've just had the guys in from Urban Outfitters,' my heart leaped just a bit more. Here was someone who had direct contact with the global retail chain that I yearned to be involved with. I felt another physical surge go through my body: a great hope that Michael would like the concepts in my bag.

After he had carefully read and signed the confidentiality agreement, I quickly started my presentation. I could tell he was the sort of guy to make up his mind straight away, so I tried to rattle on at a pace. I brought out the mock-up of 'The Little Book of Romantic Gestures', then placed the product samples on the table one by one. Michael picked up the 'Bottled Sunshine' prototype while I kept talking.

'That's neat,' he said.

Hurrah. Good start.

I kept lifting out the ideas one by one from my bag and Michael would periodically pick one up and say something positive. Now and again he'd comment about a difficulty with producing an idea, like the problem of having a real date in a packet (it would rot), but on the whole he was enormously positive. I was over the moon. By the time we'd stopped chatting, the whole table was covered in my romantic gift prototypes.

Even though the reaction to these ideas was overwhelmingly positive, I had to stop myself from getting excited. Experience has taught me to try to keep my emotions in check, but sometimes it's hard. I've had so many meetings where the person in front of you says all the right things, then you get an email a few days later saying nothing is quite right. It's upsetting.

I understand why this happens though – it's often hard for someone to criticize your idea when you're in front of them. They don't want to offend. The problem is that because they are polite and say they like your idea, you then get your spirits up only to have them dashed later on. So while I was pleased that Michael seemed to like the ideas I presented, my hopes weren't raised too high.

But then something great happened that allowed me to let my spirits soar just a little bit more. Michael did three things that gave me reasons to be hopeful that this deal would actually come to fruition. First, he excitedly asked members of his team to come in to see the prototypes on the table. Second, he asked me what sort of a business deal I'd want. Finally, he asked me to leave the product concepts and proposals with him so he could discuss them with his team more fully. He even set a deadline: 'Can I keep these until next week Shed? I'll give you some answers then.'

I normally wouldn't let the prototypes out of my sight, but this time I had a good feeling about Michael and the company. He'd given me a concrete time-frame for a response which I greatly appreciated.

My half-hour was up. I scribbled a quick inventory of the concepts I'd left behind, then drove back to my flat. I was on cloud seven. I wouldn't let myself be on cloud nine until we signed a deal. So I waited.

I called him a week later, full of anticipation. Michael explained he needed more time to make a decision and speak with his partner.

'Fair enough,' I thought, but it wasn't the 'Yes' that I'd hoped for.

'Sorry I can't give you an answer now,' he said, 'but the team are really hot for your ideas – and if we go for them, we'll work hard to make them a success. I'll be able to tell you next week for definite Shed.' I took great cheer from this. It was a very positive step and felt close to success, but I firmly stopped myself from getting too excited. Until some signatures were on some contracts the champagne would stay in the fridge. It ain't over until the Fat Lady *signs*.

Unfortunately, because of his crazy schedule of trade fairs, Michael still hadn't made any decisions a week later. I was told to ring him back in a month's time. Once again I felt the familiar mixture of frustration and hope that seems to permeate anyone's journey on the way to a goal. I couldn't just expect everything to stop for me, but the wait was agonizing, wondering whether after so many dead ends this company would pick up my ideas and turn them into a real-life product.

It would be a further two months before I saw Michael again.

He called me in to meet his partner Jonathan, an energetic, fresh-faced and fast-talking man in his late thirties. The guys told me that they'd had my Romantic Gestures prototypes sitting in their office staring at them, but they'd just been so busy it had taken this long for them to have time to deal with them.

As we talked, I took the opportunity to pitch my full slate of product concepts. I brought out a thick, ring-bound document I'd been working on for months. It was packed with dozens of ideas for novelties, toys, giftware and confectionery.

Things seemed to be going well when they informed me that they were definitely interested in developing some of my product concepts, but that it was too early to commit to anything just yet. Michael explained that they were planning to visit China the following month and that they'd take some of the ideas over to check their feasibility. Good news.

At the end of the next month, I called the guys at Worldwide Co and Jonathan told me that he and Michael had just returned from China after a successful trip. Even though they weren't entirely sure about the sales potential of the Romantic Gestures range, Jonathan had found a factory in Hong Kong that could make one of the other products I had shown them in the last meeting.

They had laughed when I'd showed them the idea for the novelty toy called Designer Beaver, involving a picture of a woman's naked torso and some iron filings – as described in chapter 3.

It was great news that there was finally some real progress with *that* product, but I soon realized that once again the Romantic Gestures range had failed to get off the ground.

Months went by. Just like all the other times when I'd tried so hard to make something happen and it hadn't come off, I felt a mixture of frustration, disappointment and weariness with the whole process. It's a time when the demons inside take over.

'Maybe you should give up with this range Shed. Maybe the reason the ideas aren't getting off the ground is simply because they're not good enough . . .' These inner voices are very convincing.

So I did give up. Well, perhaps more accurately, I stopped trying for a bit. I'm pretty sure that I'd never actually give up on any project, because (as we all know) sticking at something is the only true 'secret' to success. When you stop trying, then it goes without saying that there won't be progress. But, little did I know, a lucky break was just around the corner.

Just over five months after I'd sent the second batch of 'Romantic Gestures' books out to more publishers (and they'd all been rejected), I happened to stumble across an opportunity that would unexpectedly lead to a result.

While I'd partially given up on sending the book out to publishing houses, I was still willing to explore other avenues. I discovered that a huge 'gift and home products' trade fair was coming up. Maybe, just maybe, there would be a company there who might be interested in my Romantic Gestures range. It was a long shot, but worth a try.

The day of the fair approached and I wasn't really feeling like a trek to Birmingham's National Exhibition Centre. The demons chattered noisily: *'This fair will take up a whole day – your day off – so why bother? It's likely no one will be interested in your ideas anyway . . .'* I was very close to listening to them, but fortunately I snapped out of it.

I caught a train to Birmingham. I was amazed when I eventually arrived. The fair was spread over a large number of huge hangars, and I needed a little map to get round all the stalls. Among other things, I never knew there were so many giftwrap companies in the world.

After visiting dozens of stalls and walking what seemed like miles, I became rather excited when I happened upon a stall for Summerdale Publishers. The tasteful mustard-yellow-covered walls of their cube were lined with shelves displaying lots of 'Little Books'. Ha. Possibilities . . .

I immediately wondered whether my 'Little Book of Romantic Gestures' would fit in to their stable of titles. I needed to find out more, so I turned to approach the smartly dressed lady hovering nearby.

Now, when I tell you this story, it may seem that it was easy for me to just go up to the person behind a stall and ask them if they'd be interested in my book. In fact it wasn't.

I'd spent hours walking around the huge NEC arena looking at everything from coloured silk ribbons to intricate leather handbags and even stained-glass 'suncatchers'. Whenever I saw a stand that even vaguely looked as if it may be a company that would produce something like the Romantic Gestures range or the little book, I would pounce. More often than not, I'd be greeted with a polite but negative response. All the companies were there to sell their wares, so the last thing they wanted was someone trying to sell *them* something. It was very demoralizing.

So when, at the end of the day, with heavy feet, I spied the stall for Summerdale Publishers, I nearly didn't even speak to the person looking after it. Lucky I did.

The smart company representative was very polite and welcoming. I whipped out the mock-up of my own little book and she jotted down the details of the correct person at Summerdale I needed to write to about it. This glamorous lady told me that the commissioning editor at Summerdale was a woman called Jennifer Barclay. At the time, I simply thought I'd been given yet another name of someone to send my book out to. My hopes weren't high.

The next day, though, I sent a letter to Jennifer and bundled it in a padded envelope with one of my mock-ups for 'The Little Book of Romantic Gestures'. Embarrassingly, the letter contained a typing error that I realized I'd made only after I sent it off. I misspelt one of the first sentences in the letter, writing that I had 'visited your stall yesterday at the Spring Fairy'. Fairy! Blimey. It comes to something when you send a letter to a publisher and you can't even write properly. Given that I made that mistake, I'm very surprised that they even replied.

Months went by again, and both the book and the Romantic Gestures range faded from the forefront of my consciousness. I began to shift my concentration to other challenges I was obsessed with at the time, like creating my own money – which you can read about in the next chapter. All the while, I firmly believed that the book wasn't going to be published in the near future as it seemed all the opportunities had come to nothing. But, little did I know, my earlier efforts had sown a seed of hope. It had been hibernating for a while and now, like a spring flower, it was miraculously about to bloom. Something wonderful then happened out of the blue.

Just when I'd given up hope, an email arrived that sent my spirits soaring. Scanning my inbox as I do every day, I noticed an address and subject that I didn't recognize. I quickly realized that it wasn't one of the dozens of junk mail messages for impotence or X-rated house-wives I regularly receive, and quickly opened it. It read:

> Dear Sheridan,
>
> Thanks very much for sending us a copy of the mock-up for your little book of Romantic Gestures. It's lovely and fits nicely with the kind of gift book we publish. We might be interested in buying the rights to the book, although we tend to think a more general theme of creative gift ideas (rather than focusing on the romantic gesture) might do better.
> What do you think?
> Best wishes,
>
> ## Jennifer Barclay
>
> **Commissioning Editor and Rights Manager**
>
> **summerdale** *publishers ltd*

Wow. Wow. Wow. This was the first time anyone had taken any interest in publishing anything I'd written as an actual book, so naturally I was completely thrilled. There's a lovely sensation that comes when it seems that you've reached a goal – your stomach lurches a tiny bit and your heart skips a little beat. It's a fantastic feeling.

I immediately jumped on the phone to Jennifer, trying not to sound too needy and excited, although I was most certainly definitely both. She asked me what I thought about the idea of altering the book's main thrust from something that concentrated on 'romance' to a book about creative gift ideas.

I was so pleased that someone was finally interested in the little book, I would have considered any suggestion.

'Yes – great idea,' I said. 'I'm really into the whole concept of "creativity" anyway, and it'll give the book a wider appeal maybe . . .'

We chatted for a little bit more and I promised to send Jennifer a list of title suggestions for the new book and some more sample ideas.

Wham! The phone went down and my mind starting racing.

Superb, superb, superb. I was close to my first publishing deal. Even though I'd hardly managed to write *War and Peace*, getting this book published meant a lot to me.

For the rest of the day, I feverishly scribbled ideas and new titles for the book. I tried to skew any gift ideas I came up with away from the purely romantic, making them more generally suitable presents for anyone, whether they are in love or not. That night I sat up late compiling the work I'd done. I felt it was important to show Jennifer that I was doubly keen to maximize this exciting opportunity, so I wanted to get any new ideas to her quickly.

Here are a couple of ideas I sent – see if you can spot where I suck up to the publisher:

EVERYONE'S A WINNER
Award someone a trophy for just being them. Most trophy shops sell generic trophies – get one engraved with a suitably personal message, like 'Jennifer, Best Commissioning Editor Ever'.

MAKE YOUR MARK
Give someone their very own person-alized bookmark. Simply cut out a piece of card in a bookmark shape and cover it with cut up photos, cartoon strips or a message that means some-thing to both of you. You can even get it laminated at a print shop if you want a really professional finish.

A few days later Jennifer said she'd shown her team my title ideas and new concepts. Thankfully, she still sounded keen, saying that she preferred the title *Presents Money Can't Buy* from the list I'd sent her. Great.

I still couldn't quite believe that this was happening. 'So are you still interested in publishing?' I asked, the incredulity in my voice slightly audible. I know you're meant to be confident in these situations, but there's always the niggling feeling that what you've done isn't quite good enough.

'Yes, yes – I think we will . . .' Jennifer said.

Wonderful!

I swiftly turned the conversation round to 'the deal', asking Jennifer about what sort of publishing arrangement we'd come to regarding the sales of the book. Obviously, I was sure the book would set the literary world on fire, so it was important to get the money side sorted.

Jennifer outlined a deal structure that sounded fine to me. At that point, she could have told me that I'd have to pay *her* in order to get the book published and I would've considered it.

'So what happens now?' I asked.

'I'll send you a contract, you deliver some drafts and then we'll publish it next year,' she said.

Well, that's exactly what happened. I worked hard on my 'Little Book', rewriting draft after draft. Eight months later, it was a real thrill when it finally hit the bookshops. It was gorgeous how the publishers had given my little book of ideas and doodles a complete makeover. They'd made the pages a lovely shade of cream and given the drawings a colour wash, making them leap off the page. Plus, they'd bound the book, *Presents Money Can't Buy*, in a sumptuous chocolate-brown hardback cover that felt waxy. It was lovely to the touch.

I always find it incredible how a team of experts can run with the germ of an idea and then totally transform it into something that's so much better than the original concept.

The book had gone through quite a transformation. The original concept was about romantic gestures . . .

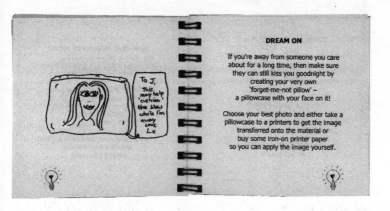

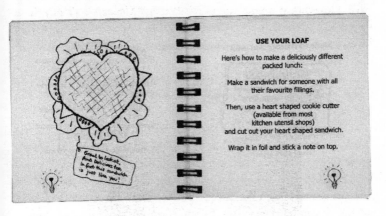

. . . and that got broadened by the publisher into gift ideas for *Presents Money Can't Buy* . . . and that got polished into the final version . . .

USE YOUR LOAF

Here's how to make a deliciously different packed lunch gift: make a sandwich for someone with all their favourite fillings. Then use a shaped cookie cutter (available from most kitchen utensil shops) and cut out your special sandwich in a heart shape. Wrap it in foil and stick a note on top.

DREAM ON

If you're away from someone you care about for a long time, then make sure they can still kiss you goodnight by creating your very own forget-me-not pillow – a pillowcase with your face on it! Choose your best photo and take a pillowcase to a printer's to get the image transferred onto the material. Alternatively, buy some iron-on printer paper so you can apply the image yourself.

So the book was out and that was great. But the spin-off product range hasn't made it off the ground (as of yet, I hasten to add – I'm not ready to give up . . .).

However, a short time after I signed the contract for the Little Book, I got a call from Jonathan at Worldwide Co to say he was ready to go into production with the Designer Beaver novelty toy. We discussed what sort of look we were going for on the packet and he commissioned two of the designers he worked with – Lucy and Tobie of the design company Two Create – to turn my prototype into a shop-ready product. Just three weeks later, he sent me the first design. It was a work of art. In fact, it was far too beautiful. The designers had created a very realistic women's torso which we both felt was a little too explicit. We were looking for something a lot more 'end of the pier'.

With this feedback, the talented designers set about creating a second version. What a version it was. It was an exciting moment opening the email. Up flashed a wonderful interpretation of the idea, one greater than I could ever have hoped for.

The idea had transformed my prototype into this stunning finished article . . .

How fantastic! Fannytastic?

Soon afterwards, a huge shipment of Beavers arrived from Hong Kong and Jonathan started showing them to his clients, hoping they'd place orders for this new item. Jonathan told me that he was delighted with the finished product and that he thought they'd provide great stocking fillers for busy shoppers looking for cheap and amusing gifts that Christmas. Now all he had to do was convince his client list of retailers to think the same way.

Within the week, Jonathan called with some surprising news. Lots of the young buyers he'd met with liked the product and had placed orders but, more amazingly, the Designer Beaver seemed to appeal to people across the board.

'One older lady I work with,' Jonathan began, 'she's very prim and proper . . . and she runs a gift shop in some country village – well, she ordered a dozen. I couldn't believe it!' he said, joy audible in his voice.

I was doubly pleased at this development, because initially Jonathan had been unsure whether saucy novelty gifts would have a big market. To be fair, I was pretty unsure myself. I mean, how many people really need a Designer Beaver or even a Butt Plug? It's not exactly like inventing the lightbulb.

Jonathan had taken a big leap of faith by going forward with the Designer Beaver, not only because he had to invest heavily in the first batch, but he also had to create a new branch of his company to house a more 'adult' type of item. Cleverly, he had called this company offshoot 'Coming Soon Ltd'.

Three weeks later, I came tantalizingly close to having another of my dreams come true.

Jonathan rang.

'Good news on the Beaver front Shed,' he said excitedly. 'Guess what?'

'What?' I said, hoping that there was a possibility that one of my ambitions was about to be fulfilled.

'I went out to dinner with the guys from Urban Outfitters last night and showed them the Beaver – and they loved it. So they've now just got to show it to their top bosses and then they'll place an order!'

Wow. Getting a product into Urban Outfitters' stores had been something I'd dreamed of for a long time. Whilst I sat slightly dumbstruck on the other end of the phone, mumbling my delight and thanks, Jonathan continued.

'So if you've any other product ideas Shed . . .'

'Yes Jonathan,' I replied. 'I'm sure I could think of a couple!'

A few weeks later, I called Jonathan to check on the progress of the Beavers. He told me they were selling well, which was good. Then I asked if there was any news about Urban Outfitters taking the Beaver. I was very much looking forward to telling my friends that one of my ideas had made it into the fashionable retailer.

'Ah . . . right . . . uh . . . no. I just heard from them yesterday actually, Shed. They didn't go for it,' he said. 'They just thought it was a bit rude, and they want to move away from smuttiness,' he explained.

Shame. I was disappointed not to get my Beavers into Urban Outfitters, but still, the product had been successfully manufactured and was now selling in lots of other shops. That was a good result for me. Plus, because it was a relative success, selling thousands of units in the first six months, the ball was now firmly rolling on the product-design front and, having built up a good connection with a manufacturer and distributor like Jonathan, it made it so much easier to pitch him new ideas.

The idea for the next product I launched happened to strike me when I was buying a sandwich for my lunch one afternoon from the slightly upmarket food and clothing store Marks & Spencer. After picking up a free-range egg and watercress on wholemeal bread from the chiller cabinet, I went to pay at a nearby checkout. I sighed to myself as I realized there was as a long queue for the till, which would mean a wait of a good few minutes. I duly popped myself at the back of the queue, ruminating (as I always do when I'm in a line) how civilized we are in this country to practise the art of queuing.

Having the sort of mind that gets bored easily, I impatiently looked around for any source of stimulation. As my eyes scoured the people and shelves near me, I was drawn to a colourful flat-pack of novelty candles hanging on a hook a few feet away. The candles spelt the words 'HAPPY BIRTHDAY', each letter having its own little cocktail stick protruding from its base and a wick from the top. The simple idea was for the candles to be placed in line on a cake and then the colourful message would happily burn away.

This product immediately sparked my curiosity. Because the letters were all separate, I began to wonder whether the letters could be rearranged to spell something else – maybe something a little less conventional. I can't do anagrams in my head, so I didn't know whether the words 'happy' and 'birthday' would yield a coherent message if the letters were scrambled, but I did know that the idea of a birthday message that was a bit more edgy appealed to me. What if the candles spelt a message that wasn't so traditional?

The fire now lit, I jumped on the train and brainstormed ideas for new candle messages all the way home while eating my egg sand-wiches. Once I'd got back to my flat, I found some photos of similar 'Happy Birthday' novelty candles and (with the aid of my photo-editing software) started to cut out and move the letters to create my own new messages.

Once I had a few ideas down, I emailed the concept to Jonathan. The phone rang soon after.

'Yeah, I like the candles Shed!' he said.

'Oh, superb,' I answered, excited.

'We actually sell the "Happy Birthday" ones already – I'm sending you a pic – so we should be able to make your ones pretty easily,' he continued.

My email pinged seconds later. This was the picture he sent:

After querying why the message on the cake seemed to spell 'BIRTHDAY HAPPY' rather than 'HAPPY BIRTHDAY' ('Yes, well done Shed,' was his reply – he was used to me being challenging), I discussed with him how quickly we could get some new messages made.

Over the next few weeks, Jonathan and I teamed up again with the talented designers Lucy and Tobie, then just a few months later the candles hit the stores.

Our alternative birthday candles came in three messages: '*LOST COUNT*', '*21 AGAIN*' and the vaguely insulting '*YOU'RE OLD*'.

Since their launch, the candles have been a big success. It seems that people like the slightly cheeky messages we created. It shows you that sometimes just slightly twisting an idea that already exists is all you need to do to produce something new.

And so, it was lucky there was a queue in Marks & Spencer that day, or these novelty candles would never have seen the light of day. And wouldn't that have been a tragedy for the world . . .

Now riding high with two products I'd made with Jonathan at Worldwide Co, six months later I went in to pitch to him again. Most of the new product ideas I presented were knocked back for one reason or another, but one of them wasn't. It would prove surprisingly challenging to make though . . .

I'd had the idea for this new product while sitting on my arse watching TV. I always slightly berate myself when I'm being a couch potato, just lolling in front of the goggle box, because there are always so many projects I should be working on instead of just surfing the channels. However, because I work in the TV industry, I can always convince myself that because television production is a fierce passion of mine, I constantly need to be up on what's going on in the industry. Great excuse to watch the tube, eh?

It was during a period of unfruitful channel hopping that I became focused on the television remote control I held in my hand. I looked hard at all the buttons and functions and then instantly remembered a joke image that someone had once sent to me years before on email, the type of mindless, amusing picture you get sent from your work colleagues or friends.

I recalled that the image had been of a remote control and that the creator of the image had used image manipulation software to replace the functions of a real remote with amusing functions. One button with a plus and minus next to it was labelled 'BREASTS' – the idea being that the user of this remote would point at someone (presumably a woman) to make their breasts bigger or smaller. The recollection made me chuckle, and as I cradled my real remote control in my hand, I began to wonder whether I could produce an authentic-looking remote control as a novelty product that people might buy.

I began writing functions for a remote that could 'control a woman' and also one that could 'control a man'. The differences in gender are always fascinating and this exercise let me explore my assumptions and preconceptions about the two sexes. Even though it's always dangerous to generalize about any social group (we're all individuals with our own personalities and free will after all), in order to make an entertaining gift I needed to take advantage of common stereotypes so that customers would instantly connect with the product.

After working on the idea for a while, I called a couple of my female friends for their input. It was vital to ensure that any functions on the 'Control-a-Man' remote were what women wanted from men.

Once I'd mocked up the ideas for two remote controls, I sent them over to Jonathan, Lucy and Tobie, who then collectively made the ideas better. We included functions on the Control-a-Man that reflected men's failings, like 'GET HINT', 'MULTI-TASK' and 'TALK ABOUT FEELINGS'. The 'Control-a-Woman' functions were (predictably) much more basic because they had to convey what a typical man wanted, and included buttons such as: 'REMOVE CLOTHES', 'COOK', 'CLEAN' and 'FORGIVE'. Yes, the finished articles were full of grotesque clichés and potentially offensive generalizations. I'm sure my Nobel Prize will be on the way soon.

Once we'd also created some beautiful 3D visualizations, the search was on for a manufacturer. This was to prove a big challenge because we wanted our novelty remotes to look exactly like the real thing, complete with buttons that pushed in when you pressed them.

I spent days and days trying to find companies in the Far East who could make such a gift, but it proved amazingly difficult. It seemed that a double mould of this nature, coupled with the silicon and plastic materials needed for the case and buttons, would make the product much too expensive to produce.

Eventually, Jonathan had the brainwave of trying to source a company already making real remote controls. This may seem obvious looking back, but we normally dealt with toy, stationery and novelty-product companies for all our gifts, so this was actually a new direction for us. He found one such company in Hong Kong. This factory produced a mind-boggling array of remotes in all shapes and sizes, many for well-known brand names. The manufacturer was eager to help with our build. But, once again, even though the investment was much less than that quoted by our normal sources, the cost of building the new moulds for the factory line meant that we wouldn't have been able to sell the product for the price we wanted to. If the final selling price was too high, then no one would buy the new joke remotes. There's only so much you can charge for a gift product that actually has no real function . . .

I feared the remotes would never make it to market, but an interesting twist was about to occur. The Hong Kong manufacturer who ran the remote-control factory contacted us to say he might be able to work out a deal after all. The situation had changed, he explained, because he had been immensely impressed with the blueprints for the remote controls that Lucy and Tobie had created. He was now prepared to go halves on the tooling costs, provided we were happy that the precise shape and button conformation of our remote control could be used to make real remotes for his other clients.

This surprised and delighted me in equal measure. The thought that this guy in Hong Kong, with his huge expertise in remote controls, would get excited about one we'd designed, was thrilling. To my untrained eye, our remote didn't seem groundbreaking in any way (though of course it was lovely in its own right), but the remote control manufacturer was sufficiently satisfied that our model offered him and his customers something new compared with the dozens of options already in his catalogue.

The deal now firmly feasible, we went into production. Six weeks later, the novelty remote controls hit the shelves:

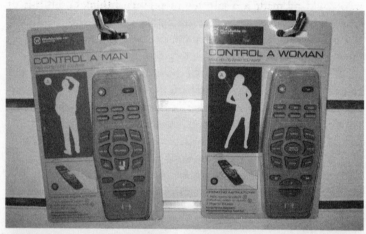

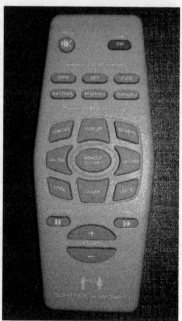

The finished products looked pretty great. They looked exactly like a real remote control, even having a section on the back for batteries. This was needed because, even though our remote didn't actually work (if I *was* able make a remote control that gave a woman an orgasm and made a man listen more, then I think I'd be able to retire), the mould was of course also going to be used for real electronic household goods. Therefore, on our versions, the battery compartment is glued down.

So, who knows, perhaps one day you'll be using one of our bespoke designed remote controls to work your stereo or even control your garage doors. Now there's a thought.

The novelty remote controls proved to be quite a hit when they were released. Not only were they featured in a couple of newspaper articles in the run up to Christmas, they also made one of my long-held ambitions finally come true.

A month after the first batch had arrived from Hong Kong, I got a call from my partner-in-crime Jonathan.

'Hey Shed – I think I'm going to make your day!' he said cheerfully.

I had an inkling what the good news could be, but didn't want to tempt fate.

'Go on,' I said, excited.

'Well . . . we just found out today that Urban are going to take the remotes!' he replied. 'Loads of them, in fact!'

This was great news. To hear that I'd finally cracked getting one of my ideas into Urban Outfitters was a total joy. My childish remote controls had made it into one of the coolest high-street chains in the world. To me, this was the equivalent of being granted a 'By Royal Appointment To Her Majesty The Queen' stamp of approval. It was the ultimate validation, like winning the Oscar of the novelty-product industry, and I was over the moon.

My adventures in product design had been most successful. From the starting point of a romantic gesture for my dinner date, I had managed to manufacture and sell a number of brand-new products.

What's next?

Well, the next chapter is about an exciting way to make money.

Here's another remote control I've created just for you.

Press the button for the next chapter.

As this remote control has as much functionality as my novelty ones (i.e. none), you might have to turn the page as well ...

Did you just groan then?

Apologies.

'*Say that again . . . You want to do what?*
Print your own money!? That's preposterous!
The Queen, Her Majesty, the head of the British monarchy,
*has **her** face on banknotes . . . but you?*
Your arrogance has reached a whole new level!'

Print Your Own Money

An intriguing experiment in 'perception'

It makes the world go round. Oh, and it's the root of all evil. Although strictly, *the love of it* is actually the root of all evil. Yes, I'm talking about the basis of our capitalist society, the units of exchange we use to obtain material goods – MONEY.

Do you have any *cash* near you right now? Have a quick look. Maybe you've got some coins nearby, or perhaps some notes to hand? If you do, briefly examine the money and weigh it in your palm.

If you don't, then just imagine you're holding a banknote between your fingers.

Look at the numbers that show how much the cash is worth.

Now, stop for a second and consider how much the money is *really* worth. By that, I mean you should think only about the materials the coins or notes are made of and make an estimate of how much the object costs to make. The notes are most likely made of some kind of paper. Paper! Even though the note may proclaim it's worth a certain amount, its actual real value as paper with a watermark, printed with coloured ink and containing a bit of foil here and there, is minuscule.

I've always been completely fascinated with the concept of money – not high finance or currency markets so much, more the bizarre concept of 'cash' in its physical form.

When I was seventeen, I remember being completely blown away by something I heard while attending a History lesson at school. That's not a sentence I ever thought I'd write, I must say. Nevertheless, it's true. The lesson in question covered the 1920s Depression in America and our teacher was explaining how 'the rate of inflation' – the gauge of how much 'money' is worth – got catastrophically out of hand. Because confidence in the American economy was low in the years after the First World War, the value of the dollar plummeted – and that made prices conversely sky-rocket. If a loaf of bread cost 5 cents before the war, as soon as the public no longer valued their dollars so much, the bread started to cost much, much more. And so the spiral continued – the currency was seen as worthless, therefore you could buy less and less for the same amount.

As our History teacher explained how this economic crash devastated America, he instructed us to turn over the page in our text-books so we could take in a passage written by someone living at the time. The person described how the US economy had got into dire straits, sending inflation into an upward spiral, making money virtually worthless. Then I saw the image that would stay with me for ever.

Underneath the text was a grainy black-and-white photograph. It showed a busy street scene and in the centre of the picture was a middle-aged man wearing a long, dark overcoat. He was pushing a wheelbarrow, the contents of which astonished me. The metal wheel-barrow was full to overflowing with a huge mountain of banknotes. I stared intently at the wheelbarrow full of cash. It was an unusual, arresting image. My immediate thought was 'This man must be rich.' However, our teacher then dropped a bombshell that shocked me.

'Inflation had got so bad at the time this photo was taken that money came to be worth less and less. This man needed all that money in the barrow just to buy a loaf of bread.'

As this information sank into my teenage brain, it blew me away. Questions flooded my mind. How could all that cash be worth so lit-tle? Surely money had a fixed value? Who decided what that cash was worth?

These questions led me to investigate the concept of money and exchange rates. I learned how the early practice of trading involved simply swapping objects. When you wanted something that someone else had, you just swapped it for something of equal value. This practice was eventually replaced by the use of coins made from precious metals and later by coins and notes that simply *promised* to pay the owner of the monetary unit a certain amount.

As I researched these subjects in my textbooks, I reached a surprising conclusion:

> An object (be it a banknote or a product)
> is only worth a certain value
> if people **agree** it's worth that value.

If a certain object or product is rare, then it is more likely to be perceived as valuable. That's why clever diamond companies hold tons of their diamonds back so that the market isn't flooded with the actual quantity they've mined. There's a huge store of natural diamonds on our earth. But if everyone thought the gem was 'common', then it would lose its value. So why pay a lot of money for a diamond? Well, quite frankly, you shouldn't. Not because it's rare. They're not. Because it's beautiful? Maybe. But these days artificial diamonds can be made that are just as stunning, so it would seem sensible to spend less money and buy one of those! The 'natural diamond' industry is a clever con trick.

All these mixed thoughts about 'value' and 'price' bubbled in my brain for years. The inspirational trigger for a new challenge came from an unusual source. One day I saw a newspaper article describing a new type of currency that was appearing in the world of online computer gaming. A rash of innovative new adventure games had recently hit the internet, involving clever game-play in which the user accrued points that let them 'buy' weapons and powers for their characters. It took a player a long time to earn enough points to buy the extra firepower, but once they had acquired this benefit, they would have an advantage over other characters (also controlled by other human users) in the game. Since the computer characters could interact with each other, it was possible for one character to give another character their weapon. This situation, in a virtual game world, spontaneously led to an unexpected effect in the real world. One day, an experienced player – some bright, enterprising spark – got the idea to sell his character's virtual weapon for real cash. It worked like this: money changed hands between players in the real world and then both players would log on to the game at the same time, and the selling player would make his character pass his weapon to the buying player. And so, a remarkable outcome occurred. A weapon that didn't really exist was sold for real money that did exist.

A fire was lit within me. And boy, did it burn brightly. If something 'unreal' could be sold for cash, could I do the same?

I quickly became consumed with the idea of launching my own currency. Questions flashed through my mind. Was it legal? Would it work? I was eager to find out the answers to all these questions, but not through considered thought or research – just by going ahead and doing it. I didn't know whether it was possible to launch my own currency, but I knew I was eager to find out.

There and then I decided to create my own money. First, I needed a name for my own unit of money. As I considered possible names in my head, it seemed to me that there was really only one choice for such a self-centred project. Each unit of money would be called one 'EGO'. It even sounded similar to real units of currency, like yen, pound or euro.

The excitement was now accelerating fast, so I immediately found an image of an African banknote on the internet and altered it on my computer. I produced my first prototype EGO banknote:

Being fully aware that my graphic-design skills are woefully lacking, I sought professional help. I immediately contacted Lucy and Tobie, the two talented graphic designers I'd worked with so successfully in the past. Once again, I desperately needed their design flair and invaluable enthusiasm.

At the time, I still hadn't actually met Lucy and Tobie, although we had collaborated on the phone and through email for months. It's amazing how you don't really need to be in the same room as someone in order to work with them these days. But I'd always wanted to meet them, as I got the impression that they were both fiercely bright and very fun people. It's also a much more rewarding and powerful experience to meet face to face. I arranged to visit them the next week and fired off an email outlining what I wanted on the banknote. I asked for the note to be covered with images relating to my life and inspiring messages I believed in.

They sent me back some sketches that afternoon:

Will have polysymmetric patterns in background (type of geometric tessellating pattern).

Silver foiled Shed Logo?

Artist Impression of you! Illustrated in dots.

Archimedes in bath

Walt Disney (will actually find out what he looked like!).

The day of our banknote meeting arrived and I hopped on the tube to Old Street where I found Lucy and Tobie's home office. They lived in a gorgeous basement flat full of contemporary furnishings.

Lucy spread various different paper samples out on a sexy curved glass table and we went through them one by one. Some were called 'wet' papers because they had a very slippery, almost latex-like feel. In the end, we went with a paper that had a fine grain running through it that also didn't tear easily.

I then got even more excited when Lucy told me about the extra printing features available, such as metal foil stickers, holograms and sequential serial numbers.

My own cash was running low at this time, and I was very concerned that the budget for this job was going to spiral out of control, meaning that each EGO would actually cost a lot of real money to make. But luckily, Lucy had a brainwave. She mentioned that as she'd talked with paper companies, they had seemed intrigued and a little bit amused by the idea that someone wanted to print their own currency. Lucy suggested to me that maybe they'd sponsor the note. It was a good idea.

Tobie then asked me to don the suit I'd brought so that he could take some photos of me for the front of the banknote. He crouched down to take the shots and pointed the camera up at my face. By taking the picture from below, my pose miraculously took on an even more pompous and regal look. After posing uncomfortably for a while, I left the designers to get on with creating the rest of the note.

One of the symbols Lucy and Tobie included on the EGO was the image of a full English breakfast on a plate. This was to represent my time working on *The Big Breakfast*. Their attention to detail was wonderful. They went shopping for the perfect plate to place a breakfast on because they realized that the plates they had in their flat were far too contemporary and that the breakfast plate for the note needed to be more 'characterful'. Unwilling to compromise on any part of the project, Lucy popped out to a number of 'pound shops' she knew and eventually found a plate she was happy with.

Once they had the perfect plate, they spent one Sunday morning cooking the perfect English fry-up, put it on the plate and then snapped away.

All this for an image that would take up an inch on the banknote. Amazing . . .

We took great care over the other details on the note too. I included the image of Walt Disney (one of my inspirational idols) on the back, a picture of a lightbulb to convey 'the power of ideas' (my passion) and had the names of all my family embedded through the background pattern of the note too.

As the design developed, we realized that it was becoming a sort of graphic résumé of my life. Therefore it seemed appropriate that maybe it should contain other details, like my telephone number (as the banknote serial number) and email address (written very small on the back). In this way, the banknote could also double as an effective business card.

We plugged all these details in and worked on the note until we were all happy with the final proof. This was then sent to a specialist printer in Brighton who ran a rare German press that could give the sharpest images and most authentic banknote colours.

The finished note was a triumph:

As a business card, the notes certainly caused a stir. People would always remember them and sometimes even stick them to their desk. As a PR exercise they were a hit.

But I wanted to stay faithful to my original mission to see whether I could produce something that had no actual value that people would buy for cash.

I decided to try to sell my EGO banknotes on eBay.

I uploaded some photos of the note and wrote out a sales pitch:

NEW CURRENCY – CONTEMPORARY ARTWORK 'THE EGO'
by Artist & Entrepreneur: 'Shed'

＊ A chance to purchase a unique limited edition work of art banknote **＊**

MONEY FOR NOTHING

HAVING BEEN INTRIGUED for a long time about the true 'value' of money (it's only paper after all), I recently read a magazine article about virtual treasure won in computer games being sold for real money online. The idea of an object that only exists on a computer screen being sold for real cash ignited my imagination so much that it forced me to question the concepts of 'value' in our society today and the idea of money as a means of exchange. It seemed to me that money was only worth something if everybody using it agreed it was worth something.

LAUNCHING A NEW CURRENCY

I decided to find out if I could launch my own currency and give it a real-world value.

I've had two thousand high quality notes made and each one is worth one 'EGO'. My aim is to find an exchange rate for the EGO – in other words, how much people think each note is worth. As with any currency, the exchange rate is only a measure of what people believe the cash is worth. So eBay is a great way to see how much value you and others decide to give this original denomination. At the end of the auction, the winner will also get a free EGO thrown in.

As my career develops and my profile rises, the value of an EGO will exponentially rise. In this way, the currency will develop an exchange rate, being worth more as my reputation grows.

WHAT YOU GET WHEN YOU BUY AN EGO

Each note is a work of art, beautifully designed with intricate detail by Lucy Nunn and Tobie Snowdowne, founder partners of leading design consultancy 'Two Create'. The note contains many symbols and messages connected with my life, some hidden and some more overt. The television represents my time working in the media and the fried breakfast represents my time working on the morning show 'The Big Breakfast'. The back of the note displays images related to my philosophies about ideas creation, portraying my idol, Walt Disney, plus some life mottos.

The notes measure five inches by three inches and are a limited edition of two thousand. Only one thousand are available to buy. They are litho printed on high quality 105gsm Tyvek paper and hot foil blocked with the Talent Shed logo. The notes are sealed meaning they are water resistant and feel silky to the touch.

Thanks for your time and have a good day.
Yours, Shed

Amazingly, I found I could sell many of the notes on eBay. All sorts of buyers bought an EGO. Some were just curious to see what I'd done, some were even banknote collectors from around the world. An art student from Glasgow bought twenty notes for £15 and, remarkably, one auction went to £5.50. But quite a few notes sold for the starting price of 10 pence as well.

At the end of the month, I was able to calculate an average selling price for each banknote, which in turn became the exchange rate for my new currency. After one month, the EGO had an exchange rate of 1 EGO to 0.74 British pounds. That's 74 pence to the EGO. Even though this was less than they had cost me to print, I was still astonished that anyone who didn't know me would want to buy an EGO note.

And so the main part of my banknote ambition was now fulfilled. I'd launched a new currency, plus it had a real world exchange rate.

What's more, the beauty of the notes got recognized by a number of eminent organizations, garnering a write-up in the prestigious magazine *Design Week* and winning an award given by a leading fine-paper manufacturer.

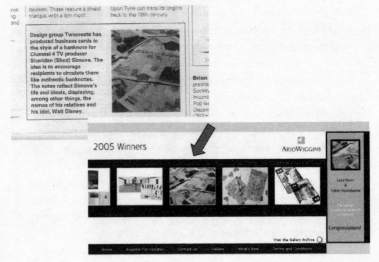

The second part of my ambition for the currency is going to continue throughout my life. My hope now is that the EGO will rise in value as time goes on and that one day (if the demand is there) I may print a batch of five or ten EGO notes, each showing images relating to events in my life that have happened since the first EGO release.

Who knows, one day I may even accept them in exchange for the products I make . . .

‘*It's one thing to get a silly little "gift book" published,
but quite another to get a book about
your "ideas" on the bookshelves . . .*

*Three things to remember, just three:
One:
No one is going to find a book about your
ideas interesting – don't you realize that in the grand
scheme of the universe, you are just a flea?
Two:
It will take you far too long to write a book anyway –
hours and hours of dedicated focus – and even then it may
not be any good!
Three:
You'll never persuade a publisher to read it,
let alone publish it!
Do you know how hard it is to find a publisher?
And how many people you're competing against?
Oh, just give up now . . .*’

IDEA 11

How I Got This Book Published

I was determined to work with the best so I had to 'wow' the best

Here's a surprise. I thought it would be easy writing this book. You know how sometimes you read a book and it seems like the author effortlessly oozes every sentence and all the words flow like smooth gravy from a jug? Well, bollocks to that (if you'll excuse my language): that's not the case for me. My gravy is lumpy and it keeps sticking to the jug. I've found it a big challenge.

They say everyone has at least one book in them. What would yours be about? Me, I've always dreamed of getting a 'real', proper book published. I don't really count *The Little Book of Presents Money Can't Buy* as fulfilling this dream because, even though it was incredibly tough to get a publisher to release it, it's still a small gift book. My ambition was to get a full-blown, one-inch-thick paperback on to the bookshelves. The fact that you're reading this means I've finally done it. Hurrah. And it took ages.

While I was writing I was earning a living by doing development work for the BBC and working on *Celebrity Big Brother* and the main *Big Brother* programme every time they aired each year. I was also trying to launch a lot of the ideas in this book during the same period so, as you can imagine, it wasn't plain sailing to find the time or willpower to write a book – especially when I wasn't entirely sure if anyone would be interested in it . . .

As I sat in my flat, typing these pages into my computer night after night, getting this book published seemed like a dream that was simply miles away. But if *I* can make such a big dream happen, then that means you can make one of your big challenges happen too.

I think it was my Dream Number 3 to get a book published – that's the dream just before 'Dream 4: Have a threesome with two Scandinavian blondes' and just after 'Dream 2: Create a worldwide toy craze'. Yes, at thirty-three years of age I am full of dreams – and 'crap', some would say. Well, you're allowed to have lots of dreams aren't you?!

How does an 'unknown' like me (as opposed to a celebrity) get a book published? The challenge is this: it's very difficult to get the attention of a publisher because there are so many people sending in books and even ideas for books. These days it's easier than ever to access a computer and write a book, so more and more people have a go – and quite right too. Unfortunately for a new writer trying to get published, though, the effect of this proliferation of authors is that every day publishers around the world receive far more books than they can physically publish. Not only that, many publishers won't even take submissions from new authors. After numerous phone calls, I discovered that it's common practice for publishing houses to commission a book in house or give an idea to an author they already know.

So this time the challenge was clear. How could I raise my game and make a publisher notice me so they would want to publish the book you're reading right now?

I figured that once a publisher had actually engaged with me and read the book, then a simple decision could be made: either they'd like or dislike what I'd written. The problem was that the publishing world was turning out to be as difficult to break into as an impenetrable showbiz party, so I decided to concentrate my efforts on getting *noticed*, in the hope that maybe I'd be invited in to the 'party'. A strategy began to form.

I reasoned that I needed to enlist the help of an expert from inside the industry to champion me – a 'friend of the host to take me into the party' I suppose, if you'll let me stretch the party analogy just a bit more.

I followed my old rule: if you're not in an industry, then find someone who is the master of that industry and cut them in on the deal. I decided I would have to find a literary agent who would believe in me. Hopefully, they would then champion me to their trusted publishers. Well, that was the plan at least.

I could have picked any literary agent to target at the start, but I remembered a man who'd caught my attention when I'd seen him on a television programme two years earlier. I happened to watch a marvellous TV show about a brand-new author – a middle-aged lady from a council estate – who had found massive success. It featured a wonderfully charismatic literary agent, a red-cheeked fellow with bright blue eyes and a boundless passion for writing and (most significantly) new talent. The programme showed how he'd cleverly engineered a bidding war for one of his clients. I was captivated.

'Wow – that man is awesome! I must work with him!' I thought. But, two years on, I couldn't even remember the name of the programme, let alone his name.

Around this time, I was lucky enough to be working at the BBC developing new programmes, so I had access to an incredible computer system that allowed me to call up any show they'd ever broadcast. I punched in the details of the programme I'd seen and after a few refinements of the search, a screen popped up with the correct information. Bingo. The marvels of modern technology.

I sat down to watch the show again, this time armed with a notepad. I fast-forwarded to the bit I was interested in and quickly discovered the agent's name: Darley Anderson. His name suited the charismatic persona I saw on screen – I thought he sounded like a character from a Mills & Boon romantic novel: '. . . and Darley gently picked her up in his manly arms, lovingly ravaged her and then left on his enormous white steed . . .' Or something like that.

Gripped with discovering Darley, I tapped his full name into the internet, instantly found his contact details and began to form a plan of how to impress him. I figured that this man would have many manuscripts flying at him from all angles, so I needed a way to break clearly through his usual day and get him to notice me among the other authors vying for his time. I hit upon the idea of combining the method I'd use to interest Darley with a way of providing the cover for this book at the same time.

I already had an idea for the front cover. The whole area of design has always fascinated me and I had fantasized for years about what the cover of my first book would look like. Oh, what a dream to see it in the shops! As this book is about 'ways of making things happen', I thought the cover could perhaps reflect the way I got the book published. So first I needed a name for the front and then I needed a stunt to photograph for the back.

I tackled the name challenge first. I considered calling the book 'My Struggle', a dubious double reference both to the challenges I've had in making all the ideas happen and also to Hitler's first book, *Mein Kampf*, which means the same thing in German. I didn't think it was a hugely sensible move to compare myself to one of the most hideous men in history. As you know, I don't mind a bit of controversy, but I thought I'd best draw the line at a gag involving a man responsible for mass genocide.

So I had a rethink. Believing that self-promotion and positivity are always the way forward, I hit upon the idea of calling the book 'NUMBER ONE BESTSELLER'. Because this book is about having a vision, and persuading others to take notice of that specific vision so they'll want to come on the journey with me, I thought it was an appropriately cheeky title. In an ideal world, I dreamed that when someone saw the front cover on the shelf or heard about the book, they might think it actually *was* a number-one bestseller and therefore purchase it, which in turn would cause a marvellous positive feedback loop until one day it actually *was* the number-one bestseller – well, I can dream, can't I? And anyway, childishly, I also noticed that when I saved this book on my computer, the name *Number One Bestseller* neatly abbreviated to *NOBS*. So that sealed it of course.

Once I'd decided on a title, I had to formulate a cunning plan to get me close to Darley the literary agent. I wanted to make him notice me, realize my passion and, at the very least, read some sample chapters. My ultimate dream was that once he'd met me and read something I'd written, he'd take me on as a new author and secure a fantastic book deal for me.

The inspiration for a way to get Darley's attention came while I was in central London, walking down Oxford Street. On the pavement in front of me I spotted one of the poor souls who hold up advertising signs all day. The most well-known sign of this kind is the much-parodied 'Golf Sale' board. It's a simple concept: a man (or woman) stands in the middle of a busy street with a pole attached to a huge placard bearing an advert. The sign often features an arrow, which helpfully points in the direction of the store having the sale or selling the goods. Every time I saw a person holding one of these signs, I always wondered how they felt just standing there with a placard while life passed them by. But the actual idea behind this unusual form of advertising is very clever.

Because the sign is held by a person standing on the pavement, it's free for the shop to place their advert in the middle of a busy street, whereas traditional billboard advertising would be astronomically expensive. Plus, the ad isn't illegally posted. The only downside is that some poor sod (normally a foreign student wanting to earn a few pounds) has to stand there just holding a sign all day.

I decided to make my own portable sign, one that would get Darley's attention so he'd notice me and hopefully take me on as a new author. On one side I'd place the name of the book and on the other I'd write a personal plea asking him to meet with me.

I spent a while planning the design of my sign. It was actually great fun, because I adore typography. The way a word is written can say so much and the difference a typeface can make totally excites me. Perhaps I need to get out more.

The huge availability of fonts on the internet has meant that, now more than ever, a large number of people, including myself, can have fun with the way words look. However, just because you have access to the tools doesn't automatically mean you're an artist (as my efforts testify). That's why I'm so admiring of designers. They strive to make our day-to-day environment a more beautiful and interesting place.

As I'm not professionally trained in design, it was more difficult to overcome a few hurdles that cropped up with my particular sign.

I wanted to make it personal, but also eye-catching. I encountered the first challenge: what font should I use to print out the title, 'NUMBER ONE BESTSELLER'?

Now then: fonts. Useful, beautiful, communicative fonts. The plethora of fonts available these days is almost like another wonderful language in itself. For me, it's comparable to the way you use the inflection in your voice, but in a visual rather than an auditory way. Here's what I mean. You can speak the sentence below in a number of different ways and the meaning will change:

Yes Shed, I did read your book

You could say this phrase in a very angry manner, with as much venom and bile as you can muster, or it could be spoken in a cheerful way, with a song in your voice – or even perhaps with a sad, despairing tone (this one will probably be played out when I meet my high school English teacher of course).

Typefaces can perform a similar function, thus:

YES SHED - I DID READ YOUR BOOK

YES SHED, I DID READ YOUR BOOK

Yes Shed, I did read your book

Taking the different styles of the type above, the top version could infer that the statement is implying that the book is wonderful, the middle one that it is 'a horror' of a book and the third one that it is rather childish. Anyway, I'm being a font geek. Apologies. Back to the sign . . .

Deciding on which font to use for the sign to attract my chosen literary agent was proving surprisingly difficult. I just couldn't bring myself to pick a font – they all conveyed so much and yet didn't seem right for the sign. I did think I was losing my mind at one point after surfing the net for hours, clicking over and over on various font sites.

I stopped the madness and decided on another route. I downloaded a free program from the net with the plan to design my very own one-off font. Yes, that would be great. Then I could make it convey what I wanted it to say. Well, that was the theory. In practice, I still couldn't settle on one particular design. I thought about creating a font out of my handwriting, but jettisoned that idea, reasoning that I could just write the sign myself freehand instead. I wanted something a bit more professional looking, but still with a personal touch.

In the end, the lucky font was Antigoni Medium. It hardly seemed worth the fuss: the letters are formed in a very simple design and it's certainly not the most memorable typeface ever. But I liked its clean, uncomplicated lines. Sometimes simple is best.

I also had another idea that I hoped would make the title just a little bit more interesting. If you have an aversion to cheesy sentimentality, then you may want to skip the next bit.

I wanted to recognize the people in my life who've helped me on my journey so far – all the people who've had a positive effect in my life. So I made a list of their names, sticking each one on to the poster.

Once I'd designed it, I took the placard template down to a printer where it was gloriously blown up to eye-catching dimensions. On the way back home I bought a floor mop complete with a detachable wooden handle from the lovely man in my local ironmongers who always sat with a carpet of dogs at his feet. Yes, I was ready to go.

I removed the handle from the mop head so I could attach it to my double-sided sign. As I gathered the parts of the sign together, a myriad questions raced through my mind. Would Darley actually see the sign? Would he think that someone who'd created such a gimmick shouldn't be taken seriously as a writer? Would he stop and talk with me? Would he tell me to sling my hook?

Given that I was making rather elaborate preparations for this 'meeting', I desperately wanted to phone Darley's office to check he'd be there the next day, as I was worried that I'd turn up only to discover that he was out on business. But I had a problem. I couldn't risk calling and asking whether Darley was going to be in the building because that would elicit too many questions and may tip them off that I'd be turning up.

In the end, I decided on a compromise. I would call up, but only to gather *some* information.

I rang and was greeted by the voice of a well-spoken young lady. 'Hello, Darley Anderson. How may I help you?' she said.

'Oh, hello there,' I started.

I purposely didn't give my name and continued speaking at a rapid pace, hoping my momentum would stop the lady asking too many questions.

'I wondered if you could help me please. I'm planning to deliver something by hand tomorrow morning and wondered what time you opened.'

My plan was at least to find out what time I could expect Darley to go into work.

The lady on the phone hesitated only for a fraction for a second and I wondered if she thought this phone call was slightly odd, but, as hoped, the rhythm of the call carried us through.

'Nine thirty,' she replied.

'Thanks a lot. Cheers – goodbye,' I said hurriedly and put the phone down. The first part of the plan was done.

The next morning I woke up early, pleased to see it looked like a sunny day, dressed appropriately for the weather and then gathered my kit ready for the mission ahead. My sports bag bulged with the following:

- 1 x printed directions to Darley's office
- 1 x large sign
- 1 x mop handle
- 1 x roll brown tape (for affixing sign to handle)
- 1 x bound manuscript
- 1 x copy of my CV
- 1 x digital camera
- 1 x jumper
- 2 x small bottle of water
- 1 x *Reader's Digest* (in case I was bored waiting for Darley)

As I loaded all this into my little Smart car I had a fleeting pang of doubt. I did feel slightly worried at the prospect of standing outside someone's office holding a wooden stick with a huge sign attached. But I knew I had to do something unusual if I was to capture the literary agent's attention, so I steeled myself and set off.

I made good time, arriving at the correct address around 8.20. I was surprised to find Darley's offices located on a leafy suburban street lined with quaint terraced houses on either side. I was also highly relieved with this spot, because its quiet location meant that there wouldn't be a huge number of commuters or businesspeople flowing past me. This was good for two reasons – with potentially fewer people seeing me with my sign, I'd be less embarrassed standing there like a lemon; and, more importantly, I had a much greater chance of spotting Darley as he arrived for work.

I parked my car outside Darley's office and pumped some coins into the parking machine, gathering my thoughts. The first job was to assemble the sign, as it had been too big to fit into the car when attached to the handle. I struggled with the brown tape as I tried to stick the handle to the board while propping it on the bonnet of my car. The tape kept getting stuck together and I became flustered as I rushed to assemble the sign, worried that Darley might turn up at any moment.

Just as I'd got the handle firmly attached, I noticed a builder's van pull up nearby and park a bit further down on the other side of the street. Two young guys in overalls got out and started to walk towards me. I quickly whipped my camera out and grasped the opportunity in front of me.

'Excuse me, mate,' I called out to one of the builders.

'Yes mate?' he replied quickly.

'I wondered if you wouldn't mind taking a picture of me please. I've got this sign . . .' I trailed off.

'Yeah – no worries, mate, no probs,' he answered.

I hopped across the street to take my position in front of Darley's office and proudly stood with the sign next to me. The builder glanced at me and that was the moment my mission failed.

The top of the sign had Darley's name printed on it in large block capital letters.

'Darley Anderson?' the builder said, surprised.

'Yeah! That's right, yeah,' I said. 'I'm going to wait for him . . .'

Then, a spanner in the works. Quick as a flash, the builder spoke.

'Oh nah – he's on holiday mate. We're doing his work – he's on holiday.'

'Serious?' I asked, looking at the other guy, hoping the first bloke was winding me up.

'Yeah. We're going in today to do some stuff for him. He won't be back till next week I think,' he said, looking at his colleague for confirmation.

'Ah no!' I laughed, tickled by the fact that I'd turned up with no chance of meeting the man I wanted to accost.

'Yeah. You want to leave it a week and come back next week sometime,' the first builder advised.

'Oh . . . cheers guys! Yeah – thanks. I'll have to come back then,' I said. But I still wanted proof that I'd been there, so I continued: 'Can you take a picture anyway. I'll write about this,' I explained.

'Yeah – no probs,' the builder shrugged cheerfully, and he pressed the button. This is the photo he took:

I thanked the builders, took my sign apart and jumped back in the car. Ah well.

Of course, I was naturally frustrated by this outcome, but I realized it was funny too. Knowing how I'd prepared hard for the stunt, got myself psyched up, travelled over to Darley's offices and then stood outside with a massive sign, only to discover the man I wanted to see was actually in another country, was tragically comical.

'You'll look back and laugh about this very soon,' I told myself. But at the time, I just had to drive home rather forlornly, with my roll of brown tape, yellow sign and mop handle.

I'd just have to come back next week and try again.

Six days later, I was back outside Darley's place of work. It was another gloriously sunny day, perfect for standing outside someone's office with a hand-made sign. After assembling the placard, I took my position outside his door and waited. Just like the first time I'd made the trip to his offices, I'd planned ahead by bringing a *Reader's Digest* to keep me entertained while I stood there waiting. I was very grateful for the company of the mini magazine as time ticked on.

I stood outside the office with my sign for just under an hour before there was any progress. During that period, I realized that I'd never spent any considerable amount of time simply watching a street before. (Well, I suppose it's not the sort of thing you do unless you're an undercover cop or a mentally ill stalker.) The experience was surprisingly fascinating. As people's curtains were drawn open and they left their houses, it felt as though I was witnessing an amazing soap opera involving all these different people's lives, which of course I was. One middle-aged man came out of his house, dressed only in his dressing gown, to let his dog have a wee. Another smart lady in a suit looked as if she was late for work as she rushed down the road. And a taxi picked another woman up, her leg completely bandaged, presumably to go to some sort of medical facility. As I stood rooted to the spot, I tried to work out what each of these people was really like – what they did for a living, what their dreams were, what their houses were like inside and where they were going that day. It was hugely intriguing.

Eventually, my silent vigil paid off – but not exactly as I'd planned. I kept my eyes peeled for any movement down the street, hoping that Darley would arrive in a car. Instead, just before 9 a.m., a young lady approached on foot. She was well dressed, wearing a smart black skirt and cream blouse. I'd been scrutinizing every person who'd walked up the street to check whether they were Darley or someone who looked as if they worked with Darley. This lady was the first one who looked as though she could.

I quickly stuffed my *Reader's Digest* into my back pocket and stood up straight next to my placard. As the woman got closer, I could see her looking at me with the sign, slightly warily. She got closer and closer until it seemed she was definitely travelling to my location. 'Here we go . . .' I thought.

The smart young woman stopped about a metre in front of me to take in the sign. Our eyes met and I smiled. I could see now that she had shoulder-length brown hair and a round, pretty face.

'Hello!' I said, trying to break the awkwardness of the situation.

'Hello . . .' came the polite, but slightly guarded reply.

The woman moved to walk past me and up the steps to the door of her office. I now knew for certain that she worked with Darley. 'Say something, quickly,' I willed myself.

'Is Darley going to be in today?' I checked.

She turned round while getting her keys out of her bag.

'I'm not sure . . . uh . . . today . . . He works from lots of different offices so he might not be here today,' she replied.

'Brilliant! That's great – me standing here then . . .' I started to say, trying to inject some levity into the somewhat strained situation.

This brief conversation was already rather stilted and we were talking over each other, so she didn't hear my sentence fully. The woman seemed (understandably) cautious about this complete stranger turning up out of the blue with a bright yellow sign.

By now she'd opened the front door to the office. She turned round again and asked, 'Have you sent in a manuscript?'

'No – but I have got one . . .' I replied.

Pause.

The strangeness of this exchange was excruciating.

'What's your name?' I asked, seeing she was about to go inside.

'Zoe,' she replied. I was sure I could see a smile on her face.

'I'm Sheridan. OK – thanks. Cheers,' I mumbled as Zoe disappeared into her office.

'Nice to meet you,' came the reply. And the door shut.

I collected my thoughts, wondering what to do next. I was still standing on the pavement with my sign on a stick, feeling rather out of place. This feeling was exaggerated now that I'd made contact with someone from Darley's office.

I stood there wondering what would happen next. Would Zoe come back out? Would she call Darley to warn him that there was a nutter outside? If he was coming in at all, how long was Darley going to be?

I decided to carry on waiting. I didn't have any closure yet and there was still a job to do.

Soon afterwards, the door of the office opened. Zoe had come out to see me. I noticed she was carrying a chunky silver camera in her hand.

'Hi!' I said, relieved to see her.

She let out a small laugh. 'Darley may not be in today, so I thought I'd take a photo for him,' she said.

'Oh – OK. Thanks,' I replied.

Zoe positioned herself in front of me and pressed the button a few times. I was pleased when she said, 'This is classic . . .'

Once she'd finished, I asked her what I should do next.

'Should I wait for him?' I asked.

'No, I don't think you should. Do you have a manuscript?'

'Yes, it's in the car,' I replied, pointing at my vehicle across the street.

As I went to cross the road, the handle of my sign caught on the pavement and the main placard whacked me on the head. Marvellous. What an idiot. 'I must be making a thoroughly professional first impression,' I thought.

Zoe pretended not to notice.

'What's your book about?' she said.

'It's about making ideas happen . . . and adventures,' I answered.

'OK – sounds interesting,' she said.

I retrieved the thick, bound manuscript from the passenger side of my car, along with a covering letter and CV, and handed it to Zoe.

'Great – I'm Darley's assistant, so I'll show these to him when he comes in – and the pictures too,' she said encouragingly.

Good news.

'Are you a writer then?' she continued.

I longed to say 'yes', but wasn't sure whether my previous publishing deal for *The Little Book of Presents Money Can't Buy* qualified me to call myself a 'writer' just yet.

'Uh . . . not yet,' I blurted.

'Is this your main job then?' Zoe questioned.

'No, no. I work in television and I'm a product designer mainly, but I've been working on this for two and a half years,' I said, trying to impress upon her that this book was so important to me.

'Oh cool. Television?' she said.

I briefly explained my background and Zoe seemed interested. I hoped that my past track record might give her a reason to think my book might be worth a look.

She repeated that she'd give Darley the manuscript. I thanked her for her friendliness; we said our goodbyes and then Zoe crossed the street to return to her office. The sign was swiftly dismantled and I jumped into the car, my mission accomplished, if not completely to plan.

Back home, I began to wait for Darley to call. He didn't. The next day he didn't call either. Or the day after. 'No worries,' I told myself. 'I'm sure he's very busy. You'll just have to be patient.'

After a week, there was still no news. I called Darley's office and was told 'Thanks for calling – I'll let Darley know you called' by the polite assistant who answered the phone.

I heard nothing the week after that and the week after too. Even though I called again, I didn't even get a call back to let me know if my manuscript had been read.

It was disturbing to realize slowly that I hadn't made the impact I'd hoped for and that now I was being treated like all the other authors who'd sent in a manuscript.

I was hurt and disappointed that I didn't hear from Darley or anyone at his office. I cursed myself that I had just handed over the manuscript without actually meeting him. The aim of the placard stunt had been to meet Darley in the flesh and at least make a personal impression on him. Instead, he'd been handed my manuscript by his assistant. Even though Darely may have seen the photos of me standing outside his offices with the placard, we hadn't actually met. Therefore, to him I was just another wannabe author whose work had to be placed on the pile. Of course, I *was* indeed another wannabe author, but I hoped my personalized targeting would have made me stand out from the crowd and persuaded him that perhaps my book was worth a closer look than normal.

After nearly two months of hearing nothing, a letter from Darley arrived. The envelope bore his name, so I guessed what was inside. I paused for a second before tearing it open, hoping that the missive would bring good news. A part of me knew that it was more likely to be a polite rejection. I figured that if he'd been interested Darley would probably have called me by then.

My eyes scanned the letter. Underneath a beautiful letterheading showing the name of the agency in delicate type was the phrase '*Our Writers Mean Business*'. This immediately triggered memories of a similar slogan I'd heard many times during my TV work that never failed to amuse me: '*Comedy is a Serious Business*'. But as my eyes moved quickly downwards over the letter, and picked out certain phrases like 'two problems' and 'I'm definitely not the agent for you', I knew there was no chance of my laughing in the near future.

The letter was very polite and well written. Darley apologized for taking so long to reply and explained that to take on a new writer he must either 'absolutely fall in love with a book' or be '100% convinced of its bestsellerdom'. Alas, he explained, neither of these was the case with my book.

That door was clearly closed to me.

I reluctantly had to concede that I needed an alternative plan to get the book published, and decided the only thing I could do was to send it out to publishers and agents. I hated the idea of this cold-calling approach, but I didn't have any other leads at that time. I still felt I needed an experienced agent who would champion my book, so I bought the *Writer's Handbook*, a wonderful compilation of everyone involved in the publishing business. I picked a dozen agents I thought sounded as if they might like what I'd written, and I started the slow process of writing to each of them and sending out the manuscript.

Slowly but surely the rejection letters started to arrive. After two months, I was getting knocked back from all corners.

All the while, it kept me going to think that many hugely successful authors had been knocked back when they first attempted to get published, like ex-lawyer-turned-writer John Grisham. He tried to get a deal for his first book, *A Time to Kill*, and was rejected by fifteen publishers and thirty agents. It went on to sell millions of copies worldwide. The world-famous *Animal Farm* by George Orwell also got turned down by both British and American publishers. One publisher even remarked that 'It is impossible to sell animal stories in the USA'. When it was finally published, Orwell's story would turn out to be one of the most important books in recent history. Even J. K. Rowling of Harry Potter fame got knocked back numerous times before someone saw the book had potential.

Now, I'm not comparing myself to these incredibly talented people. All I'm saying is that these are yet more comforting and re-assuring examples of how sometimes in life the powers-that-be turn something down that eventually becomes very popular.

Helped by these tales of rejection, I ploughed on, sending manuscripts out each day. I got some cracking rejections, including this one which surprised me because it was from a literary agent and didn't make grammatical sense:

LITERARY AGENTS

With compliments

Many thanks for the offer but regret the work does not show us a profitable readership. Do try elsewhere in case we missed something and forgive this note copy forced by the volume of offers we receive. Best wishes.

After twelve publishers and three literary agents had turned me down, I began to question whether there was a specific reason I wasn't having much success. I called up one of the publishers who had written a personalized letter of rejection and asked if there was anything I could change.

'Well . . . the title isn't very good, Shed,' he said.

'Go on,' I prompted.

'The title "NUMBER ONE BESTSELLER" doesn't describe what the book is about. You need to change it.'

After putting the phone down, I thought hard about what the publisher had said. I concluded that he had a fair point. I sat down and wrote lists and lists of new titles, but (foolishly, stubbornly) kept it the same.

I sent out dozens of copies of my manuscript on compact disc and when this brought no response, I high-tailed it down to the printer so I could print it out into a heavy, three-inch-thick bound copy, which I then posted out. All this wasn't cheap, but I was completely driven to get the book noticed because I hoped that once it was out in the real world, it may just kick-start some exciting new opportunities in my life.

I explored all avenues and contacts, cheekily imposing on friends, relatives and work colleagues to push the book forward to anyone in the publishing world they knew. It's always great to have an 'in' with someone who can help make your goal happen – a personal link is the best way, of course, but a recommendation is the next best.

I was still drawing blanks from all corners. My only personal link to a publisher was the company who'd published my *Presents Money Can't Buy* gift book. I sent them the manuscript for the book you're reading and they quickly passed on it, saying they'd enjoyed it but it just wasn't their type of thing.

My break eventually came from a slightly more oblique route – a sort of guardian angel you could say.

Five years before, I met the person in question just after I'd won the commission for the documentary that landed me in hot water – the 'Back to School' programme. As I'd always wanted to get a book published, once 'Back to School' was given the green light by

Channel 4, I immediately asked the channel bosses whether it would be possible to launch an accompanying book about my experiences when the show aired.

I was quickly introduced to a charming and brilliant woman called Mandie Howard, a big player in the Channel 4 consumer-goods department. Mandie and I got on well from the moment we met and she said she'd definitely consider publishing a book about the programme. The actual arrangements for the book would be sorted out after I'd finished filming in the school and before the documentary went to air. This was wildly exciting for me, and at the time it seemed that all my dreams were coming true at once. As you know, the dream of the programme being aired didn't quite turn out to plan, and so consequently there could be no book to accompany it.

So, when I was at my wits' end, racking my brains for someone in the book business to help me, I remembered how Mandie had been a smiling face when I approached her all those years ago. I didn't know if she still worked at the channel, but a couple of phone calls confirmed that she was indeed still thriving at the company and was now head of a big division that encompassed books and other Channel 4 spin-off merchandise. Good news.

I called Mandie up and luckily she remembered me. Once I'd explained my challenge to get the book you're holding off the ground, she told me to send the manuscript in.

A few weeks later she rang me and asked whether I'd mind if she sent it to a guy she knew at a publishing company she worked with. This was brilliant news, and I couldn't hide my feelings when she asked me.

Mandie picked up on this excitement and swiftly made sure I had a reality check, not wanting me to set myself up for a fall. She stressed clearly that the publishing guy was simply a contact of hers she thought may connect with the book and that there was no guarantee anything would come of it.

Months went by and I was still no nearer to getting the book published. Periodically I'd hassle poor Mandie, asking her if her contact had got back to her. She exhibited the patience of a saint, always dealing with me so kindly and explaining to me that these things took time.

Eventually, Mandie called.

'Hey Shed. Doug – the guy I gave your manuscript to – he wants to meet up . . . The three of us for lunch,' she said.

This was a great development.

'Oh that's superb, Mand! Yeah – sure,' I replied.

I then asked Mandie whether Doug liked the chapters he'd been sent, but she told me that she didn't know. She added that, once again, I shouldn't get my hopes up because this was simply a meeting for Doug to get to know me and didn't necessarily mean anything in terms of getting the book published.

'He might just want to see if you have any other ideas, Shed,' she told me.

Oh, I hope not, I thought.

I was very nervous the day I was to meet Doug The Publisher. To make matters worse, I'd woken that morning to discover a large, subdermal eruption right on the tip on my nose. I had a whopper of a zit on my conk. Argh.

I manically fretted that this huge bump would lose me the deal. Nightmare scenarios flashed through my mind. I imagined meeting Doug and him saying to me: 'Yes, Shed, I *do* like your book and I *would* love to publish it, but there's just one small – well quite . . . big thing, actually: I simply can't work with an author with such a hideous face . . . I mean really, what would the publicity head-shots look like? So I'll have to decline I'm afraid . . .'

I met Mandie and Doug in a posh Indian restaurant round the corner from Channel 4. They were very polite and no one mentioned my bulbous red nose. We chatted amiably for a long while, with no one broaching the subject of the book either. My mind burned like a fiery vindaloo, eager to talk about it.

Finally, Doug got the ball rolling during the main course. Relief.

'Hey Shed, so I enjoyed your book,' he started.

'Thanks,' I said, my heart soaring.

'Yeah, I've been thinking about showing it to some of my team.'

'Really? . . . Really?' I checked.

'Yes, it's just the first stage though,' he replied.

The fact that someone in a publishing company thought the book actually might work was a great leap forward in my eyes.

Doug continued, 'There's just one thing though.'

It's my zit, isn't it? I thought.

'The name,' he paused. ' "NUMBER ONE BESTSELLER" – you should change it.'

Doug went on to explain that in the crowded book market, a book needed to be easily categorized and the title couldn't be too oblique because both the sales force and the customer had to be able instantly to get their heads round what the book was about. The title needed to explain what was inside. This all made good sense of course.

I left the restaurant as pleased as I could be, knowing that a big publisher liked what I'd written but that I was still way off from landing a publishing deal.

Back home, my list of alternative titles came out again and was furiously added to. I kept being drawn back to just one title for the book and I suggested it to Doug when I called him a few days later.

'How about *Ideas Man*?' I asked. 'Because sometimes people call me that.'

A small pause and then Doug answered, 'Yeah – I like it.'

Phew.

From then on, another set of challenges began. I wanted to prove to Doug that I was worth his time and effort. If he was going to put his neck on the line for me, recommending the book to the company board, then I felt I had to prove myself worthy of his effort.

I decided to send him a unique gift that would put me in the forefront of his mind, at least for a minute. I knew he represented loads of authors and was constantly being approached by new ones, so the aim at that point was just for him to remember me.

I started brainstorming for something unique to give to Doug. I thought about the traditional gifts that are sent by people to someone working in an office. They are broadly three types: flowers, chocolate and alcohol.

Now, flowers didn't seem quite right for this occasion – I was trying to impress Doug, not woo him. A box of chocolates didn't seem powerful enough, so I focused on the other option – booze.

It would have been easy to send Doug a bottle of champagne or even a decent red wine, but I needed something special. As I sat thinking about what booze I could send, my thoughts turned to stronger liquor. And then I recalled a brand I'd been fascinated with for years – Absolut Vodka. This company produced an iconic bottle of vodka which had letters printed straight on to the bottle, plus it also created adverts that were works of art. The bottle shape was so distinctive that for years the company released beautiful ads made by various artists and designers which sometimes showed lovely representations of the bottle, or visual gags using the bottle, rather than the actual product.

This design classic fired me. Not only was the transparent bottle gorgeous, the name Absolut has great word-play possibilities because it's a word that can be used for emphasis. I decided to try to replicate my own version of this brand.

It took a long while, but I found the exact fonts to mimic the 'label' on a real bottle of Absolut vodka. Once I'd designed my own version of the label, the next challenge was to mimic the original bottle itself.

I visited my local liquor store and purchased a number of cheap bottles of generic-brand vodka (not a usual trip for me). I then boiled a kettle, poured boiling water over the glued-on paper labels and carefully scraped them off with a knife and scrubbing cloth.

Once I'd chosen a suitable 'naked' bottle, I then tackled how to place the lettering on the bottle. After much thought and experimenting, the solution I came up with was to print the words backwards on a sheet of clear acetate used for overhead projector presentations. I then glued the acetate to the bottle. Although the acetate was visible if you looked very closely, the overall effect was that the lettering was printed on the glass. It looked pretty good.

I sent Doug the bottle of vodka. This is what it looked like:

The bottle was very well received. Soon after I sent it, Doug called me to say thanks – he loved it. He also added that he wanted to pitch the idea for my book at an acquisitions meeting attended by fifteen power-players in the company. You can imagine how pleased I was.

I knew this was my big chance to be published. The meeting was the make-or-break point. I had to impress the people in that meeting or my book would be rejected and I'd hit another brick wall. It was an internal company meeting that I couldn't attend, so I knew I'd have to do something to show the assembled decision-makers that I was completely passionate about working with them.

I immediately put together a lengthy proposal, explaining exactly what the book would be about. I knew each person would have limited time and I had to grab their attention quickly, so I tried to bring some of the chapters to life with brief descriptions and simple visuals, like this one for the first chapter:

CHAPTER 1
HOW A PIZZA CHANGED MY LIFE

To land my first job in television,
I sent a pizza to the boss of a large
TV company. The pizza had a
message pinned to the underside
of the pizza box.

In the proposal, I also included marketing ideas for how we'd promote the book, figuring that I should try to bring as much to the party as possible. I even designed some mock adverts for bus stops.

I never for one moment believed that my book would ever b
given the budget for bus-stop advertising; I just wanted to prove t
the team that I was keen to promote the book in any way.

After I'd finished compiling the proposal, I sent each person
attending the meeting their own shiny presentation pack, which
included a copy of the proposal plus a goody bag containing a packet
of 'Clitoris Allsorts' and an EGO banknote.

Then I nervously waited.

On the day that the meeting was scheduled, I found it hard to
concentrate. When I phoned the next day to hear the news, I was told
the meeting had been cancelled and put back a week. A week seems
nothing now, but back then I was devastated. After years of waiting,
I was so hungry to get a deal.

The next week the meeting did happen.

I didn't want to hassle Doug too much, so I waited two agonizing days before I called him.

'Hi Doug – how's it going?!' I started.

'Hey Shed, great – yeah, your sweets went down well with the
team,' he said.

That's good news, I thought, but did they like the proposal?

'And they liked your book – they thought it was great.'

Oh joy of joys. Sing hosanna and crack open the champagne.

Doug then went on to explain that the members of the board and
the boss of the company had heartily approved my book and that
they'd be making me an offer to publish. After three and a half years
of writing and pitching, it was everything I'd wanted and more.

As this happened, I experienced feelings of intense relief mixed
with extreme delight. Notice that the relief came first. After trying to do
something for so long, the first thing I felt wasn't pleasure at succeeding,
rather it was relief at not having to carry on pushing, fighting . . . trying.
Oh, and then the elation came very soon afterwards.

I then found myself plunged headlong into a thrilling ride until
the launch of the book. As soon as the publishing contract was
signed, a new family of talented experts suddenly popped up around
me. I got invited to numerous meetings with dozens of brilliant people who all wanted to make the book a success. It was like entering a
competition and winning a ready-made team of experts, each with a

niche skill in a certain area like marketing, sales or design. Totally thrilling.

Heading up this crack team was an amazing English rose of a lady in her mid twenties named Emma Musgrave. Emma became both my editor and publishing guru, guiding me through the rewrites and plans for the launch. As Emma is hugely well read and highly respected in the publishing field, I frequently felt guilty that this literary giant was having to deal with such fripperies as having to ask me for clearer 'Clitoris Allsorts' pictures and checking my additions to the 'Designer Beaver' chapter. With admirable patience and constant encouragement, she deftly and calmly helped me through the process of getting the book into the shops.

So that's how you're reading what you're reading now. It shows you that with very little writing talent, a few stories and a team of superb people around you, you can get a book out on to the shelves. And that goes for any ambition you have. If I can do it, then so can you.

Thanks a lot for being with me through these journeys. Now, if you're interested, I'd like to offer you an opportunity to be part of the next book . . .

The Next Chapter

Could you feature in it?

IN MY NEXT BOOK, I'm going to give you a brief update on any interesting progress that I've made with the projects in this book, plus I'll also describe even more adventures that I've embarked on. And this is where you come in. I've got a lot of ideas that need expert help. They include:

- A brand-new bottled-water brand

- A completely fresh magazine idea

- An innovative e-greetings format

- A children's meal concept

- A neat website idea involving printing clothes

- A new advertising strategy

- A great movie script

- A unique minicab business

- An original board game

If you are an engineer, web designer, businessman, magazine publisher, distributor or simply someone who believes you'd like to bring these ideas to fruition and share in their success, then please contact me:

www.ideasman.co.uk

Let's make something new . . .

My Favourite 'Go For It' Quotes

Cut them out and stick them up to inspire you . . .

> If you can dream it, you can do it.
>
> *Walt Disney*

It is better to have enough ideas for some of them to be wrong, than to be always right by having no ideas at all.

Edward de Bono

Creativity comes from a conflict of ideas.

Donatella Versace

I don't know the key to success, but the key to failure is trying to please everybody.

Bill Cosby

It is on our failures that we base a new and different and better success.

Havelock Ellis

You've achieved success in your field when you don't know whether what you're doing is work or play.

Warren Beatty

To follow, without halt, one aim:
there's the secret of success.

Anna Pavlova

What's money? A man is a success if he gets up in the morning and goes to bed at night and in between does what he wants to do.

Bob Dylan

Many of life's failures are people who did not realize how close they were to success when they gave up.

Thomas A. Edison

Success is the ability to go from one failure to another with no loss of enthusiasm.

Sir Winston Churchill

Don't be discouraged by a failure. It can be a positive experience. Failure is, in a sense, the highway to success, inasmuch as every discovery of what is false leads us to seek earnestly after what is true, and every fresh experience points out some form of error which we shall afterwards carefully avoid.

John Keats

Nothing in the world can take the place of persistence. Talent will not; nothing is more common than unsuccessful men with talent. Genius will not; unrewarded genius is almost a proverb. Education will not; the world is full of educated derelicts. Persistence and determination alone are omnipotent. The slogan 'press on' has solved and always will solve the problems of the human race.

Calvin Coolidge

You must keep sending work out; you must never let a manuscript do nothing but eat its head off in a drawer. You send that work out again and again, while you're working on another one. If you have talent, you will receive some measure of success – but only if you persist.

Isaac Asimov

THANK YOU FOR READING THIS BOOK
I hope you enjoyed it

Yours,

Shed

Now, maybe go and start something
you've been meaning to do for ages . . .

TRANSWORLD PUBLISHERS
61–63 Uxbridge Road, London W5 5SA
A Random House Group Company
www.rbooks.co.uk

IDEAS MAN
A CORGI BOOK: 9780552155502

First published in Great Britain
in 2008 by Bantam Press
a division of Transworld Publishers
Corgi edition published 2009

If you're reading this page, then good on you – you must be someone very inquisitive
with a bright mind who likes the minutiae of life. I salute your greatness. Shed.

P. 4: head illustration courtesy of Two Create; p. 91: *ITMA Review* reproduced by kind
permission of the ITMA; p. 153: *Sky Magazine* courtesy News International, background
picture to article courtesy Scope Features; p. 252: *Sun* front page courtesy News
International; p. 253: *Telegraph* front page courtesy Telegraph Group; p. 256: *Sun* courtesy
News International; p. 257: *News of the World* page courtesy News International; pp.284–6
Little Book of Presents Money Can't Buy courtesy Summerdale Media Group.

This book is a work of non-fiction based on the life, experiences and recollections of
Sheridan Simove. In some limited cases names of people, places, dates, sequences or the
detail of events have been changed solely to protect the privacy of others. The author has
stated to the publishers that, except in such minor respects not affecting the substantial
accuracy of the work, the contents of this book are true.

Addresses for Random House Group Ltd companies outside the UK
can be found at: www.randomhouse.co.uk
The Random House Group Ltd Reg. No. 954009

The Random House Group Limited supports The Forest Stewardship Council (FSC), the
leading international forest certification organisation. All our titles that are printed on
Greenpeace approved FSC certified paper carry the FSC logo. Our paper procurement
policy can be found at www.rbooks.co.uk/environment

Typeset in Berling by Falcon Oast Graphic Art Ltd.
Printed in the UK by CPI Cox & Wyman, Reading, RG1 8EX.

2 4 6 8 10 9 7 5 3 1